# Toads

## More Amusing Farmyard Tales

### Lynnette Barlow

i

ISBN 978-1-8382249-8-1

Cover design: Philip Barlow
Illustrations: Lynnette, Philip & Saffron Barlow
Corina Atkins and Kieth Tovey.

Featuring: John Owen

Published by Hampshire Oak Publications

Hampshire Oak
Publications

# Toads in a Hole

## More Amusing Farmyard Tales

For 'The Aunties',

Terrie, Diane and Candy.

With many thanks for always being there.

Disclaimer:

The title of this book in no way reflects our
view of the beautiful
*Ynys Môn,*
or
Isle of Anglesey, North Wales.

Let the reader read on.

# Preface

As a sequel to A Handful of Toads, Toads In A Hole continues to tell of the often amusing adventures of a young family adapting to farm life on the beautiful *Ynys Môn* or Isle of Anglesey, North Wales during the 1990s.

During our previous three years as novice sheep farmers we had learned so much about the local culture and even attempted to learn the Welsh language. We had explored the beaches and beauty spots of the Island and befriended a host of interesting people of diverse origin who were to widen our horizons with their fascinating life experiences. Those experiences make up many of the sensitive and often humorous tales told in this book.

# Chapters

# 1 Bleating the Odds

Bursting into the room, Philip threw open the door to the medicine cupboard and rummaged about in it noisily. Bringing the box of medicines to my nicely cleaned kitchen table, he tipped out all the contents and caught up a sizeable brown bottle.

"This is it!" he exclaimed triumphantly, holding it up to the light for examination, and after grabbing a large plastic syringe, he started back toward the door.

"What is it?" I asked, looking between him and the mess left on the table.

"Calcium borogluconate," he replied impatiently, "but I think she is already dead!" And with that, he disappeared back outside. I assumed he was talking about one of the sheep and not one of our neighbours, and as all the female members of the family had been accounted for that morning, I continued in my mission of filling lunch boxes with apples and cheese-filled bread rolls and chunky squares of cake.

It had been a challenge for me to adapt to life as a sheep farmer, especially as I was previously only used to town life. My husband, Philip, grew up as a country boy, and it had been his dream to be a farmer, so with three young children, we had moved from the south of England to the beautiful Isle of Anglesey and had striven to integrate into the charming Welsh culture. We had lived on the farm for three years and added two more dear little girls to our family. I had put every effort into a way of life that was totally strange to me; the absence of roads and streetlights, of traffic and next-door neighbours and the odd silence of mountain life, save for the sounds of bleating sheep, was something that, as a 'townie', I had learned to adapt to, and was actually beginning to enjoy.

"I hope she will be all right," Philip said a few minutes later when he came back indoors to wash his hands and rinse the syringe at the kitchen sink. I hoped so too, whoever 'she' was; I

1

had just finished tidying up the debris on the table and was not relishing having to do it all again. He was still watching out of the window at the inert woolly figure tucked in the shelter of the stone wall leading to the top fields. Two young lambs hovered beside her, their little tongues protruding with each call they made to their mother to wake up; it was a sad sight.

"What is the matter with her?" I asked as I closed the lid to the last lunchbox and started wiping down the draining board at the kitchen sink.

"Milk fever," Philip stated emphatically. "Not enough calcium in her diet to keep healthy and give her what she needs to feed her twins."

"Is she dead?" I asked as I watched those poor little lambs poking at their mother's teats in the hope of getting some nourishment and normality back to their young lives. The clock ticked ominously on the wall and threatened to alert us that it was almost eight o'clock and time to leave for school.

"Oh, look!" Philip gasped. "She's getting up!" Sure enough, the previously comatose ewe was struggling to her feet and then stood shakily for a moment while her two offspring took advantage of the situation and dived under her belly in search of a good meal.

Philip's smile widened as he watched the ewe regain control of her legs, take a few small steps and then bend her head down to graze. He felt like a 'miracle worker', it was against the odds that she survived, a proud moment and a successful start to the day.

A spectacular sight greeted us a few days later when we drew back the bedroom curtains on that chilly Saturday morning.

"Snow!" I proclaimed. Yes, the fields of *Ty'n Llain* wore an enchantingly thick white blanket. The day was unusually still, with not even a light breeze to disturb the silvery humps of snow clinging to the bare, black branches of the gnarled hawthorn trees. That may not sound particularly special to those who are used to a regular dose of that winter wonder, but for Anglesey, it is a rarity. The sweep of the Ocean Gulf Stream that washed up from the Southern Seas usually keeps the Island at a relatively mild temperature throughout the year. It could get extremely windy at times, but apart from that, the climate is reasonably comfortable, with temperatures never overly hot and rarely below freezing point during the daytime. However, dense grey clouds hung low that morning and muffled all sounds outside as we gingerly opened the window and sniffed at the cold, fresh, clean air.

Thump! A snowball hit the window and showered us with its crystalline powder. Our boys had already discovered that exciting white gift and had been waiting in the vegetable garden for us to wake up.

"Right; this is war!" Philip called back and attempted to gather a handful of snow from the window ledge. "OK, after breakfast," he conceded as Daniel and Joshua reappeared with more 'ammunition'.

"Can we go sledging today, Dad?" asked eleven-year-old Daniel that morning, between mouthfuls of porridge, his eyes bright with excitement and anticipation.

"Sledg-ing! Sledg-ing!" chorused Amelia and Joshua in support of their elder brother's suggestion.

3

"I think we should, don't you, Mummy?" Philip replied as he swallowed the last of his tea.

"Too cold for me, I'm afraid," I answered, peering through the kitchen window at that wintry sky. "You all go sledging while I stay with the babies and prepare lunch."

"Hmm, I don't know about that though, all of our slopes have a lot of big rocks, and someone could get hurt," Philip mused as he considered other possibilities to indulge his offspring. "Just a minute!" his frown lifted as he rose from the table, walked over to open the kitchen door and gazed out at the long, steady slope where our neighbour's field joined our boundary. "Yes, I know; how about we go sledging on *The Coeden*?"

"Ooh, do you think Wyn Rogers would be OK with that?" I asked sceptically. I had never met our neighbour but I knew that he was very fussy about the presentation of his fields, and he always kept them well-fertilised and lush green. His farmhouse was situated about a mile away over the top of the mountain if you took a straight line, but it was quite a few miles by road.

"Please, Daddy, please!" the children begged.

"You stay with me, Saffron," I stated, not that she understood their plans at only two years old. "We can watch them through the bedroom window and maybe make a snowman in the back garden after Amber has gone back to sleep."

The children's faces were a picture of exhilaration as they sped down the slopes of *The Coeden* on their plastic sledges, and their squeals of delight echoed across the sleepy valley. Saffron and I sat by the bedroom window, watching them for some time as I nursed baby Amber and rocked her to sleep in her crib.

My thoughts drifted back to the excitement I felt as a child in the early years following the Second World War when my sisters and I awoke one morning to see snow covering the street. The wickedly cold and ferocious Arctic wind, known as the 'Beast from the East', frequently assailed the eastern side of England, and

4

overnight, it had driven a mountain of snow onto our garden. I recalled a hurriedly-eaten breakfast that morning, followed by my mother's meticulous preparation of we girls to battle with that white counterpane. However, when she opened the back door, there was no garden, just a snowy barricade that had completely blocked the doorway. Nevertheless, our mother was determined that, after all her efforts at preparing us, we were going out to play, so she beat a large hole in the snow drift for us to exit. And play we did; we rolled down the sloping garden, quilting the pristine whiteness with the patterns from our anoraks. We built snowmen and threw snowballs at each other until our noses reddened and our mittened fingers grew numb, as children do wherever the winter unfolds its burgeoning clouds and drops its snowy bounty.

I remembered the magic of that night when our youngest sister, Candy, was about to be born. My sisters, Terrie, Diane and I had been awakened and hurried into the cold, still February night. In the light from the new streetlamps, the snow had sparkled with a million diamonds and twinkled like a sprinkling of silvery stars fallen from Heaven to guide us. It crunched under our feet as we made our way to our car, one of very few seen at that time on the new council estate carved out of the wheat fields of the Medway Valley. Then there was the thrill of climbing onto the black running board of my father's Humber saloon with my heavy woollen coat wrapped over my nightdress and smelling the comforting aroma of the leather upholstery. As we sped toward our grandparent's home, we watched the rapidly passing houses built for families celebrating the end of World War II. We children born at that time were among those who became known as the 'Baby Boomers'. It was a privileged time of rebuilding and innovation, with television and motor cars becoming available for the average household.

So, here were my own children in the 1990s, laughing and playing in the snow but under very different circumstances. The last few weeks since we had received permission to continue building the barn had been hectic; with our capable builder, Chris Chivers, Philip had worked feverishly to finish its roof. He had constructed two doors to fit into the doorways that had stood stark and open for the previous ten months; those ten months had been an irritating test of our patience. We had been shocked when the council stopped the completion of our barn, despite ardent protestations that the owl holes set above the arched door were not crosses and that we were not building a chapel. Philip had been relieved to begin moving several farm implements from the tiny old stone barn into the new barn and hanging his tools on the walls. He had even ordered a truckload of hay bales, now carefully stowed in the hay loft. What he was not allowed to do in the new barn was to house animals!

*'Unfortunately, rules regarding the housing of animals have recently been changed. Therefore, any new buildings intended for housing any form of livestock must have the express permission of all neighbours within a quarter-mile radius of your house.'*

Thus read the clause at the end of the official letter from Llangefni County Council announcing the decision to lift the ten-month ban. Although those new regulations defeated the purpose of the new barn, it was hardly likely that we would invite all our neighbours to consent to our housing animals in it, and risk suffering rejection. Therefore, in concession to that new ruling and constantly looking over his shoulder for the reappearance of the dreaded building inspector, Philip had constructed three sheep pens in the old barn in preparation for the upcoming lambing season.

Tearing myself away from watching my family playing happily on those snowy slopes, I was considering returning to the kitchen to start making lunch when I noticed the tall figure of a man with

6

a shotgun silhouetted against the grey sky on the crest of *The Coeden*. I held my breath; 'It must be Wyn Rogers', I thought in alarm; 'what would he do?' We had heard through our neighbour, John Owen, that the farmer had threatened to shoot our dogs if they came on his land again; I hoped that threat did not extend to human intruders! The man stood stock still, watching the happy but oblivious troupe of trespassers, and then, after a few minutes, I breathed a sigh of relief as he strode back toward his home.

"Do you think Mr Rogers would mind that we had been sledging on his land?" Daniel, ever conscientious, asked as everyone returned to the kitchen, flushed and exuberant after the morning's activity. As he entered the back door, Philip looked behind him at the shallow grooves cut into the snow on the previously unspoiled slopes of *The Coeden*.

"No, Daniel," he answered his son reassuringly. "We have done no harm, and I am sure he would never even notice."

The snow did not last long, and Saffron's snowman in the back garden quickly melted as the weather grew a little milder. She spent some time searching for it and wondering who had stolen it, but other distractions soon took her interest.

Daniel, who had started at *Ysgol* Sir Thomas Jones Secondary School in Amlwch the previous September, was pleased to return to his school routine while Amelia and Joshua recommenced the school year at Llanfechell Primary School.

Although he had found his school years challenging and had left school virtually illiterate, Philip was keen to resume his Horticultural studies at Coleg Pencraig after the winter break and was doing well. Bryner Jones and Alan Savage were excellent tutors, and Philip thrived under their direction. Bryner Jones was true to his word and was always mindful of keeping Philip up to speed with the gist of the subject, especially as he was teaching Agricultural Accounts and Agricultural Management in the Welsh language. Alan Savage, teaching Amenity Horticulture, maintained

7

the cheerful enthusiasm that had put Philip at ease during his first interview with him the previous autumn. His new term project was to prepare peat 'plugs' for flower seedlings, some of which he wanted to plant in our ploughed field. Having purchased the seeds and equipment through the college, Philip had created one thousand plugs each of Statice, Helichrysum and Gypsophila. It sounded like a lot of hard work ahead for us come the spring; what was more, he was about to start on another planting project before that.

"The Anglesey County Council have a tree nursery and is giving out free trees to anyone who will promise to plant and care for them," Philip announced that news just as soon as he arrived home from college one evening, which struck a chord of dread in me. I was still reeling from our winter tree-planting mission three years earlier. I knew it would happen sometime since the rumblings of the proposal had been surfing at regular intervals ever since then. "Yes, I heard about it at college," Philip continued, undaunted by the fact that his announcement had met with resounding silence and a noticeable absence of enthusiasm. "The council is encouraging tree planting in this area, which is certainly needed. Now, where is it? They said it is advertised in the Anglesey Herald somewhere. Ah, yes, here it is. 'Anyone interested, please contact………'"

That weekend, Ms Barbara Stravinsky from the Anglesey County Council came to visit and agreed that the 'bog field' at the lower corner of our boundary, which was too wet for sheep to run on, would be an ideal place for a tree plantation. They decided that Black alder, Hairy birch and Goat willow would do just fine, while Beech and Norway maple would be best for the drier areas. The delivery arrived within the week. Since my earlier attempts at tree planting in the frozen soil had proven somewhat ineffective, Philip prudently decided to take sole responsibility for establishing the new copse and had all three hundred of the various species planted by the following weekend. He was exuberant that his arboreal plan had finally come to fruition.

While planting the last few trees, he heard the whirring sound of three Mallard ducks flying at tremendous speed. The ducks swooped in an arc very close overhead, plunged, and crash-landed into the reedy edges of *Llyn Bwch*, the lake just thirty yards from where he was working. A Peregrine falcon in hot pursuit narrowly missed the ducks and sped away into the distance empty-clawed, like a thwarted robber.

"Phew! Close one!" Daniel remarked when his father related that drama at tea time.

"A Peregrine falcon is the fastest creature on Earth and it can dive at a speed of more than two hundred miles per hour!" Philip informed us knowledgeably. "You should have heard the whooshing of his wings when he was diving!"

"'The swift do not always win the race'," I said, quoting the ancient adage.

"Poor little ducks, I'm pleased they got away safely," nine-year-old Amelia contributed passionately.

"Well, once the ducks landed on the lake, they had beaten the odds and the falcon knew he was defeated; he could hunt over the water but not on the water, or he might drown," Philip explained and then sat thoughtfully for a while before saying: "That falcon must live on the sea cliffs somewhere not too far away; they often nest on the coastal cliffs and rocky ledges. Maybe we should take a walk to see if we can find their nesting places; how about next weekend?"

"I will come with you, Dad," chorused a host of volunteers.

"I wonder why our part of the Island is so devoid of trees," I pondered as I joined Philip to admire his handiwork in the bog field. "Benllech, Dulas and the Moelfre area are all quite well-wooded with all sorts of trees; is it just that it is more sheltered from the wind there?"

"Perhaps we should ask our local 'Oracle'," Philip suggested. "I am sure he will have a tale to tell about that." Our friendly but mischievous Welsh neighbour, John Owen, who had been watching the tree planting from his farm at *Bryn Awel*, came to pay us a visit the following Saturday afternoon.

"That's a good job you have been doing there, Philip," John congratulated him. "Yes, we need more trees in this part of the Island."

"We wanted to ask you if you know why there are so few trees around here, John," I ventured as he shared a *panad*, or cup of tea, at the kitchen table with us.

"Ah! Now that is a good question," John answered after washing down his ginger cake with a good draw on his tea. "It was the Romans," he began. "Yes, the Romans came here and invaded the Island." Another mouthful of tea kept us all in suspense.

"They hated the Druid religion, and as trees were sacred to the Druids, the Roman armies cut them all down...the groves that is...and the Druids."

"So this area was once all forested, John?" I asked. Daniel, Amelia and Joshua were raptly interested; they loved their trees and the little tree house Philip had made for them amongst the few Sycamores lining the lane.

"That's right, and they have never really recovered," John affirmed. "Apart from that, with the trees gone, there was no helter from the wind, which made it difficult for new trees to survive."

"Hmmm, I can believe that!" Philip replied. "But I think our trees in the bog field should do all right; they are in a more sheltered spot down there."

"Yes, Philip, they should do very well there," John agreed. "Anyway, I came to tell you about the robbery at the *Swyddfa Post.*"

"What?" we all gasped. "Not the Llanfechell Post Office surely?"

"No, no," John assured us, "the sub-Post Office here in Mynydd Mechell."

"Oh, my goodness! Was anybody hurt? Did they get away with much? Poor Ted and Brenda!" John was suitably pleased by the response from his captivated audience. The little local Post Office just occupied the front room belonging to a couple from Manchester who lived on the 'Mountain Road'. They sold a few stamps and kept a post box outside for Dewi the *postmon* to empty when he passed each day.

"Ted was sorting out a few things behind the desk when a motorbike pulled up outside, and a yob burst in, still wearing his helmet. He whipped out a large knife and shouted at Ted to empty the till," John related.

"How scary! What did Ted do?" We all asked, and John started to laugh.

"Ted was not at all fazed; he's a hard city man who knows how to deal with young louts. He called out to Brenda and said, 'Hey, Brenda, look at this. This hoodlum thinks he is going to rob us!' So Brenda came charging out from the back room with a baseball bat, and the lad ran back out the door with Ted chasing after him threatening to beat him with the bat. He got back on his motorbike and took off at high speed, empty-handed. You can be sure they won't see him around here again!"

11

# 2 On the Brink

When we arrived at my parents' home for Sunday lunch, my father was watching the televised news reports on the Gulf War. Regular updates about the war being fought against Saddam Hussein of Iraq due to his invasion and annexing of Kuwait had occupied centre stage for over six months. Although it was raging many miles away from us, it was as though it was happening locally due to its constant news coverage. Since the United States and the United Nations were involved in countering the attack, there was National anxiety that the United Kingdom might also be drawn into the conflict.

I could tell that my parents were anxious; it had been less than fifty years since their first-hand experience of the devastating effects of World War II. My mother, Doreen Hearne, and our grandparents would frequently relive those difficult times and the horrors and hardships of war-time living in the stories they told. They had lived in the historic city of Rochester in Kent and very close to the Short Brothers' riverside factory that constructed the Sunderland Flying Boat aircraft for The War Effort. Therefore their city was the focus of attack from the enemy bombers that would often fly overhead at night. The sirens would sound, the family would rush down to the air-raid shelter that Grandfather had dug in the garden, and they would spend the night there until the 'all clear' siren would sound, usually the following morning. Then they would hurry back up to the house to inspect any damage to their home - if it still existed! Then they would check on their neighbours before preparing for school or work, carrying their gas masks in pouches around their necks. If the air raid occurred during the daytime when the children were on their way to or from school, they were instructed to run to the nearest shelters where they could be sure of being welcomed and protected.

My father, George William Baker, was enlisted into the army at the age of eighteen and trained as a radio operator. He worked with the spotlight team that directed their lights to reflect off clouds to illuminate the terrain ahead of the troops without silhouetting their own men. He was among the soldiers that landed on the Normandy Beaches, France, on D-Day plus 1 in June 1944. He and his comrades had been shocked by the carnage still evident on the beachheads from the previous day's terrible battle. The devastation and destruction inflicted on the French countryside before their arrival was still etched on his memory all those years later. So now, the younger generation of innocents seemed on the brink of active involvement in another war. No wonder they were worried.

However, that particular day was unseasonably mild, bright, and sunny for a February day on Anglesey, so a walk around the clifftops to blow away the winter cobwebs was in order. While I stayed with Amber and my father in his home in Cemaes Bay, Philip and my mother decided to take the dogs and our four older children on the scenic coastal walk with the hope of spotting the Peregrine falcons. The starting point for our team of 'twitchers' was to be the car park by Llanbadrig church. That tiny church was said to be founded by Saint Patrick, the patron saint of Ireland, about 440 AD after he survived shipwreck on the rocks of Middle Mouse Island or *Ynys Badrig*.

The sea air wafted clean and fresh, giving a sense of freedom and clear-headedness. As usual, Lucy was full of pent-up energy, and Daniel struggled to keep her pace as he was towed along rapidly by her lead. Although she enjoyed her life and was my mother's enthusiastic walking companion, she would have made an ideal sheepdog. Lucy was white with red-brown ears and patches across her smooth coat and built like her father, Tweed, a working collie from Bethesda in Snowdonia. In contrast, her mother, Jill, was a smaller dog with a long, red-brown coat, while her ruff, socks and tip of her tail were creamy white. Being well trained as a sheepdog on our farm, Jill needed only a word to make her stay obediently 'close' beside my mother the whole way around the clifftops. Border Collies are such a beautiful breed of dog, loyal, trusting and intelligent, and for Jill, her work is serious business rather than play. Mother may be in command in the home, but out in the fields, the sheepdog considers herself second only to her master.

Amelia and Joshua were keen explorers and bounded ahead of the rest, watched by their little sister, Saffron, who had the prime viewing position on her Daddy's shoulders. As they walked the well-worn footpath that followed the undulating, rocky coastline, there was no need to worry about adders, which would have been hibernating at that time of year. Middle Mouse Island, named after its mouse-like shape, loomed closer as the group strode onward, and the swirls and eddies of the sea, racing between land and Island, reminded them of the danger of that fast-moving tide that had claimed the lives of so many.

Hardy Welsh Mountain sheep nibbled at the sparse brown-top and red fescue grasses beside the pathway that descended toward *Porth Llanlleiana*, the most northerly point of Wales. There, they came across the stone-built ruins of what was originally a convent but later converted to porcelain works. Now, however, it was no more than a shell of what was once a grand and carefully constructed building, overshadowed by a tall, well-preserved chimney. Standing there for a few minutes, they marvelled at the sight of the Curlew as that beautiful bird skimmed the wet, boggy marshland objectively with its purposeful wing beats. The melodious strains of its trilling blended harmoniously with the flutelike call of the Lapwing, which flapped its irregular wingbeats across the clear blue sky.

Watching creatures of such diverse habits occupying the same airspace without discord, Philip thought of what humans could learn from Nature, particularly given the terrors of the Gulf War raging at that time.

On that pleasant day on Anglesey, however, the members of our family group skipped happily along in their bird-watching pursuit. As they continued on to *Porthwen*, warning signs stood at intervals along the footpath reminding walkers not to stray off the path because of the mine shafts.

"Look out for porpoises and dolphins, everyone," Daniel called out. "Uncle Paul said we might see some along this coast."

Eventually, they came across a small track which tumbled down through the undergrowth of gorse and blackberry towards two tall, red-brown and square-shaped brick chimneys that towered regally over three large beehive-shaped kilns. Along with several roofless buildings, those structures formed the remnants of the Porthwen brickworks, built during the Victorian era but now unused.

It was fascinating to see evidence of the hard work and industry of a bygone age. That location looked as though it had been ideal in its day for barges to come into the bay on the high tide bringing in coal to fire the kilns and to carry away the special quartzite refractory bricks for lining industrial furnaces and kilns. The brickworks sat on a small platform carved into the side of the sea cliff that terminated in the extraordinary form of a natural rock arch, while the pale, sandy beach curved horseshoe-shaped around the azure blue water of the bay. Jill and Lucy pounded over the soft sand, chasing after small stones the children threw for them to retrieve. After a welcome picnic, it was time to return home. Although that time they did not see any Peregrine falcons, dolphins or porpoises, everyone was satisfied with their day.

Back home in Cemaes Bay, some exciting news awaited them the Gulf War had ended! We were all so relieved. Although sadly many lives were lost, thankfully, no more of the world's young men would be living under the threat of being called upon to fight in that war. Celebrations were in order; a long drink of water for the dogs, lemonade for the children, a glass of sherry for the ladies and a welcome tumbler of whisky for the men. Chicken sandwiches, strawberry trifle, ice cream and homemade cake finished the evening nicely. It had been a well-spent winter's day and a happy start to the year.

What had *not* been a happy start to the year was Philip's anxiety over being unable to give our sheep enough nutritious herbage to sustain them during their pregnancy and the subsequent nursing of their lambs. Although he had carefully reserved the grass in the lower fields since the previous summer a fierce winter storm had swept in from the Irish Sea, covering the fields with a salt spray and 'burning' the grass to an unpalatable dry, brown. So it was necessary to take all the vegetable peelings into the fields for the sheep to sort through and increase their serving of sheep pellets, especially for those ewes carrying twins.

Bleddyn Roberts had not received Philip cordially on his previous visit to *Tyddyn Gwyrdd* a few years earlier to purchase red diesel for our tractor. Nevertheless, Philip was pleased to see a sign outside that farm on the Mountain Road advertising 'Silage for Sale', so he hoped he would be a welcome customer this time. He was pleasantly surprised by the warm welcome from Mr Roberts and wondered whether his friendliness was genuine or was he merely being a good salesman? The cordial interaction continued between the two men when Mr Roberts arrived later that day at *Ty'n Llain* with a large silage bale on the back of his tractor, tightly embalmed in black plastic.

"Hmmm; Welsh Mountain sheep, eh?" he commented as his eyes scanned our fields. "Had any trouble with lambing?"

18

"Very little; these ewes have given us very few problems," Philip replied. He knew that the sheep he had seen grazing on the lush, green fields of *Tyddyn Gwyrdd* were not purebred but 'Speckle faced Mules', a cross between the Welsh Mountain ewe and the Border Leicester ram. Mr Roberts was a talented, seasoned farmer; nonetheless, Philip felt sure there must have been a good reason for his unusual friendliness. He felt something was not being said here, but if Mr Roberts had any concerns, he was not eager to share them.

Philip was eager to reveal his treat to his hungry ladies just as soon as Mr Roberts and his tractor had trundled back down the lane. He eagerly cut away at one side of the black plastic wrapping, and then stood back at a suitable distance with the self-satisfied smile of a generous benefactor, anticipating a stampede of appreciative ewes. The first sheep delegated by the flock to investigate walked suspiciously toward that ominous-looking black hulk, sniffed at it and walked away. A few more ewes decided that nothing terrible had happened to their companion, so it was safe for them to investigate for themselves.

'Give them time to get used to it,' Philip thought to himself, and, satisfied that the flock would now be well fed he hurried off to the barn to tend to some necessary duties. When he returned to the field a few hours later, his heart sank; not one sheep was interested in the silage bale.

"There was an unpleasant smell from that silage," Philip said as he helped me gather the washing from the line while flashing disappointed glances at that bulky dark shape in the middle of the field. "Do you want to go over and take a sniff?" I didn't fancy sniffing any more unpleasant smells than necessary, but I put the washing basket inside the kitchen and walked over to the silage bale to give him my verdict.

"Ugh! It smells like vomit!" I uttered involuntarily.

"Yes, that is what I thought." Philip concurred.

Was it usual for silage to smell like that, we wondered? Perhaps the bale had been over-ripe, or were our Welsh Mountain sheep just too fussy? Or had we been duped again for being novice immigrants? Either way, they never touched the stuff, and eventually, Philip had to dispose of it while the sheep remained on the brink of starvation.

"I knew something like this would happen!" Philip stated unceremoniously one Sunday afternoon while I was preparing the evening meal.

"What has happened?" I asked, and several other members of the family, who were helping to set the table for dinner, also turned puzzled looks toward their father.

"It must be 'twin lamb disease'," he replied with a mixture of distress and irritation. "I knew she was carrying twins from when she had her scan; I wish I could have persuaded her to eat that silage; now she looks as though her lambs must have died inside her!"

"Oh, no! Where is she?" I answered, feeling for him, especially as I knew he had worked hard to avoid such a situation.

"She has taken herself off and separated from the rest of the flock, which was the first thing that alerted me. When I approached her, she stood still and didn't attempt to run away."

"Does her breath smell of 'pear drops'?" I asked, remembering what Philip and Sally, the vet, had told me when they had first scanned our pregnant ewes together.

"Stank like a car paint shop! And her nose is streaming too; I must ring Sally and ask for her advice." He finished washing his hands at the sink and marched out to the telephone in the hallway, still drying his hands on the kitchen towel. Daniel had already started serving glasses of milk to his siblings as they sat around the kitchen table with a packet of biscuits to stave off their hunger until tea time.

"Glucose!" Their father announced as he returned to the kitchen a few minutes later and helped himself to a biscuit and the cup of tea I had placed on the table for him. "Sally recommends that I feed her glucose to help revitalize her and then get all the flock onto some better pasture; I should have some glucose here…." and out came the box of medicines again to be sorted through on the kitchen table amongst the milk and biscuits.

"Ah yes, this looks like the stuff!" Philip exclaimed as he held up the packet of white powder and read the label. "It says to mix it in a jug with warm water and pour it down her throat. OK, let's hope this works."

"Do you want me to help you, Dad?" Daniel asked, rising from the table and reaching for his anorak, which he always kept hanging on the back of the kitchen door next to his father's wax jacket.

"I don't think you would like to see what I will have to do, Daniel." Philip grimaced at me as he headed back towards the door, indicating that he would need to perform some sordid operation, so I was relieved that he didn't ask for my help either. I ventured outside once or twice to look for signs of his grisly task having ended, but against the darkening sky, I could see his silhouetted form bowed over the rear end of the sick ewe as he 'cleansed' her of the remains of her dead lambs. Oh, to be a farmer! It was late in the evening that my poor husband came back indoors to search in the fridge for the bottle of 'Neomycin' antibiotic to inject the ewe.

"I gave her the maximum dose of antibiotics and she is in the barn now with water, fresh hay, and a bucket of sheep nuts for when she is feeling a bit better," Philip said as he sat wearily at the table with a well-earned beer. It was just as well that I had already fed the children and sent them off for their baths and to get ready for bed, as Philip had no stomach for food that night. "Sally recommended that we buy some 'molasses sheep lick' from

21

Llandeusant Watermill. I will pick it up tomorrow and get some more sheep nuts too."

Thankfully, despite having been on the brink of death, the ewe survived, although there would be no lambs for her that season. Although we could not afford to rent better pasture, the sheep loved the 'sheep lick', which came in the form of a giant dark brown 'lollipop', the size and shape of a dustbin lid. It contained molasses, barley and all the nutrients necessary to help restore their health while waiting for the onset of the spring grass.

# 3 A Rocking Weekend.

"Nut pouches!" was the first observation Granny Lucy made when she met baby Amber for the first time, and yes, it was true, three-month-old Amber had the chubby cheeks of a cute little hamster.

It had been a long drive for our visitors to come from the chalky hills of Oxfordshire on that blustery spring day. Philip's sister, Linda, wanted to construct a rockery in her garden, and *Ty'n Llain* was an abundance of rocks to spare. It was an opportunity to send her family with Granny and her dog, Emmie, tying in collecting those rocks with a camping holiday.

"Granny tricked me!" declared twelve-year-old Timothy with indignation.

"Really? What did she do?" I asked as I looked accusingly at his grandmother, who sniggered unrepentantly at the memory.

"She said 'We are coming up to the Welsh border; have you got your passport ready?'"

"Oh, Mum, you didn't?" Philip grinned at his mother.

"She did!" Timothy maintained. "And when I said I didn't have a passport, Granny said I had better hide under a blanket in case any policemen came along. I was really worried, so I stayed there for ages!"

"You poor little boy! So, now you know you don't need a passport to come to Wales from England, don't you, Tim?" I sympathised. Philip could not help a chuckle at his mother's mischief.

"We don't need special treatment," Linda's husband, John, insisted. "The two boys and I will be happy to camp somewhere on your land." So Philip found them a comfortable niche for their tents, sheltered from the wind in a far corner of the top fields. John, Timothy and young Toby happily set up camp while Granny rightly stayed in the comfort of the home.

23

Collecting the right-sized rocks was a fun mission for everyone involved, although some were so large that they were more like boulders and had to be rolled down the sloping fields toward John's waiting trailer.

"These rocks are enormous!" John commented. "I can't work out how they got up here; it's not as if they could have rolled down from a higher mountain, as you are almost at the top."

"Yes, I wondered that myself. It seems that Anglesey has a fascinating geological mix," Philip replied. "It is thought that this region was covered in snow and ice during the Ice Age. I wonder if a glacier could have pushed the boulders uphill before it, and when the ice melted, it left behind the evidence for us to deal with." Peeling off the blue tarpaulin cover from the trailer, the two men laid it out carefully on the field beside the new barn, then wheeled the wheelbarrow up to the first pile of rocks to be loaded. When Philip returned to the trailer no more than five minutes later, he was surprised by what he saw.

"Hey, John, look at this!" he said, smiling broadly. John loaded another rock into the trailer and turned around to see why Philip was laughing. Within just those five minutes, about twenty inquisitive ewes had come to investigate the tarpaulin, all standing on it, sniffing it and wondering if it was edible.

Granny Lucy has always been an adventurer and a keen archaeologist, so we created a list of sites that we thought would be of interest to her and the *Trefignath* Burial Chamber at Trearddur, south of Holyhead, was first on our list. Philip had acquired a small antiquated handbook on the Ancient Monuments of Anglesey, which sold for the princely sum of sixpence during the 1950s. According to that guide, the Burial Chamber was a Neolithic construction consisting of a continuous, 45 feet long rock-built passage containing three or four burial chambers. It was made from enormous upright stone slabs, and topped with a couple of giant capstones. As we stood and looked at that ancient edifice mostly uncovered from its original mound of earth and stones, we thought it to be a marvellous feat of engineering. Created without the aid of modern technology, it had stood the test of time and weather for centuries, and here it was, free for anyone to visit. The same was true of most ancient monuments discussed in detail in our little guidebook: 'Access: At any time and without charge.'

So we visited various points of interest, such as the two structures built close together, near Bodedern village, known as the *Presaddfed* Burial Chambers. One of the chambers had collapsed, but the other still had a capstone measuring twelve feet by eight feet, supported on four uprights.

Next, we visited the Neolithic remains of the Bodowyr Burial Chamber toward the south of the Island, which had a domed capstone measuring eight feet by six feet perched precariously on top of huge, upright, rectangular stone slabs. The unanswered question arose every time: how did they manage to get those enormous capstones up on top of the burial chambers?

South Stack lighthouse has sat proudly on a small, rocky island close to the towering sea cliffs on the north-western corner of Anglesey, shining as a lifesaving beacon for over one hundred and eighty years. Its powerful light can be seen for at least 27 miles or

44 km as the first beacon to warn trans-Atlantic sailing ships and steamers of the hazardous, rocky Anglesey coastline. Strong March winds are usual for much of the British Isles, but when we arrived to visit the lighthouse, we found the winds were at severe storm level and far too dangerous to walk down the zig-zag steps built into the cliffs. We took a quick look to acknowledge the effort we had put into visiting the place before retreating to the lee of the headland, where we investigated the site of the *Cytiau Gwyddelod* or 'Irish Huts', otherwise known as the Holyhead Mountain Hut Circles.

According to our faded blue guidebook, the huts are the remains of a settlement occupied from the second to the fourth century A.D. Although the original area would have amounted to 15-20 acres, only twenty huts remained when our guidebook was published. It was fascinating, standing amongst those ancient dwellings, trying to imagine what life would have been like back then for that hardy little community.

Those small huts, some round, some rectangular, were nestled amongst the crisp, brown bracken left from last year, which rippled in the wind. Sage green lichen clung to the irregular stones of the low hut walls beside splashes of indelible white patches from previous generations of that plant. The walls gave an insight into the individuality of the builders. Some huts looked like they had been thrown together haphazardly, with some rocks placed vertically instead of the expected horizontally while other constructions indicated the conscientious work of meticulous craftspeople.

The roofs of the circular huts would most likely have been thatched and supported by a central pole. We could make out what appeared to be hearths in the centres, while stone slabs may have been the situation of beds and seats. Could those villagers have been Irish settlers, as the name indicates, who were later driven out by the Celts? From where did they get their drinking water and food? And why live there, where the wind was often fierce and the land unsuitable for crops? Maybe it was due to the availability of metal? What tales those Hut Circles could have told.

"Here it is!" Philip suddenly called out and everyone rushed over to see what he had found; maybe an ancient body, exposed after centuries of interment? But no, Philip and Granny Lucy were searching for the *Spathulate fleawort* or South Stack fleawort. One of the rarest plants in the world, it is a sub-species of the field fleawort and is only seen on Holyhead Mountain, especially around South Stack. Philip had spotted the spear-shaped leaves of a plant they hoped would be the specimen they were searching for, or were they being optimistic? They discovered a rash of those plants, which, if they were the South Stack fleawort, would grow low and produce a burst of small, bright yellow 'suns' from a single stem. They would be in flower between April and June, roughly the same time as puffin nesting season; we were there just a little too early to see that rare plant in all its glory.

That night, as we gathered around John's campfire in the top fields, we had so much to discuss with the discoveries we had made that day. Daniel, Joshua, Timothy and Toby enjoyed helping John and Philip gather scraps of wood from around the farm, pulling out any dead wood from the hawthorn trees to drag it up to add to the fire. The cousins had been shy of each other when they first met that weekend but were now starting to relax.

27

Inspired by the exciting archaeological explorations of the afternoon, or perhaps just because they were enjoying being boys out in the wilds and up way past their bedtime, they started laughing and whooping around the fire. Granny Lucy, cheeky as ever, made a gibe at their expense, upon which Daniel stopped his frivolity and thought for a moment.

"It's hard to fly like an eagle when surrounded by turkeys," he sighed. His Granny considered that comment briefly as she warmed her hands on her steaming mug of tea before replying:

"Well, at least I am popular at Christmas!"

As the air grew colder, everyone snuggled together, wrapped in warm coats and blankets, eating hot, buttery, foil-wrapped potatoes baked in the ashes of the crackling fire. The moon rose like an enormous quartz bauble set in its phosphorescent haze and hung benevolently over the contented group as the fire sent flaming tongues of red, yellow, and orange, licking high into the night sky.

# 4 'Dig for Victory!'

"I cannot think where they have all come from; there were no weeds there before we had the land ploughed over, and now they re everywhere!" Philip complained. Our neighbour, Leslie, shook is head in commiseration as he leaned over his garden gate and ooked down at our recently planted strawberry fields. We had ound Leslie and his wife, Heulwyn, to be an amiable, reclusive ouple who lived in a small caravan at the back of *Bryn Llyn*, a small onverted cow shed and the home of Leslie's elderly parents.

"Doo! Doo!" Leslie replied thoughtfully. We had grown used to is expressions, most of which were his own rendition of the Velsh word *Duw*, meaning 'God', which seemed to cover most ecessary responses.

"The strawberries are growing well, but I have to hoe around hem regularly because of the weeds, and I can't even see the loughed area where we want to plant flowers," Philip continued with irritation. "Has that field ever been ploughed before?" Philip sked, hoping Leslie could fill him in on the history of *Ty'n Llain*.

"Oh yes!" Leslie took the pipe from his mouth and pointed it oward the strawberry fields. "Them fields were ploughed over by hy Mam and Dad during The War!" Philip was surprised.

"Did your parents own *Ty'n Llain*, Leslie?" he asked.

"It was in my mother's family for years," Leslie explained, eturning his pipe to the corner of his mouth.

"I thought you were born in South Wales?" Philip replied, trying o make sense of Leslie's revelation. Leslie jerked his head in the irection of his parents' cottage behind him.

"Mam met my Dad in South Wales before The War while he worked on the docks loading coal into the cargo ships." Philip waited expectantly for further details while Leslie continued to ean on the gate, chewing on the end of his pipe and gazing heditatively into the distance. "Fell down into the hold of one of he ships and broke his back! Doo!" Leslie added after a few more

29

moments of contemplation. "Couldn't keep his job after that. Me and my sister were born by then, so they decided to bring us back to live here."

"So, what about the field?" It was not easy trying to get the full story from Leslie, but Philip felt he had the answer to the mystery of the weeds, so he persisted.

"'Dig for Victory' they called it," Leslie stood up stiffly, stretched his back and made a grab at his flat cap, which was challenged by a sudden gust of wind. "Every farm had to have a

field or two set aside for The War effort. So my parents were sent a man with a tractor and a plough to turn over the land and given some seed *tatws* to plant. It was a hard life for them, but they had to produce a good crop to feed the soldiers or the land would have been taken away from them." Philip was quite surprised to hear that participating farmers were allotted the use of tractors at that time and wondered if they had to be tow-started like our old Ferguson 35.

"So, that field has not been ploughed since the end of The Second World War?" Philip exclaimed, returning his attention to his strawberry field. "That's over forty-five years ago! Seeds dormant in the soil for four decades, that is amazing!" He was fascinated by that information and decided he would watch to see if those 'weeds' really were a product of wildflower seeds that had lain dormant for all those years, just waiting for a plough to turn over the soil and bring them to the surface to be able to germinate.

Philip's studies at Coleg Pencraig in Llangefni were going well, which he enjoyed immensely. He brought home three thousand little peat plugs of flower seedlings in early April, including Statice, Gypsophila and Helichrysum. Row upon row of them we planted together as a family, and when I stood up to stretch my aching back, Philip reminded me of all the revenue we would make from selling the flowers in the summertime.

The colony of Black-headed gulls returned to roost in the reed beds of *Llyn Bwch* while we were planting the flower seedlings, and we were reminded of what a noisy crowd they made. They screeched, cheered, chattered and argued like a team of football supporters, but it was music to my ears as it meant spring had arrived.

To contribute to his coursework in Amenity Horticulture, Alan Savage had given Philip the assignment of designing the flower border at the college entrance. Philip thought long and hard about that assignment, and his musings reminded him of his research on the history of Anglesey. *Môn Mam Cymru*, or Anglesey, Mother of Wales, was the esteemed title by which the Island had been known for centuries. It had long been the 'bread basket' for Wales, its fertile land being considered capable of providing food for the whole country. Therefore, to make his flower border feature a fitting representation of that ancient, honoured service, he dug over the designated area and sowed cereal seeds of wheat, oats and barley. As their green shoots began to appear, Philip planted amongst them flowers grown from seed, such as one would have expected to see as natural companions to the crops in years gone by. With the azure blue of the cornflowers, the scarlet bursts of the poppies, and the fire-red pheasant's-eye with its feathery leaves, the presentation offered an appropriate welcome at the college entrance, telling the tale that Philip wanted to be remembered.

Alan Savage was delighted with the effect; however, the new age of computing had recently bloomed, with computers becoming increasingly popular and widely available. Coleg Pencraig became divided between its original purpose of teaching Agriculture and Horticulture and the new studies in computing or Information Technology. Therefore, the symbolic agricultural presentation Philip had created at the front entrance received mixed reactions from students and tutors, depending on their reasons for attending the college. Which of them would gain the victory? Time would tell.

"That ewe is not looking good," Philip commented when he arrived home one evening. "I think she is suffering from magnesium deficiency."

"How do you know?" I asked as I joined him at the kitchen sink to look through the window at the sheep in question. I had noticed her behaving rather strangely when I checked on the flock earlier in the day, but I thought nothing more of it since then.

"Well, just look at how she is staggering about and her legs are trembling," he pointed out.

"Oh, dear, she was not that bad when I saw her earlier. She does not look good, does she?" I had to admit.

"No, the symptoms of Hypomagnesaemia or Grass Staggers can come on quite rapidly," Philip explained, and his fears were confirmed as the afflicted ewe began to arch her back and then stretch her legs out in front of her. "I must do something and quickly, or she will die!" On cue, the ewe collapsed in a heap on the ground while her bewildered lamb looked on. "What do we have in the way of magnesium?" he asked urgently, and I reached hastily for the medicine cupboard. I usually kept some 'Milk of Magnesia', that old standby for upset stomachs that my mother had always administered, but there was only a drop left in the bottle. I made a mental note to buy some more.

"Epsom Salts; do we have any of that in the house?" Philip asked urgently.

"Yes, but she would not like that; it tastes really bitter." I screwed up my face at the memory of the last time I had indulged in that unpalatable product for intestinal discomfort.

"We are not talking about how it tastes here, Lynnette; we are talking about survival. She is one of our oldest ewes," he rebuked. "Please get me a funnel and a jug of warm water to dissolve the salts."

"Right, yes, funnel, jug, warm water….," I muttered, producing them as rapidly as possible. The ewe looked worryingly moribund as we approached, and her lamb skittered off to a safe distance to watch as Philip raised its mother's head, inserted the funnel into her mouth and poured in a substantial dose of the dissolved medication. The ewe opened her eyes, shook her head violently and rose to her feet. I understood her reaction to the dosing and sympathised with her. Philip was delighted and smiled broadly at the results of his ministrations, especially when she began to gallop around the paddock. Her lamb cowered against a stone wall as she thundered past while all the rest of the flock scattered in alarm. The ewe did another circuit of the paddock, and her eyes bore a crazed look as she passed us for the third time. However, the smile on Philip's face began to fade and then disappeared when she finally came to a grinding halt in front of us. She gave Philip a wild and accusative glare and abruptly dropped dead at our feet! We were shocked! We stared open-mouthed and disbelievingly at her inert form, willing her to revive, and neither of us said a word for a few minutes. We looked up at her poor orphaned lamb, and after a while of turbulent emotions, I broke the silence:

"I told you that stuff tastes awful!"

It was sad to have lost a good ewe despite our best efforts. But, with a lot of coaxing, we managed to get her lamb accepted by one of the nursing ewes. However, the vigil of checking for lambing ewes in difficulty continued throughout April. Philip had parted that morning, leaving me with instructions to keep an eye on one of the ewes he had brought down to give birth in the barn. It was a hectic Monday, with all that Mondays often bring for busy homemakers, and it was also my day for baking the cakes and bread for the week. The expectant mother in the barn seemed contented enough when I peeped in before starting my kitchen missions, so I became immersed in domesticity until after lunch when I put the two little girls to bed for their afternoon nap. That was a big mistake!

When I looked into the barn, the ewe was in distress, with only the large, swollen head of her lamb having presented. I felt enormous guilt that I had left her for so long, but I felt confident that I could help deliver the rest of the poor creature, as I had previously succeeded in similar situations. However, this lamb looked further gone than usual, its lolling tongue and puffy eyes told a sad story of hopelessness. When I attempted to slide my carefully washed and soaped hand into the birthing canal, I discovered that the neck of the lamb had also swollen to such an extent that I could not get more than two fingers inside. There was no hope of pushing the head back inside the mother to grope for the front legs, and that head was not coming any further forward without them. After about half an hour of trying, I was near to tears with self-reproach and pity for mother and lamb, so I decided that it was time to call for help.

I was relieved that Carl was home to answer my distressed telephone call. Our two families had been through some crises together and were always there for each other.

"I will be right there," he assured me and slammed down the telephone. I knew he would be with me within the twenty minutes it would take him to speed from his home in Cemlyn.

"Aaw, Lynnette," was all he said when he appeared at the barn door. I had not thought about my appearance until that moment, but I must have looked a mess, slumped in a defeated heap in the corner of the barn with straw in my tousled hair, streaks of grime down my face from rubbing away the tears and with aching arms from my efforts at midwifery. I saw the evidence in the mirror when I left Carl to do his best to help the ewe while I went to the house to make him a cup of tea and to check on Saffron and Amber. To my great delight and surprise, when I arrived back outside, he had successfully delivered a live lamb and was ready to go home. It was a victory, and I could have hugged him! Instead, I gave him a carefully-wrapped, newly-baked fruit cake as a gesture of thanks.

"Did you keep a check on that ewe in the barn today?" Philip asked that evening.

"Yes, she had a stocky little male lamb," I smiled in return, and then my conscience got the better of me, and I related the truth of the day's events. When we next met up with the Mackenzie family, Carl was still suffering from the effects of his difficult assignment, with his hand bruised and bandaged. But he bore me no reproach and laughed it off as all part of neighbourly friendship.

However, I had learned another lesson from that experience: Always have a cake baked in case of an emergency!

# 5 Mid-summer Miracles

Philip stared at the paper before him as he sat in the exam room at Coleg Pencraig, Llangefni, and his thoughts returned to the last time he was in this situation, twenty-five years earlier.

On the particular day that came back to his memory, young Philip had found it impossible to make sense of those confusing black marks on the paper and the white spaces between them that ran like rivers down the page. He had looked out of the window, past the red brick school walls with their metal railings at the fields of Funtley Hill beyond, wishing he was out there, running free, instead of sitting in the classroom with that awful eleven-plus examination paper in front of him. The teacher, Mr Thompson, had looked at him sternly from his desk just a few feet away. Philip had picked up his pencil to show willing and rubbed at his eyes in the hope of seeing more clearly, but the black marks began to swirl in an anticlockwise direction, his head swam, and he felt he would tumble from his chair with dizziness.

That day had started well enough – for Philip, that is. He had been walking up Funtley Hill, or Fontley if you talk posh, toward Funtley junior school, built like most of the houses and buildings in Funtley, from the red bricks from Funtley Brickworks, when he had found himself following the school headmaster. Mr Gilbert was a tall, dignified man with a shiny, bald head who always wore a grey suit, a crisp, white shirt, a stylish tie, and shoes polished to a chestnut brilliance. Philip quickly tucked in his shirt, then bent down to tie his shoelaces and attempted to smooth down his wayward crop of fair hair as he followed Mr Gilbert from a safe distance. He was not an unkind man but an impeccable contrast to Philip's rather wild, untidy presentation, and he had frequently commented on Philip's need to smarten up. Suddenly a seagull swooped overhead and landed a 'missile' on the top of Mr Gilbert's gleaming bald pate - Splat!

37

Mr Gilbert looked up at the sky for the offender, and the deposit started to dribble down the back of his head. Philip watched as the man wrestled with his trouser pocket and pulled out an enormous, snowy-white handkerchief to mop up the damage before looking around to see if anyone had witnessed his embarrassing dilemma. Philip had quickly turned away, pretending that he had not noticed.

As he chewed on the end of his pencil in the school examination room later that morning, Philip tried to suppress a giggle at the memory, and Mr Thompson had given him another hard stare. The examination paper was still there on the desk in front of him, and according to the clock on the wall, Philip had been sitting in that uncomfortable position for at least half an hour without even adding his name to the top of the paper. He recalled the frequent whacking with the slipper, bamboo cane or the long blackboard ruler for his 'stubbornness' during his school years, but it was not for want of trying. He had not been invited to take any more exams before being dismissed from secondary school, virtually illiterate, on the day he turned fifteen, a casualty of what was to become known as dyslexia.

Now, however, at thirty-six years old, he was a mature student. He had worked hard to learn to read and write, and this day he was determined things would be very different. The insignia 'City and Guilds of London' at the top of the exam paper meant so much to him. How he hoped he would gain some qualification or mark of achievement this time.

During that anxious week in June, Philip sat exams in Phase I and Phase II Amenity Horticulture, Phase III Agricultural Management and Phase III Agricultural Accounts. Phase I was straightforward, consisting of multiple-choice tick boxes. Phase II had questions based on maths and plant identification, which he found easy since memorizing the botanical names of plants was one of his hobbies.

Although his writing was still hardly legible, and his spelling bore scant resemblance to the English language, he had at least improved his reading skills over the years and had discovered that if he put his finger on the page, the words seemed to stop reeling. He also found it advantageous to shade the page so that the spaces between the print were less likely to turn into those unhelpful white rivers that trickled off the page and washed away the words.

A week after the final exam, Dewi, the *postmon,* arrived in his *Post Brenhinol* van. He cheerfully handed Philip one or two bills, a flyer advertising the date of the annual Agricultural Show held at Gaerwen, and a large, stiffened, brown envelope containing the anticipated exam results. After thanking Dewi and wishing him a good day, we hurried back to the kitchen with a combination of excitement and trepidation. Philip opened the envelope and pulled out three papers bearing the legend:

NATIONAL EXAMINATIONS BOARD
FOR AGRICULTURE, HORTICULTURE AND ALLIED INDUSTRIES.

He was stunned by the results. He had attained three Certificates with Distinctions and one pass with a Credit for Horticulture, Phase I, Phase II and Phase III; all achieved in only nine months!

The pleasant voice on the other end of the telephone was unfamiliar, and I rightly assumed that the man wanted to speak with Philip.

"Philip!" I called across the farm gate, "A Doctor Robert Whitbread from Bangor University is on the phone, and he wants to talk to you."

"I don't know him," Philip frowned as he came out from working in the barn, unhitched the gate and closed it behind him. "Did he say what he wanted?"

"No, just that he wanted to talk with you," I replied, hurrying ahead of him with Saffron in my arms to check on the soup I was preparing for lunch.

"Well, I never!" Philip exclaimed after finishing his telephone conversation in the hallway. "Doctor Robert Whitbread is the Dean of Science and Professor of Biology at Bangor University. He saw the article about my exam achievements in the Anglesey and Holyhead Mail. He wants me to meet with him and is inviting me to enrol at the university starting in September."

We were both stunned!

"I am amazed that you would make me this offer, Doctor Whitbread," Philip said honestly. But how can I accept entrance into the university when I left school with no qualifications?" The tall, dignified man sitting opposite Philip at his tidy wooden desk in his immaculate, roomy office at Bangor University smiled reassuringly.

"Are you referring to the Entrance Matriculation?" Doctor Whitbread responded. "Your achievements at Coleg Pencraig make you well qualified to attend the University." Philip was taken aback by those encouraging words, especially after all the years of being labelled the school Dunce. Rubbing at his moustache, he studied the man as he considered this bizarre situation as though it were a dream come true. Doctor Whitbread raised his eyebrows and smiled expectantly at Philip.

"Does the offer of studying Plant Biology with us appeal to you, Philip?" he asked.

"Very much so!" Philip nodded emphatically. "I am fascinated by plants, but right now, all I want is a good job; I really should be earning a living to feed my family." Doctor Whitbread looked a little disappointed, but he leaned back on his high-backed leather chair, fixed Philip with a kindly look and pressed his cause.

"So, do you have the prospects of such a job?"

"I have an interview next week for a job that I have long wanted. If that interview is unsuccessful, I would certainly like to take you up on your very kind offer," Philip assured him. "However, I am not in a position to be able to afford to pay for university fees, so I wonder how that would affect your proposal."

"Yes, I had considered that matter," Doctor Whitbread replied. "I believe the W.D.A. (Welsh Development Agency) financed your course at Coleg Pencraig?" Philip nodded in response. "Then you should continue to qualify for a grant from the County Council to cover all university fees. You would also receive a subsistence allowance, which you could top up with a student loan if necessary."

"That sounds very tempting," Philip admitted.

"Excellent!" Doctor Whitbread slapped his hands on his polished desktop and rose from his seat. "We must make a visit to the Head of Plant Biology, who I would assign to be your personal tutor."

Chris Marshall warmly welcomed the two men into his small, cramped room as though he had been expecting their arrival. His smile was as warm and sincere as that on the face of Doctor Whitbread.

"Do sit down, Gentlemen," he invited, gesturing to two wooden chairs before seating himself in front of what was possibly a desk hidden beneath a mound of papers, books, and an eclectic array of other stationery items. The two tutors seemed as much of a contrast as could be imagined, yet they seemed to accept their differences as though they did not exist. Chris Marshall adjusted his wire-rimmed glasses, pushed up the sleeves of his off-white linen jacket, and his eyes creased with a warm smile as he leaned forward expectantly.

"Mr Barlow is interested in our offer, but he has an interview for a job next week," Doctor Whitbread explained. "If he is unsuccessful, he would consider joining us and will let us know in

41

due course." Chris Marshall looked from one to the other and ran his fingers through his wild, white hair.

"Oh, I see," he responded.

"I am very grateful for the offer to study here, Mr Marshall," Philip quickly added, noting his look of disappointment. "It very much appeals; but I really need a job to feed my family."

"Well, for your sake, I wish you all the best, Mr Barlow," Chris Marshall replied cordially. "However, we feel that your practical experience and work ethic could be of great value to us in helping our undergraduates to be enthusiastic in their studies and to understand the practical application of what they will be learning."

"I will certainly be back in touch," Philip assured as he shook the hands of his possible future tutors and took his leave.

There was a lot to talk about over dinner that evening, and we all listened with interest as Philip recounted every detail of his interview. After all, it is not every day that one is invited to attend university!

"Would you like to take up the offer, Dad?" Daniel asked. Philip paused to think before answering while a large forkful of steak and kidney pudding dripped thick, rich, brown gravy onto his plate.

"You know how I love to learn, Daniel, and I have thoroughly enjoyed this year at Coleg Pencraig, but how can I keep your Mum in the manner to which she has become accustomed, on just a student allowance?" Philip asked, grinning at me across the table. I raised an eyebrow sardonically. He knew that coping with life on the farm on such a small income had been particularly hard that year, yet I had managed to budget our meals within a few pennies of his subsidy. Apart from trying to keep pace with my household responsibilities and the needs of the family, I had five orphan lambs and fifteen acres of sheep fields to check over daily. I had never worked so hard in my life! Philip thought it wise to change the subject.

"So, how about you, Daniel? How is 'Linda Lipstick'?" he asked. Philip had been impressed by Daniel's glamorous Welsh teacher with her crown of thick, blond curls. Daniel laughed and scooped some of the boiled nettle and cabbage into the remaining gravy on his plate.

"She is very kind; she says my Welsh is good, and I have done well in my tests," he replied.

"Yes, so she said at Parent/Teacher evening," his father agreed. "Mister Williams said you are doing very well in his History lessons too." Daniel smiled, pleased that his father was happy with him; he had always been a bright boy who enjoyed school. Joshua watched me expectantly to see what was for dessert, and he smiled broadly when the chocolate cake arrived at the table, accompanied by strawberry ice cream.

After cleaning up the kitchen and bathing the babies, ready for bed, I made up the bottles of milk for Amelia and Joshua to feed the lambs while Daniel went to help Philip in the barn. Some of the ewes had produced their lambs quite late in the season, while some had given birth to twins and would only accept one of them. Others had been elderly ewes who had lived just long enough to supply the vital colostrum to their newborn lambs and had then slipped quietly away to a much-deserved 'sleep'. As John Owen had predicted, the ultimate essential tool for any shepherd was a spade; "because sheep die!"

Mid-summer day seemed to go on a lot longer on Anglesey than anywhere else we had lived, so with the older children bathed and sent upstairs to get ready for bed, I drifted outside to enjoy the ambience of that beautiful evening. Leaning over the field gate, I watched the sparkling waters of *Llyn Bwch*, alive with the chattering and squabbling of the colony of Black-Headed Seagulls as they battled over nesting spaces. I looked back toward our house and then returned my attention to that exquisite lake, bristling with life, sound and activity, and the thought occurred to me, not for the first time, that we were missing out on a stunning view because of the lack of windows on the front of the house. Philip was so engrossed in sharpening the jagged iron teeth on the blade of the hay cutter just outside the new barn that he did not notice me watching him as he worked. I announced my presence, and he jumped at the sudden intrusion to his concentration.

"Philip, what would you think about our building an extension on the front of the house?" He looked at me blankly as though I had just dropped from the sky; I guessed he had a lot on his mind, and 'extension' was not at the top of his list of priorities. Nevertheless, it was the seed of an idea that I hoped would germinate. I decided to wander down to the strawberry field to check on the progress of those plants. Philip had made it his evening duty to hoe around them since his initial concern about the overgrowth of weeds/wildflowers that threatened to overtake them. They looked healthy enough, like rows of little soldiers proudly displaying their dark green uniforms, and to my delight, I spotted the first succulent-looking, fat, round strawberries.

The long jersey skirt I wore around the farm had often been of use for collecting flowers or garden produce, for wrapping up little lost lambs or tearful children with grazed knees, and that time, I filled it with delicious strawberries for an evening treat. Gathering up my skirt, bulging with my scarlet treasures, I smiled happily at the three little faces watching me from my bedroom window. I did not need to beckon them twice; one twitch of the head and they instantly disappeared. By the time I reached the field gate after pausing to display my harvest to Philip, Daniel, Amelia and Joshua in their pyjamas, dressing gowns and rubber boots, all assembled excitedly around me.

We all sat together on our favourite rock in the top fields with our feast of strawberries, ready to watch the sun slide down into the Irish Sea when Philip suddenly gasped.

"What is that shape in front of the sun? Is it a cloud or a mountain?" he asked as if *I* was likely to know if he didn't. "You know, I think that could be the Mountains of Mourne," he answered his own question. We looked up to see what he was staring at, and sure enough, there was a shape like the hump of a camel that we had not noticed before, silhouetted against the setting sun.

"On Ireland?" I asked, licking crimson juice from my fingers.

"It must be," Philip replied excitedly. "That means the sun does not set in the Irish Sea, as we have always thought, but behind Ireland! If we see it again tomorrow, we will know they are mountains and not clouds, which will only be viewable from here around Mid-summer evening." And yes, they were still there the following evening. According to Philip's chart of the Irish Sea, it was Slieve Donard, the highest in the Mourne Mountain Range, just over eighty miles away, to the northwest and far further than we thought we could see from our vantage point. It was another magical Mid-summer miracle.

# 6 Queen of Bones

My sister, Diane, has the remarkable ability to aspire to elusions of grandeur; tall, slim and regal, with a coronet of white/blond hair, she can command respect with just a look. Heaven only knows how she manages it since we were all raised the same way on a council estate in the Medway Towns. However, the truth is that she is extraordinarily successful at any project she undertakes. If Diane organises a garden party, a holiday or a building project, she will have the best weather and her plans will always come to fruition. Of course, there was that one occasion she would probably have liked to put to the back of her mind.......

'The Hog Roast' was meant to have been the highlight of Diane's catering accomplishments. Her garden looked splendid; not a blade of grass was out of place, and no bedraggled gladiolus was to be seen bowing an aged visage across the pristine flower borders. Perfectly pressed white linen tablecloths covered the long table on the carefully groomed patio, decorated with vases of freshly-picked roses, set amongst an array of fine china crockery. Gleaming crystal glasses surrounded decanters of ruby port and sweet sherry on silver trays while a collection of beer casks sat on the hired bar. The bouncy castle was blown up enthusiastically by several manly guests and some of the children had already claimed the first turn at dressing up in their inflated sumo wrestler outfits. Squeals of delight issued from the participants as they careered into one another, bouncing off and rolling around, laughing helplessly. Diane's husband, Michael, and his brother, Danny, set up a coconut shy and prepared a 'Lucky Dip' for any successful contenders. That proved quite popular, although they had to chase away one or two overly-zealous young lads who managed to shatter a couple of coconuts instead of just attempting to knock them off their stands.

The dessert contributions from the visitors were set indoors on the kitchen table, tempting many young fingers to 'sinfulness'. As

the hours ticked by, there was still no sign of the ma
commissioned to bring the hog roast. Diane had eventuall
managed to track him down on his mobile phone – he was in th
emergency department in the hospital, poor man. He had a
accident and Diane's hog roast was splattered somewhere acros
the M4 motorway! As ever, Diane had risen to the occasion; sh
pulled her bank card from her purse and handed it to her sister
with the nonchalant words:

"Buy something; I am going upstairs to wash my hair!" Wit
that, a marauding band of hungry ladies swarmed into the house
took control of the kitchen and produced a wonderful spread fror
whatever they could find while waiting for the 'cavalry' to retur
from the supermarket with the meat. The ensuing festivitie
proceeded well after everyone had been well-fed, with enchantin
melodies produced by a small ensemble of guitar players.

I have always enjoyed spending time with Danny's wife
Vanessa, as we share an interest in the 'holistic' approach t
health, healthful eating habits and natural medicine. Vanessa is
qualified reflexologist trained in homoeopathy while m
experience in that field amounts to no more than what I hav
learned through motherhood and much reading on the subjec
The two of us spent almost the entire afternoon discussing ou
most recent discoveries, which we related in an almost constar
and enthusiastic dialogue while working in the kitchen togethe
As the evening progressed, we absorbed ourselves in clearin
away the aftermath of the party as Mums do, washing and dryin
the dishes together. Our conversation moved on to how th
poisonous metal, lead, had been steadily removed from paint an
other products as there had been several cases of accident
poisoning over the years.

"But, it's OK; I've had all my pipes changed," Vanessa said i
conclusion to what had become a prolonged explanation of th
effects of that harmful element. I stopped drying the dishes th

48

she passed me and stared at her. I thought she appeared healthy enough as I looked her up and down, wondering how I had managed to miss such a grave health issue. After a while, Vanessa noticed that I had stopped working and jumped when she saw me frowning hard at her before looking around for a clue as to what she had done wrong. Silence reigned between us for the first time that day, and it took me a few moments to work out that she had been talking about the pipes in her *house* that she had changed! I turned my attention to Michael, who was rummaging in the fridge for more chilled beers for his guests.

"Have you had all your pipes changed, Michael?" I asked to cover my embarrassing misunderstanding.

"Yes," he replied. "Don't you just hate it when that happens?"

Carefully arranged garden lamps began to glow as the twilight succumbed to the navy blue night sky. The music grew louder to be heard above the shrieks of laughter coming from the *adults* who had commandeered the children's Sumo wrestler outfits and were now the ones bouncing off one another and rolling about with hysterical laughter while the children looked on. A magnificent firework display concluded the happy occasion, and the tired but happy guests reluctantly filtered homeward, bearing memories to last a lifetime. As always, the event was a blazing success.

So, when Diane, Michael and their two children, Georgia and Joel, visited us at *Ty'n Llain* some years later, I mentioned my plan to build an extension to the front of our house. Diane's eyes lit up with interest and enthusiasm for my cause, and I knew her input would be invaluable.

"Yes! You can do this!" she exclaimed excitedly. "You could build it from here, with a big window facing the barn." She then strode across the front garden, past the existing front door and touched the corner of the far wall. "And it could go all the way out to here," she enthused as she clambered over the low concrete block wall and gave a wide sweep of her arms to indicate the dimensions of the intended extension. "It could come out this far, and you would still have enough space to get your tractor past." I began to tingle with excitement as her enthusiasm became contagious.

"You could have a large picture window facing the lake," Diane continued. I joined her at our imaginary window, and we stood together, looking out from it at the sparkling waters of that beautiful lake and the view we would have from our new extension. "And then you could go up the stairs like this, from an entrance hall to the first floor where you could have an ensuite master bedroom that also looks out at this view."

We all watched with amusement as she marched up the proposed stairs, and then we turned to Philip to see his reaction. He watched her performance with misgiving, but I loved it. My suggestion to build an extension had not been top of Philip's list of priorities, but I felt that with now seven of us in the house, we really needed more bedrooms.

"Oh, I don't think we could afford all that, Diane," Philip countered. However Michael, a qualified civil engineer, supported her suggestions, and I was very grateful for their collaboration.

"Well, you have no mortgage, Philip; maybe you could take one out to build the extension and give yourselves a large, comfortable lounge, an entrance hall, an office and an extra bedroom. And I could draw up the plans for you," he assured. So the seed of my idea was being watered and showing signs of germination.

It was always a special occasion to have family come to visit, and our parents loved having their spare bedrooms filled with laughing, happy guests. Although she thoroughly exhausted herself, Mum always worked extremely hard to feed everyone. However, one day, Diane, Candy and I persuaded her to come with us to take the dogs for a walk, leaving the children with their fathers and Granddad. Diane and Michael's little ones, Georgia

50

(named after Granddad George) and baby Joel, were of similar ages to our two youngest, so it would need to be a quick walk around the bay between nursing times.

We all stood on the cliff top close to Wylfa Power station, ankle deep in the pink thrift peppered grassy tussocks. With our hair dancing around our faces in the bracing sea breeze like the legendary Medusa, we watched the contrast between the waves crashing against the rocks on the outer reaches of the bay and the tranquil, jade-green water within the shelter of the bay itself. Out in the Irish Sea, two enormous ships passed each other at a safe distance from the treacherous Skerries, likely on their way either to or from Liverpool.

"That is a very dangerous sea!" Diane exclaimed.

"Yes, many people have lost their lives to those scary waters," I concurred, and a shiver went down my spine at the thought.

"Has that happened recently?" Diane asked. "I mean, people drowning out there."

"Yes, I am afraid it has, and no sign of them has ever been seen again," Mum answered, shaking her head sadly.

"How terrible!" Diane took a step back and frowned. Mum stood still, closed her eyes, took a deep and contented breath and announced:

"This is my favourite thinking spot." We three sisters turned to look at her.

"You don't spend much time here then, do you?" Diane said cheekily before running off along the track, giggling and with the rest of us chasing after her.

The path we followed dipped down to a small, secluded beach, which would be fully submerged at high tide. Jill and Lucy sniffed around at the smells, searching for fish carcasses, while we 'fossickers' turned over large shells and boulders and tossed gnarled pieces of driftwood back into the receding sea waters. It was then that Diane made her shocking discovery.

51

"Oh, my days, look at this!" she exclaimed and we all straightened up swiftly and looked behind us at the sea as if expecting a tsunami to gobble us up instantly. Pointing up at a grassy ledge that hung, dry and untouched, just above the high tide level, she stared at us with wide, sky-blue eyes, her mouth opened in disbelief, and her face suddenly flushed with excitement.

"Bones!" she elaborated.

Sure enough, when we stood on a boulder to reach Diane's stately height, we could see a collection of bleached bones tucked into a niche at eye level. "Perhaps they were washed up here some time ago when the sea was unusually high," Diane suggested. Mum, Candy and I exchanged glances and wondered where we were going with this, but we did not have to wait long to find out.

"Quick! We must go home and ring the police!" she commanded and started back up the rough track to the clifftops.

"Well, I am not going to ring them," my mother confirmed quite definitely as she made to follow. I knew she would still be smarting from the last time one of her daughters had talked her into phoning the coast guard to report the man who seemed to be stuck on the rocks. I cringed at the embarrassing memory and decided it wise to say nothing in the hope that she might have forgotten which of her four daughters that might have been.

Meanwhile, Michael, a keen kayaker, had persuaded Philip's brother, Paul, to join him in the bay and offered to teach him some kayaking skills. As this was quite a new venture for him, Paul was somewhat reluctant and would much rather have stayed at Tudor Royal playing cards with my Dad and Philip. However, Michael had put so much effort into transporting his kayak all the way from Essex that Paul agreed to accompany him. So they drove together to the opposite side of the bay where they parked in the car park, lifted the kayak from the car roof and carried it across the beach to the water's edge.

"After you, Mate," Paul suggested with a grin, and Michael was more than happy to oblige. With one deft manoeuvre, he slid into the sturdy plastic seat, grasped the paddle, then, digging one end into the sand to dislodge himself, man and kayak sliced swiftly through the water and across the rippling bay. Michael was in his element; he breathed in the fresh sea air, which teased and whirled around him playfully. Small children ran in and out of the bobbing sea waters, splashing and squealing with delight. If he had noticed four women hastening across the cliff tops in the direction of Tudor Royal, he would have chosen to ignore them in favour of enjoying the pleasure of that leisurely and rewarding long-awaited moment.

Paul stood and watched Michael's display of capability with due respect and a degree of foreboding. With his lean but solid six-foot-three-inch frame, Paul was still not sure about this sport, and the thought of squeezing himself into that kayak and tripping round the bay was not high on his list of safe activities. He preferred bigger boats, and had served for some years in the

Merchant Navy as a cook/seaman, with some of that time on the E2, which had taken him to many faraway places. He had gained the Seaman's certificate, which qualified him to work on the vessel, *Pinnace*, a tough little boat built in 1955 and used to tidy up the seabed of World War II mines and bombs. More recently, the *Pinnace* was being used for military exercises and was now involved in the noble task of training helicopter pilots and winchmen for the Search and Rescue service. She was often seen scooting between her mooring in Holyhead port and the notoriously rough waters around The Skerries, especially during violent storms with a wind-beaten helicopter hovering above her. Paul's job was to guide the pilot to position over the boat to practice winching trainees up into the helicopter in the worst possible weather. How many distressed sailors have benefited from the courage and expertise learned from working with that brave and devoted team?

Like Philip, Paul had grown up knowing much about sea life from their father, who had owned boats for as long as he could remember. Michael Barlow was a skilled Yachtsman, Coxswain and navigator and had been the berthing officer when the tall ships came into Southampton in the early 1980s. More recently their father had received the rank of Sub-lieutenant in the Royal Naval Reserves and spent considerable time teaching his skills to Sea Cadets. Shortly after The Second World War, he served on the submarine *HMS Affray*, but that is a sad story to be told at another time.

The tide had receded even more during the short while that Michael, had been enjoying his excursion. Safely within the protective embrace of the solid harbour wall, colourful boats of all sizes and uses began to settle gently, awaiting the next incoming tide to lift them from their muddy beds. Returning to where Paul stood watching him, he extricated himself with expertise from his kayak and stood cheerfully holding onto it, ready for Paul to board. However, Michael's confidence in the ability of his beloved kayak to accommodate such a titan as his brother-in-law began to wane when Paul attempted to climb in like a gallon of man poured into a pint pot. As he lowered himself into the narrow opening, with his large hands gripping the sides for support, the kayak began to bulge, and Michael had visions of it splitting at the seams.

With Paul now 'wearing' it rather than sitting in it, the kayak became firmly lodged in the sand and it took the strength of both men and a few good, hard pushes with the paddle to dislodge it. Paul was away; he made two strong strokes with his paddle before a shallow wave washed gently in, and the top-heavy receptacle toppled instantly onto its side in the two inches or so of water. Thankfully Paul's broad shoulders prevented him from suffering damage from the lapping waters. Nevertheless, it was a humiliating experience, which endorsed his aversion to further attempts at mastering the sport.

"OK, Michael, I think this is not for me, thanks!" Paul exclaimed as he squeezed himself out of the kayak like toothpaste from a tube. Michael struggled to suppress his laughter at the sight of Paul with the kayak's rubber apron hanging from his waist like a lime-green mini-skirt. They decided it was time to join the rest of the family back at the house.

Back at Tudor Royal, Diane was anxious to telephone the police to inform them of her astounding find, which she was sure would answer many questions about those lost at sea.

"No *beebubs*, please just come quietly," she insisted. However, despite her strict instructions, within minutes, the undulating sirens of two police cars could be heard wailing down the main road from Amlwch. With their lights flashing, their tyres screeched as they pulled up and parked noisily at the front gate in Tudor Royal. With considerable embarrassment, my parents watched the ignominious departure of their daughter and son-in-law in a police car as they went to show the way to the scene of Diane's find while all the neighbours watched from their windows at the 'criminals' who had come to visit.

Shortly before the family returned to Essex, our 'Queen of Bones' received the following letter:

*'Dear Madam,*

*Regarding the bones you found on Wylfa Head.*

*Our Forensic department, having carefully analysed a sample of them, would like to inform you that you have discovered the skeletal remains of a sheep.*

*With thanks for your concern,*

*Yours sincerely,*

*The Amlwch Rural, North Wales Police.'*

"Oh!" Diane said with a majestic air as she carefully refolded the letter and replaced it in its envelope.

"Of course, they could always be wrong, but at least I gave them the chance!"

# 7 A Matter of Honour

"You know I have wanted to work in Cestyll Gardens for quite some time," Philip declared as he did up the top button on his blue and white striped shirt and began applying the 'hated' tie to his throat. "How I detest wearing these stupid things!" he exclaimed with irritation. I was well aware of his dislike of that obligatory piece of apparel for attending a formal function. However, that afternoon was his interview for the position of gardener for Cestyll Garden, so there was no choice but to present well. Since discovering the back gate to that outstandingly beautiful hidden garden while fossicking for mussels on the beach under the shadow of Wylfa Power Station, he had promised himself that, one day, he would work there.

Now two years later, he was pleased to see a notice in the Anglesey and Holyhead Mail for a caretaker for that miniature paradise, planted by the Honourable Lady Violet Vivian almost seventy years earlier. She was closely associated with British Aristocracy being the daughter of the 3rd Baron Vivian of Glynn and Truro. In her will, she donated her seaside estate, home and garden to the Nuclear Power Agency for the development of a new Atomic Power Station, on the condition that the garden should be taken care of and made open to the public for their enjoyment. Her house had been neglected since her death and had recently been demolished, however, with due honour to the legal requirement of that noble lady, her cherished Cestyll Garden continued to be maintained. Sadly, it was only open to the public just once a year, on the Spring Bank Holiday weekend.

The job opportunity was perfect timing for Philip since he had just finished his year at Agricultural College and had left with several good qualifications, which he hoped would assist in his application. Three other men were waiting for an interview when Philip arrived, and when it was his turn, he was shown into a room that resembled a Magistrate's courtroom. An array of interviewers

57

was seated on an elevated plinth behind panelled desks while he was instructed to sit on a low wooden chair in front of them. The lady from Human Resources and the three people representing Wylfa Power Station management bore cold, unsmiling expressions, looking Philip up and down intimidatingly as he took his seat. He had instant, 'flashback' memories of being a little lad back in the school classroom.

'Not at all the warm and friendly welcome he had received from those two kindly tutors at Bangor University,' he thought.

"Thank you for coming for this interview, Mr Barlow," the spokesman for Wylfa Power Station began. "We hear you have recently completed a Horticultural course at Coleg Pencraig with good results."

"Yes, I was given the 'Student of the Year Award'," Philip concurred. "All my qualifications and experience are listed on my application form."

"Yes, yes," interrupted the lady representing the Human Resources department. "But we want to know if you are a competent horticulturist capable of managing these grounds. Can you do the weed control and pruning proficiently? Do you understand the requirements of each type of tree and plant?" Philip took a breath and nodded affirmatively.

"Yes, I am very familiar with weed control, and yes, I have worked with the care of ornamental trees and shrubs all my working life……" he was about to elaborate when the lady representing Wylfa Power Station interrupted.

"Have you visited Cestyll Garden, Mr Barlow?" she asked.

"I have," Philip replied, remembering his first encounter with that beautiful garden, but he thought it wise not to confess that he had accessed it through the broken-down back gate.

"Are you fully conversant with the botanical and the common names of all the plants you saw there?" the lady pressed.

"I am quite familiar with most of the names at a species level, but I will probably need to do research for the specific cultivars," Philip replied honestly. The board of interviewers conferred between themselves, nodding and muttering, and then directed Philip to wait outside while they interviewed the final applicant.

"Rather intimidating, wasn't it?" whispered the other man, waiting in the waiting room after his interview.

"I'll say," Philip replied with feeling. "More like humiliating! Where is the other chap?"

"He was sent home; obviously didn't get the job." Philip and the other applicant sat in silence for the next ten minutes while Philip wondered how much he wanted this job compared to the option of attending Bangor University.

'Nuclear power is safe! Nuclear power is clean! Nuclear power is economical! Nuclear power is the answer to our future!' Such were the advertisements posted around the walls in the Visitor Centre of Wylfa Power Station when Philip had previously taken the tour, hoping to ingratiate himself with the board of interviewers.

"We have covered every foreseeable situation," the tour guide replied when Philip asked about the general safety of the plant, but what about the unforeseen? From the viewing gallery above the top of the very high reactors, everything below looked clean, bright, well-presented and well-maintained. However, he could not help thinking about recent nuclear power tragedies, such as the Chernobyl explosion that occurred four years earlier. The nuclear accident in Japan, just the previous February, was said to have been the worst since Japan had begun operating atomic power plants. Both of those events amplified his misgivings.

"Mr Barlow, please." The woman who appeared at the door to the interview room broke into Philip's thoughts.

"Best of luck!" the other men in the waiting room proffered as Philip was invited into the room and was stationed back into the 'seat of discomfort', ready to face the verdict of the 'court'.

"Well, Mr Barlow, we are pleased to be able to offer you the post of gardener/caretaker of Cestyll Gardens," announced the lady from the Human Resources department and the whole board of interviewers allowed him a perfunctory smile of congratulations.

"I am absolutely delighted to hear that!" Philip responded, smiling broadly in return. "However, I have one or two questions that I would like to ask before accepting."

"Yes, of course, go ahead," the lady invited.

"I gather from this interview that you are looking for someone experienced, knowledgeable and well qualified, for which I think you will agree I am well suited?" The team on the dais nodded in unison. "However, the salary you have advertised at £2.75 per hour is equal to the starting wage of an unskilled agricultural worker. Also, I would be working in almost as close proximity to the reactors as any other worker at Wylfa; therefore, I propose you pay me the same rate as the person who sweeps the floor at the power station."

"What? No! What do you mean? Negotiation was not on offer!" The board of *inquisitors* transformed instantly into shocked and verbose mayhem. While conferring amongst themselves, the members shot irritated looks of disapproval at Philip, who sat and watched them from his low chair. After a moment or two, Phil was asked to return to the waiting room. He stood silently for the next five minutes with the other applicants darting questioning glances at him while muffled conversations issued from the interview room.

"Mr Barlow, would you please come back inside?" the lady from the Resource Centre reappeared at the door and ushered Philip back into the room, where Philip chose to remain standing.

"We have considered your request, Mr Barlow," one of the men on the board announced with an ingratiating smile. "In view of your qualifications and experience, we have decided to offer you £2.95 per hour." There was a brief silence in the room as the people on the platform anticipated Philip's reaction. He looked back at them thoughtfully; he really wanted this job but felt insulted by their proposal, particularly considering that each of them would be earning a very respectable wage and that even the unqualified worker who sweeps the floor of the power station would be receiving more than double the amount he was being offered.

"I am sorry, but you obviously did not understand *my* offer;" Philip bravely stood his ground. "My terms are that I will give you everything you ask for, but I will only accept the equal hourly pay as the man who sweeps the floor of the power station." With that, he was swiftly escorted to the door by his elbow and the door was closed behind him. The two men in the waiting room looked at him in surprise. Philip straightened his tie, smoothed down his jacket and, regaining his composure, returned their open stare with a self-satisfied smile. He knew that one of them would accept the pitiful wage he had first been offered, but he hoped that man would treat the garden with the due care and respect the Honourable Violet Vivian had anticipated.

"Best wishes!" Philip said as he opened the door to leave. 'You will need it!' he thought as he passed through it and closed it behind him, along with his hopes of working in that beautiful Cestyll Garden.

Within a few days, Philip received a letter that read:

*Mr Barlow,*

*Re. Position of Gardener/Caretaker of Cestyll Garden.*
*With regret, we must inform you that we did not consider you to be suitable for this position.*

*The Human Resources Department for Wylfa Power Station.*

Of course, Philip had been disappointed by the outcome, but he knew he had made the right decision; apart from that, we had many summertime activities planned. News of his qualifications at the college had spread rapidly and he was asked to judge the village flower show held in the local school. It was a tricky business given the interrelationships of the village people, which required a great deal of tact and diplomacy; thankfully, he managed to achieve that without ruffling too many feathers. In fact, it was quite a pleasant experience to mingle with the local people, contributing to our acceptance in the community.

We were also pleased to attend two weddings over the summer months. Kay and Derek's Ruth made a stunning bride with ash-blond curls bedecked in scarlet flowers to match her bouquet. The ensuing reception party was held in their back garden in Red Wharf Bay, and fortunately, the day was a perfectly warm and sunny gift. Two-year-old Saffron was gaining much attention as she swung happily on the wooden swing hanging from a sturdy old tree, with her cousin, eleven-year-old Natasha, gently pushing her to and fro. They were the image of each other, those two girls; their babyhood had been an exhausting whirl of mischief and discovery and raising Saffron was like seeing Natasha growing up all over again. Natasha, with her lovely long fair hair and Saffron, with a thick toss of yellow/blond curls, almost stole the show.

"Oh, what lovely curls!" I heard several wedding guests exclaim. "Can I have some of your curls, please?" Saffron smiled and swung while we watched proudly.

The evening was still warm and pleasant after the reception, with several more hours left before the end of the sunshine that graced the month of July. So we wove our way homeward to where we were pleasantly surprised to discover our friend Glen Howard sitting and waiting for us on the front garden wall. Amelia said a gracious 'Hello' and disappeared indoors with Saffron in her arms to help prepare her for bed. Daniel and Joshua stayed beside us as we adults sat on the garden wall and chatted over a glass of sherry. The boys were in awe of Glen's movie star appearance in his black leather jacket, sunglasses and shiny black Mazda sports car. But they had well-deserved respect for his faithful Alsatian guard dog, Heinz, who lay obediently on the grass beside his master throughout our conversation.

There was so much to catch up on. Glen had been out of the country for a while in Saudi Arabia, training members of the Saudi Security organisation on how to use modern tele-surveillance systems. He had some fascinating tales to tell about his years in the Royal Air Force (RAF) and recent experiences in the Middle East. We thought it was the opportune moment to mention the extension we planned to build and to ask if he would do the electrical work for us, to which he readily agreed.

As the evening progressed pleasantly, with baby Amber nestled comfortably into Philip's chest and with the sherry doing an excellent job of relaxing the three of us, we grew silent as we watched the stunning colours of the setting sun reflected on the waters of *Llyn Bwch*. While we were engrossed in that captivating experience, Amelia crept up quietly beside me holding a mound of golden curls in her cupped hand. I stared hard at it and frowned; no thoughts or words seemed to make sense of this little offering. Joshua subsequently arrived and presented me with a pair of kitchen scissors, and that was when warning bells began to break through my bewilderment. In answer to unspoken questions,

aniel next appeared carrying Saffron with her head cocked
against his shoulder and her angelic little face looking somewhat
guilty. Then she turned her head to reveal a perfect crew cut, close
to a 'scalping', neatly sheared across at least a third of her head!
In that instant, no one moved nor spoke; it was like a moment
frozen and captured in a photograph. According to Glen, whose
acute sense of humour forced him to turn away in an effort to
stifle his laughter, my mouth then opened and closed several
times, my eyebrows rose and descended, and the colours in my
face alternated like a set of traffic lights, but absolutely no words
came out!

The following weekend as we attended the garden reception
celebrating the wedding of another couple, little Saffron found
herself sitting in her pushchair with her pink bonnet tied tightly
over her semi-bald head. My sister, Candy, our family hairdresser,
has an aversion to hats, especially as Saffron's coiffure was her
pride and joy. She whipped off the bonnet, stood stock still and
gaping when she saw what had happened, and burst into tears!
Saffron's curls grew again in time, but no one asked for any of her
curls again – by special request.

Over the remaining weeks of summer, Philip absorbed himself
in work around the farm. There was always plenty to do with the
sheep dipping and shearing, while work in the vegetable garden
was an ongoing and necessary task. So, the children learned to
work for part of Saturday afternoons, helping with cultivating the
vegetable patch and planting the little plants with Philip. We made
it an enjoyable time for them, with frequent breaks for picnics and
ice cream. It was a time of discovery that led them all to a love of
nature and the countryside and kept them far too occupied to get
bored or into mischief.

Joshua created his little den, which he called his 'Paradise',
among the Goat willows in the far corner of one of the lower fields
and persuaded me to come inside with him. It reminded me of the

dens my sisters and I had made among the brambles an
undergrowth in the wasteland near our home when we wer
children. Joshua has always liked the idea of 'secret gardens' an
has enjoyed making his own flower-filled niche wherever he ha
found himself.

Daniel was delighted when his carefully cultivated pumpkir
grew huge, orange and promising. That result buoyed his sense c
self-esteem and personal success, especially when they becam
suitably ripened and ready to eat during the chilly months c
autumn.

Amelia was excited by the abundant produce of the strawber
plantation; after all, she was made of strawberries. Philip had bee
managing a strawberry field in Kent while I was pregnant with he
and each night he would bring home not just one punnet but
whole eight-pound tray of the most delicious strawberries, mo
of which I devoured myself.

Before the end of the school holidays, it was time to harve
the abundant crop of flowers to dry and sell. We gathered th
Statice, Gypsophila and Helichrysum into small sheaves befor
they fully opened, bound them with ribbons and hung them fro

66

every available hook, stair spindle, door handle or window frame. Although we enjoyed the sweetly perfumed smell of 'outside' that permeated every room, the house quickly became filled with tiny flying bugs that had hidden in the flowers. However, the inconvenience of trying to encourage those little pests out through the doors and windows was outweighed by the joy of seeing the end product of our hard work so spectacularly displayed in shades of purple, pink, yellow, orange and white.

We never made any money from sales of those decorative bouquets, but what beautiful gifts they made for our visitors when we bestowed those colourful sprays upon them as they left our home. We wanted to teach our children the value of those sage Biblical words: 'There is more happiness in giving than there is in receiving', which seems to have paid off, provided that did not include giving away their hair!

# 8 The Freshman

"This is a Tephigram; see if you can work it out," Philip said one evening during his first week at university. He spread out a thin sheet of green graph paper on the kitchen table, the texture of a baking sheet and covered in faint, green, criss-crossing diagonal lines interspersed with small dots and tiny numbers. Between stirring the soup and mashing the potatoes, I managed a few cursory glances at the paper while he went up to wash and change and decided that if my mother looked at it, she could knit up a beautiful cardigan from the instructions set out there.

"So, did you work it out?" Philip asked when he reappeared and sat down at the table with his cup of tea.

"A Tephigram?" I questioned, handing little Amber a piece of bread as she sat, grumbling for food in her high chair.

"It's a Meteorological Tephigram; it plots the temperature and humidity against altitude," he smiled, and I knew there would be a story behind this. "Mr Sinclair Buchan; he is such a nice man and a good teacher. He gave this graph to each student with the instructions to try to understand it, and then we were to enter three sets of weather readings. 'Just come to see me in my office if you need help with this assignment,' he said."

"And did you understand it?" I asked before opening the kitchen door and calling upstairs to the children to come down for dinner.

"Not a bit! I guess I had the same confusion as everyone else, and some students were quite distressed about it," he replied. "But after about an hour of studying it, I decided the test was less about assessing how intelligent the students might be and more about how prepared we would be to seek help so as not to quit the course. So I picked up my paper, went to his office under the Memorial Arch at the university entrance and asked him to explain it.

"What did he say then?"

"He was quite happy to explain to me how it worked: A Meteorological Tephigram is used to plot altitude, temperature, air pressure and relative humidity all on the same page; with that, the height and base of the clouds can be estimated."

"So, do you think you passed the first test?" I asked.

"Taking up his challenge and going to his office to let him know that I had rumbled him may have helped me gain a few points. I told him, 'I know what this test is really about, and I want you to know that I am *not* going to drop out of university; I am going to stick this out, and I will be back here in your office every day if that is what it takes until I completely understand!'"

"Was he all right with that?" I asked, a bit taken aback by Philip's cheek and wondering if he would be kicked out of the class so soon.

"He laughed and said he thought I would do just fine."

"Well done! I am pleased to hear that he has a sense of humour."

"What is my alternative? I must see this through; if I drop out of university, there is no job for me, and I do not intend to go on the dole and sit here expecting the rest of the country to pay me to do nothing."

It took Philip about an hour to travel daily to Bangor, a small city on the northern end of the Menai Straits. He was impressed with the high standard of learning expected at the university; the founders were Welsh slate miners who wanted their children to have a better future, so they had sacrificed so much to ensure the establishment of the university during the 1880s. And here he was, a hundred years later, amongst the recipients of those benefactors. So a new strain of vocabulary started to invade our home, with words such as 'apical meristems', 'amphiboles' and 'pyroxenes' all explained in detail. When Philip set out graphs or technical papers on the kitchen table to enlighten me on what he had learned, I usually needed to arm myself with a cup of tea and a packet of biscuits to mop up those moments when I had absolutely no idea what he was talking about. I got through a lot of tea and biscuits.

As there are many highly renowned universities in Britain, Bangor needed to carve out a good reputation for itself; therefore, it focused on the natural resources of its location and culture. At that time, the only other university offering courses in Ocean Sciences was Southampton; Bangor and Aberdeen offered Forestry, which along with Reading, were the only other universities specializing in Soil Science. Bangor University also returned to its rich cultural Celtic roots, focusing on Language, History, Poetry, Music and Art, mainly taught in English, but with many courses available in *Cymraeg* (Welsh). Generally, Philip found the professors and tutors to be very pleasant and accommodating. They evidently loved their subjects and thoroughly enjoyed teaching them, although perhaps some would have preferred to be working on their favourite research projects.

71

Professor Tony Jones taught Geology and was clearly aglow with warranted enthusiasm for his topic. With the Snowdoni Mountain range so close and the fascinating formations of th varied and complex Anglesey geology to be explored, there coul not have been a better location to indulge in his passion. Phili found Professor Jones informative, understandable an entertaining; with his wild, 'outdoorsman' appearance, fu red/blond beard and gruff voice, he considered him Bango University's answer to the well-known botanist David Bellamy During the first week of Philip's course, Professor Jones gave th students a Geology assignment; mineral classification was th topic, involving identifying small rock samples.

"You will not be judged on the quality of your handwriting, bu it would be useful if it were legible," Professor Jones assured Phili with a measure of sarcasm before a three-hour practica examination. Philip had never understood the reason for h lifelong struggle to read and write legibly, leading to his having le school virtually illiterate. The results were posted on the notic board outside the Geology classroom a week after the exam Some students rejoiced when they saw their results, while othe walked away wearing smug smiles or a look of disappointmen Hoping he would not be among those who had failed the exam Philip looked closely at the notice board and saw a strange symbo written against his name that he had never seen before.

"Hey, everyone; I got a squiggle and a dash!" he announce "Does anyone know what that means?" Donna, one of the othe mature students, stepped forward to examine her results.

"That stands for 'Alpha-minus', Philip, and it is a very goo mark," she assured him. Philip was shocked; although he ha received pleasing results at Coleg Pencraig, he never expected t receive a mark like that at university!

Professor Jones' lectures were always well attended, and h would start each session with a classical quotation, calling upo the works of such Greats as Shakespeare, Socrates and the like. He would conclude his lectures with a difficult research assignment as homework for the students. So Philip found an appropriate saying, wrote it in his neatest handwriting and placed it on the rostrum before Dr Jones took his station before his audience.

"What's this?" Professor Jones frowned as he unfolded the paper and silently read what Philip had written. "Who put this here?" he asked, and Philip raised his hand to confess. Professor Jones read the saying aloud:

"'To the making of many books, there is no end, and much devotion to them is wearisome to the flesh.' Did King Solomon really write this?" He looked directly at Philip, who nodded affirmatively. "Philistine!" stated Professor Jones with a sardonic smile and continued his lecture.

Dr Chris Clidden, teaching Genetics and Evolution, proved to be a sensible and understanding man. Philip was concerned that these obligatory lessons would clash with his own conviction of there being a Creator, so he asked for a private meeting to discuss the matter.

"You know it takes more faith to believe in Evolution than Creation," Dr Clidden replied. Philip was surprised to hear such a statement from that learned man.

"Sorry, I don't understand what you mean," he replied.

"Well, look at it like this, the evolutionary theories I learned twenty years ago are quite different today and I suspect that in another twenty years, what I am teaching you today will be outdated. So if you put absolute faith in the current teaching, you are a fool!" Dr Clidden seemed satisfied to see the astonishment on Philip's face at his response.

At the outset of his lecture on the subject the following week, he made the firm statement: "Many who are here today will have their own ideas on the Origin of Life; my job is to teach you the currently accepted Evolutionary theory. You do not have to believe it, but you will be expected to know it." Philip appreciated his honesty and decided to like and respect the man. Dr Clidden was true to his word in not expecting a compromise of personal beliefs to pass the course.

Tall, slim and fit, Dr Adrian Bell was an energetic and animated tutor, possibly in his early fifties, with large eyes set in an angular face. Lecturing on Plant Form, Botany, Biology and Forestry, Dr Bell was passionate about the beauty and mathematics found in the branching patterns of plants. The patterns conformed to mathematical rules, including the Fibonacci series and the 'Golden Ratio', he explained. To Philip, this helped confirm his belief in a Creator. Dr Bell loved to use photographs of his excursions to French Guiana, South America, with the French botanist Francis Hallé of the French National Research Institute, where he would spend his time in the upper canopy of the tropical rainforest. He worked with a specialist team cataloguing the diversity of plant, animal,  bird and butterfly species found there to form a case against those industries responsible for destroying their natural habitat. Dr Bell's photographs were projected onto a large screen, showing a gigantic, brightly coloured, inflatable raft-like contraption with mesh flooring for the study of orchids growing in the crotches of the upper branches of the trees. The raft was dropped into place in the treetops by an enormous gas-filled balloon, then secured and anchored with ropes. The researchers used the ropes to climb up to the raft in the canopy daily and then abseiled down again.

Philip was entranced with those adventures, reminding him of the thirst for exploration he had indulged in as a small boy, growing up in the ancient Forest of Bere in Hampshire. He learned that the branches of different species always followed a specific pattern for that particular tree type, as though following a code written inside each of them. When Adrian Bell quoted the work of Francis Hallé on this subject, Philip was tingling with excitement since never before had he been able to explain his personal observations. A whole new world was beginning to open up to him, and he felt like the proverbial 'round peg in a round hole'.

Unfortunately, his slow writing speed hindered his studies, and he could not even read his own notes, so he decided to sit right at the front in the lecture rooms and focus on listening carefully to each presentation without note-taking. Quite soon after starting at university, three of Philip's tutors asked why he had not previously disclosed that he suffered from dyslexia and advised him to get along to the Dyslexia Unit. However, as dyslexia was not widely understood then and was virtually unknown while Philip was a schoolboy, the stigma of being labelled with a 'condition' sounded insulting and offensive. So he felt it was just another way of being told that he was a stupid and worthless 'dunce', and I got to know precisely his feelings when he came home at the end of that day.

"They say I am dyslexic and want me to go for tests!" he announced before even taking off his coat. "And I was just beginning to enjoy myself at the university. They are all the same; I wish I had never started this course!" Oh, dear. He must have been stewing over that word all the way home, and it looked as if it was threatening the hope of a peaceful weekend.

"Philip, do you know what dyslexia is?" I asked in an effort to calm him as I pulled the kettle across the top of the stove to make him some tea. "Our nephew, Hadleigh, has been diagnosed with dyslexia and is receiving special remedial lessons to help him improve his reading and writing. Now you know he is not stupid, don't you?" The memory of a recent conversation I overheard rang in my ears:

"Are you *sexic*, Joshua? I am; I have to have *sexic* lessons." I had nearly driven off the road, listening to the conversation between the little boys in the back seat as I transported Paul and Candy's Hadleigh home on the route to Bull Bay. In the rear-view mirror, I could see Joshua staring at him.

"Why do you need to do that?" he asked.

"'Cos I can't read and write," Hadleigh replied as though that answered all questions and then turned back, unfazed to watch the passing scenery.

Still aggravated, Philip soldiered on without going for the test for a few more weeks; however, he could not possibly have known just what an impact the results would have on him when he did submit to the test. Meanwhile, he had access to the university computer room, where each student had a keyboard connected to a monitor with a dark-coloured screen. It was a large, chunky machine with a bulbous black back, like an old television that showed only text and linked to the main-frame *Vax* computer. Unfortunately, the orange letters and the flashing cursor against the black screen often caused him to experience nausea and dizziness. However, on the plus side, albeit a one-fingered job at the outset, he could write his findings using the keyboard with this strange new technology, even being able to read what he had written.

Professor A.J. Green, a world expert on Mosses and Liverworts, was concerned about Philip's aversion to note-taking and persistently encouraged him to do so. Philip just shook his head and continued listening attentively to the lectures. He has an incredible photographic memory, a gift that proved advantageous at exam time when the students were instructed to leave their notes outside the examination room. Philip found the lectures by Professor Green fascinating, with the diversity of moss species being a frequent source of conversation around the table in the evenings.

"Did you know...?" The children listened raptly as Philip related the contents of his day's absorbing lectures, followed by detailed descriptions of the formations of his latest botanical discoveries. When it is time for a fern to distribute its spores, this is what happens...." he explained one evening before demonstrating in a way they could understand. Wrapping a small parcel of dried rice in a piece of tissue, he tucked it into his curled fingers and then 'ping!' it was launched into the air, showering rice over the table. Several pairs of eyes darted glances at me to see what I would say about the 'forbidden' behaviour of throwing food at each other at the meal table, but I made no issue on that occasion, deciding it was all for a good cause.

"I went for an examination today for dyslexia," Philip announced the minute he walked through the door one Friday evening. I stopped setting the table for dinner and stared disbelievingly at him.

"Really?" I asked; I was beginning to doubt that he would ever do it. "How did it go?"

"It was the hardest three hours of mental exercise I have ever experienced!" he replied as he slumped into a chair, shaking his red head and sighing deeply. "They tested my knowledge and coordination abilities using puzzles, IQ tests, writing, reading, and lots of questions to see my response. It was really hard!"

"So, what was the result?"

"I should receive the results next week," he replied.

It was a very long week, and I hoped daily to hear that he ha received his results. I knew how he had agonized over the matte and how long he had been bewildered about his scholasti inadequacies. The moment of truth arrived as promised by the en of the following week; Dewi, the *postmon,* sped up our lane in hi red *Post Brenhinol* van, and I intercepted him on the driveway. H always bore a broad smile, rain, wind or shine and a thick thatc of almost black, shiny curls atop his ruddy face.

"Something special here then?" he suggested as he proffere an official-looking, bulky letter bearing the insignia 'Bango University' before adding one or two more envelopes to m collection, which could only have been the inescapable bills.

"I hope so," I replied with a smile that I hoped would mask m anticipation. When Philip arrived home, the official-looking lette was lying on the table in front of where he usually sat. I was itchin to open it, but I managed self-control.

"Go on then; what does it say?" I asked. Philip took a knife fror the drawer, sliced swiftly through the top of the envelope, and h brow furrowed as he examined the sheaf of papers inside. hovered busily around the kitchen, frequently glancing to see if h had finished it, and when he finally looked up at me, his face wɛ inscrutable.

"Do you want to read it?" he asked. I grasped the missiv enthusiastically, in case he changed his mind and made a space ɛ the table in order to examine it. I read it right through once an then started again from the beginning.

"This says your IQ level is virtually off the scale, Philip!" announced, although it was not really a surprise to me.

"'In the very superior range....verbal attainments should hav been well in advance of chronological age level.....Regarding th score on the spelling test, however, writing and spelling skills a *about equal to elementary school level. From the Bangor Dyslexia Test results, it is the opinion that Philip's functioning shows a recognizable dyslexic pattern, and this disability is likely to have produced school progress difficulty even though he is an intellectually bright pupil. Philip is an extremely gifted man who suffers from severe dyslexia. He will be awarded a personal computer for home use and will be given all necessary considerations for his condition to assist him in his studies at Bangor University.'"*

Philip watched me closely as I read the report aloud and a slight smile quivered on his lips, betraying the deep sense of inner relief he felt from the results of that analysis. After all the years of bewilderment and subsequent persecution, he finally felt understood and vindicated. He was not stupid! Tears formed in his eyes and streamed copiously down his cheeks.

I rose from the table and hugged him.

# 9 Smack a Rat

"I heard rats in the barn again, Philip," I informed him one evening in December.

"Oh, no," he groaned. "They will be in the oat straw; I will deal with it at the weekend. It would be helpful if Dinky Doo gave us some assistance there, but she is not interested." I honestly did not blame her; I would not feel inclined to take my chances with a hoard of rats if I were a farm cat.

Our friend, Brian, from *Rallt Uchaf*, was still managing his farm while he and Petula had been renovating the Gadlys Hotel in Cemaes Bay. However, the field he had devoted to growing oats was too small to warrant hiring a combine harvester, so he had cut and baled the oats without threshing them, and his sheep loved it. We were pleased to say the oat straw was also a definite winner with our sheep when Philip brought home a sample to test on them. So he had ordered a hundred bales and had stacked them in the hayloft of the new barn with the help of his brother, Paul. What Philip had not accounted for was that the oats would also appeal to other, uninvited creatures, a situation that needed dealing with as soon as possible. Before the weekend arrived, Philip had some distressing news to relate that galvanized him into action.

"One of the farmworkers at Coleg Pencraig died this week," he announced and shook his head mournfully. "He was only a young chap too; they said he contracted *Leptospirosis* from rats on his farm." My face must have drained at that awful news, and my thoughts rapidly moved to our barn and the deadly beasts that had invaded it. I had heard the shocking story of a woman who had died after drinking from an unwashed can of fizzy drink. The can came from a warehouse riddled with rats, which had urinated freely and contaminated all the stock. Since hearing of that tragic account, I was always careful to wash all cans before opening them.

"OK, OK, I will deal with it this weekend, I promise," Philip reassured me when he saw the look of fear in my eyes.

After lunch the following Saturday, Paul and Candy arrived from Amlwch with their children, Natasha and Hadleigh, to give us moral support. As we were two sisters married to two brothers, our children bore such a resemblance to each other that people were often confused about which of the cousins belonged to which parents. We had always lived near each other, shared the same friends and swapped hand-me-downs according to the ages and sizes of the children. Whenever one family moved home, the other also moved to be closer to them, and here we were again, living just a few minutes away from each other. Paul and Candy's family lived in their newly renovated clifftop bungalow near Bull Bay, overlooking the Irish Sea. Our family lived on our little sheep farm near the top of Mynydd Mechell, and our parents lived halfway between us in Cemaes Bay. It was a perfect arrangement.

So, our formidable band of 'rat smackers', along with our sheepdog, Jill, for protection, prepared to evict those verminous invaders. The intrepid troop approached the barn, dressed in 'combat gear' of balaclavas and rubber boots and armed with improvised weapons of farm implements.

"Just a minute," Paul said, stopping as they reached the door to the barn. "Give me some of that baler twine; I know where those pests like to go!" And he bent down and bound the twine tightly around his trousers at the ankles. Philip knew well what Paul was referring to; it had happened while they were working together on an old threshing machine in Hampshire...

Simon Collins was a hard-working farmer who owned a two-hundred-acre farm near the pretty village of Droxford. His full-set of bushy, black beard and moustache, with heavy, dark eyebrows under a thick, flattened fringe, made him appear more like an intense naval captain than a farmer. Nonetheless, he was an enterprising person who had started building up his business as a outh by collecting and selling bundles of kindling wood, and he vas now a wealthy man. The variety of wheat Simon was ultivating on his farm was an ancient long-straw type, hollow-temmed and specially grown for thatching. He owned two efurbished antique McCormick reaper binders, adapted to be ulled by his modern John Deere tractors. They were remarkable nachines that replaced the manual work of men, women and hildren of previous times. Reaper binders had been virtually hased out by the 1950s and replaced by the more modern ombine harvester. However, these nodern machines cannot produce the wheat reed with the required straight, ndamaged form necessary for natching the roofs of the charming ottages of southern England. Simon's nachines cut, bound and spat out the neaves of wheat straw perfectly undled and tied. The wheat sheaves vere then stacked by hand into tooks' to dry thoroughly before being aded onto a flat trailer. They were nen taken to the large, open-sided arn and arranged into a 'rick' rmation with the outer sheaves arefully arranged in diagonal rmation to keep the rain from penetrating them.

The event that Paul referred to was an exceedingly cold inter's day, below minus six degrees. The ground was frozen ock-hard, the mud on the farm track had dried to a fine powder, nd the water in the puddles had evaporated, leaving a crunchy hite layer of ice over the hollows. Not a breath of wind stirred te beautiful, spiky, white hoarfrost decorating the leafless oak nd ash trees. It was so cold that the two John Deere tractors, with their trailers full of wheat straw bales for sale, got no further than the farm gate when they both stopped dead. The diesel in the tanks had congealed and turned to wax, blocking the fuel lines. So Simon had to quickly drive to town in his car to purchase some special 'anti-freeze' to thin the diesel, thus enabling them to continue their mission.

Philip and Paul worked that morning on the 'William Foster' threshing machine, formerly powered by a steam traction engine. At this time, however, it was driven by a powerful old Fordson Super Major tractor that would have initially displayed attractive bright blue paintwork on its body and bold scarlet red on its wheel hubs. However, through years of work in all weathers, it was a dull representation of its former self, covered in pigeon droppings from being housed under a beam in the barn. A shiny steel pulley on its side turned the long, stiff canvas belt that flapped up and down as it drove the main drive wheel of the threshing machine. Paul's job was to stand high on the rick, close to the underside of the barn roof and toss the sheaves of wheat with his pitchfork down onto the threshing machine platform. Then the men on top of the threshing machine would cut the sisal twine from the sheaves and feed them steadily into the reed comber where two long and spikey, counter-rotating steel cylinders whirled rhythmically at a dangerously high speed.

The machine combed out any bent or broken straws and threshed the ears of wheat to release the golden grains, which originally bounced down a wooden chute and into hessian sacks at the front. At this time, however, the grains were lifted to a modern grain trailer by a spiral auger. On the side of the thresher was a powerful blower to winnow away the chaff to burn later. The machine deposited weed seeds into a separate hessian sack on its side as poultry feed, particularly for pheasant hatcheries. At the rear, Philip's job was to rake all the bent and broken straw and feed it into a modern baler for selling as ordinary bedding straw.

84

for livestock. Then he would catch the tightly bound bundles of the straight and valuable wheat reed that rolled off the machine, which he then stacked neatly onto a trailer to be stored ready for sale to the thatchers. The threshing machine tied the bundles using two twisted cast iron fingers that would rotate and cut the string of the tightly tied reed, all mechanically. Philip marvelled at that technology, invented over a hundred years earlier; it was a Victorian engineering wonder!

The rick upon which Paul was working was a haven for wildlife, such as is often found amongst various cereal crops. So he was just about to dig his fork into one of the sheaves when he noticed a

family of tiny harvest mice snuggled into a meticulously constructed little nest. That gentle giant of a man bent down and cupped the miniature woven basket containing the ginger-coloured mother, father and little naked babies in his great hands. He carefully carried them to the safety of a quiet and undisturbed corner of the barn. The men working on the machine started shouting ribald comments at him for having deserted his post and leaving them without wheat sheaves to process. But Paul ignored the insults, climbed back up onto the rick and quietly continued the repetitious job of pitching the wheatsheaves.

About ten minutes later, above the rhythmic whirring of the threshing machine, Philip heard a high-pitched 'girly' shrieking coming from the rick, and when he turned to look, Paul was skipping about like a Morris dancer on top of it. Philip thought his brother had gone crazy, especially when he started tugging at his belt and pulling off his trousers! All the men working on the threshing machine stopped working and stared at him agog.

No one but Paul ever saw the rat that had run up the *inside* of his trouser leg, but he was to remember that experience for years to come!

Years later, on that winter day in the barn at *Ty'n Llain,* we all burst into laughter after Philip related his story. He found it hard to finish it due to intermediate hysterics, with tears streaming down his face at the memory. Everyone decided to lash baler twine around their trouser legs, just in case!

"Right, 'men'," Philip commanded when everyone had finished their rat-prevention undertakings. "I will go up top and throw down the bales one by one, and if any rats run out, you can smack them. All ready?" And with no more ado, he climbed cautiously up the ladder leading to the hayloft, where he began tossing down the bales to the carefully cleaned and swept concrete floor below.

"Fifteen...sixteen...seventeen...scream!"

Sudden pandemonium erupted as two rats scurried out from the oat bale and made a dash for the barn door with several 'killing machines' and a dog running around, biting, barking, smacking the ground wildly or just yelling loudly, depending on their age, capacity or conviction. Paul managed to immobilize one and Jill the other. There were still more than eighty bales to go, and who knows how many more rats there were in the hayloft! Six more rats were swiftly dispatched, and as the minutes ticked by, Philip was getting closer to 'rat headquarters'. His eyes flashed keenly over the remaining bales, with his rubber boots hardly emitting a sound as he crept closer and closer to his quarry. With one skilful flick of the wrists, he grabbed the last two oat bales, hurled them down to the floor below, and three cornered rats scaled the sheer concrete block walls, escaping under the eaves of the barn roof.

"What a waste!" Philip lamented several times that evening as we two families sat huddled in our blankets, drinking mugs of hot chocolate outside the barn and watching a hundred bales of oat straw lighting up the evening sky, popping and spitting as they burned. "It was such good stuff too! But I could not allow the sheep to eat it after the rats had run all over it, or they could get *Leptospirosis* and abort their lambs."

"'Course they would," Paul nodded sagely and raised his eyebrows at me as though he knew exactly what Philip was talking about. Paul was more a constructive 'doer' than a studious academic; I often thought they made a perfect team and were as loyal a pair of brothers as they could have wished for.

"If I had been allowed to keep those owl holes, we would not have had this problem; the barn owls could have picked the rats off easily before the situation got out of hand." Philip had never stopped smarting about the false accusation that the owl holes he had built into the walls above the arched barn door were crosses on an aspiring chapel.

"But they make a nice bonfire, Philip," Candy attempted to soothe the moment with a positive comment.

"Yes….." Philip heaved a sigh. "But you try telling my hungry sheep that, Candy."

The night sky darkened, and an icy chill settled on the surrounding fields. Daniel stole the odd glance at his uncle and giggled at the memory of his father's story while Philip and I looked around at that precious collection of family. We were an inseparable team of mutual supporters who loved each other dearly. The reflection of the firelight flickered on our faces as we snuggled our children close against the winter air and lost ourselves in our own thoughts. Not the least of which was that, somewhere, skulking in the undergrowth, were three toxic rats!

# 10 Lose Some, Win Some

"Don't put your shearlings to the *tup*, Philip." After losing several underdeveloped and spindly-legged lambs that winter, we vowed never again to ignore the sage advice from Mr Cledwyn Davies from Bethesda, from whom we had acquired our flock. Although those year-old ewes were physically capable of producing offspring, they were still adolescent-minded, and some made hopeless mothers. Sometimes the young ewe would turn in total bewilderment to examine the little woolly bundle that had just dropped from her rear end. She would sniff it, but when the tiny creature whimpered and staggered to its feet, she would jump in alarm and retreat to the far side of the birthing pen. However, the ewe would usually be so engorged with milk, which compelled her to allow her young offspring to feed, and gradually, they would bond.

Perhaps I became overly self-confident in my midwifery skills during those early days of my lambing experience, so there were times when my intervention was more of a hindrance than a help.

"Come on, lady, you can do this," I reassured the young ewe as I leaned over her wooden pen in the barn on that brisk spring day. She was in the final stages of labour, and I empathised with her. "Let's get this over with," I suggested as she lay down again on the fresh scattering of straw. The snowy-white head of her lamb had appeared, and its little hoofs were tucked up underneath its chin, just as they should have been. The ewe was doing well and there seemed to be no problem, but she was panting and pushing hard with the next contraction, and I was breaking out in a sweat just watching her, so I decided to give her a helping hand. However, the moment I clambered over the fencing and my feet touched the floor inside the pen, the crazy young mother leapt up and dashed, helter-skelter around its perimeter, smacking the head of her poor, helpless little lamb against each side of the enclosure. I

89

hastily retreated, and the lamb dropped to the ground; however its skittish mother seemed unaware of the presence of the new little life that now shared her space. She continued to buck and charge around as if the whole world was against her, thereby managing to trample her newborn lamb, damaging its delicate little legs. I was devastated!

Lamed and rejected by his juvenile mother, Snowy became my new 'baby'; he was the most adorable, fluffy white lamb and he even wore tiny disposable nappies. We took turns feeding him and I set up a bed for him in the kitchen beside the Rayburn. He seemed to appreciate being part of the family, contributing to the mealtime conversations to make his little presence known. As he grew a little older, I would take him out into the field and lay him propped up against the stone wall where I could watch his interaction with the other lambs from the kitchen window. He seemed happy enough bathing in the warm sunshine, but like a mother taking her child for his first day at nursery school, I willed the other lambs to accept him. Some of them would give him a cursory inspection, but, on losing interest, they would gallop away on their sturdy little legs. Snowy lasted for a few anxious months and I came to treasure that little darling, but then sadly pneumonia took him due to his inactivity. We were learning some painful lessons.

Snowy was not our only dependent lamb; we bottle-fed five others that year that were either orphaned or rejected by their mothers. They would all follow me around the farm perimeter as I checked for labouring ewes, and we would call to each other as we walked. I realized I was becoming absorbed in lamb language when baby Amber would whimper, and I would bleat back at her in return.

It was becoming a comparatively rare experience for me to take time out from working on the farm, especially during the lambing season; plus, I was stranded since Philip needed the car

90

for his daily trip to the university. So, it was a real treat when our builder's wife, Christine, also from the south of England, offered to take me out with our two little girls. I dressed up in one of my best warm dresses, ready for my trip out, but I was somewhat concerned about our Suffolk ewe, Tag, who had always been an excellent mother, and now that she was nearing the time to give birth, I did not want to be too far away. So, we decided to stay more local and take the short walk across the fields to visit Dave and Molly at *Ty'n Gorse*.

"Would you please watch Saffron and Amber for just a few minutes before we leave, Christine?" I asked as soon as she poked her head inside the back door. "I am all ready, and Amber is in her pushchair; I just need to give one more check on our Tag."

"Of course I will," Christine replied, all smiles, and her lovely clear blue eyes lit up as she sat Saffron on her lap and watched me don my padded purple jacket and Philip's tweed hat.

"I must make sure I wear this hat; it doesn't exactly suit the rest of the outfit, but it goes with the job," I said cheerily and slipped out through the door. Tag was lying on her side on the ground in the top fields when I found her; she was pushing hard, and the dark head of her lamb had emerged entirely. Its long black ears flopped pathetically over its closed eyes, and I regretted leaving her for too long before checking on her. Although Tag was tame since she had been the pet lamb of our friends, Geoff and Yvonne, she was usually quite independent when it came to lambing. As I approached her, she struggled to her feet and blundered off a few yards before lying down again and heaving. In her incapacitated state, I could examine her lamb for signs of little feet, but to my dismay, they had not presented. Tag staggered to her feet again and repeated her previous performance; I stalked her until she laid down, gasping and panting, and then I slipped my fingers into the birthing canal. One little bony knee was lodged hard against the wall of her pelvis, and I managed to free it by cupping the hoof in

91

my hand to prevent it from scratching her inside. I gave it a firm but gentle tug, and the lamb stretched its foreleg out; I was relieved to see it was still alive.

Tag grunted, rose from the grass and walked away, only managing a few feet before lying down again and straining hard. I could have done with some help to keep her restrained, but it was too late to call on our neighbour, Leslie, although I was sure he would have obliged. Still, I managed to keep her on the ground by sitting lightly on top of her and then repeated my delivery method with the lamb's other leg. So, now two long, black legs protruded from underneath the head of the listless creature. I was grateful that my dear midwives had never resorted to that tactic while aiding me to deliver my babies!

I thought Tag could manage from here, but no, for all her pushing, straining and gasping, the lamb was huge and quite stuck. As Tag rose again and started to walk away, I grabbed those two little legs as delicately as possible, dug my heels in the ground, and then sheep and shepherdess performed a 'tug of war' for the life of the little one....and I won! The lamb slid out and dropped onto the grass, and so did I. Sitting there for a few moments to regain my breath, I watched as Tag turned and began to whicker to her handsome, stocky lamb, licking him reassuringly as he responded with his healthy calls back to his mother. Could anything be more rewarding than saving a young life that would otherwise have meant digging another grave?

"Give me five minutes to get ready please, Christine?" I requested as I opened the back door with bloody gunge all over my dress and hands and with Philip's tweed hat cockeyed over my bedraggled *coiffure*. Oh, the joys of being a farmer's wife! Christine took one look at me and laughed.

"What has happened to you, girl?" she asked. "What would our friends in the South say if they could see you now?" It was true; as

I eyed my presentation in the mirror, I had to admit that this 'townie' was becoming a country lass!

As if we did not have enough already going on around the farm, we were asked to adopt a pregnant goat. Her owners were moving from their farm to a townhouse and were desperate to find a home for her; they assured us that she would make an excellent milking goat once her kids arrived.

"What do you think?" Philip asked me at dinner that evening. "Have you ever milked a goat before?"

"Heavens, no," I replied, surprised by his question. "I am a 'townie', remember. The nearest I ever got to any activity like that was being a milk monitor at school, distributing those little third-pint glass milk bottles and straws to the rest of the class."

Of course, as a little girl, I knew just where milk came from. It appeared as miraculously as *manna* on the front doorstep every morning in pint glass bottles, wearing gold, silver or red foil tops and often with tiny holes pecked out of them if the bluetits got to them first. On those bitingly cold winter mornings, when the icy fingers of 'Jack Frost' etched jagged patterns across the window panes, the cream on the bottles of gold top would congeal and rise about two inches, with its little golden cap perched on top. It made the perfect ice cream.

"Well, I could help you milk her in the evenings, but you would need to do it every morning," Philip stated as if the matter was all done and dusted.

I seemed to be in a reasonably good routine with my other responsibilities, and I had to admit that it would be nice to add the role of milkmaid to my range of farming skills. I began to picture myself proudly presenting a bucketful of fresh, creamy milk for my family to enjoy along with those wholesome bread rolls and other home bakes.

"What have they called her?" I asked, and Philip smiled on seeing a sign of my acquiescence.

"Jan, after the Mother-in-law," he replied, and his smile grew wider.

Jan's owners had already packed up and left for their new address when we arrived with the trailer to pick up the latest addition to our smallholding, and the deserted farmyard had the atmosphere of a Wild West ghost town. The wind rattled between the farm buildings, and we half expected to see the odd tumbleweed rolling past.

"Did they say where she would be?" I whispered as though some ruthless gunslinger might have been hiding behind one of those creaking wooden doors that swayed and snapped shut with each dusty swirl of the wind.

"They said to call out her name, and she would meet us here," Philip whispered back and looked around with his eyes narrowed against the noonday sun.

"Go on then; you had better call her," I suggested.

"You do it; she might respond better to your voice," Philip countered.

"Oh, all right," I cleared my throat and called out her name. "Jan, are you there?" It seemed rather silly to try to communicate with a goat that way, and Philip gave me a sideways glance, which told me he was thinking the same thing. Not surprisingly, there was no answer.

"I think you have to do it louder," Philip scratched at his beard as we looked around for signs of her approach.

"COOEE! JAN, you can come out now," I shouted, and my words echoed eerily off the walls of the buildings surrounding us. Nothing! No sign of life rewarded me for my efforts, and then,

94

ithout warning, Philip put his fingers to his mouth and gave a eafeningly shrill whistle. I jumped at the sudden and unexpected trusion into that empty establishment and gave him a hard stare. /e waited tensely, not knowing from which direction our quarry rould arrive. And then we heard the jangling of a chain and the ow, heavy shuffle of hooves scraping ominously at the concrete por as they drew nearer. I tucked in behind Philip and peered out om underneath his arm as from around the corner of one of the uildings appeared the spectral form of a very large, white animal, ugely bulbous with developing young. She stood stock-still on her layed hooves on seeing us and weighed us up and down with er slit amber eyes. A chain hung loosely from her thick, white eck, and her long, white beard quivered as she chewed onchalantly on a wisp of hay. We stared at each other across the ourtyard as though we were in a 'Mexican stand-off'.

Jan the goat turned out to be a companionable farm guest; she ever complained about being tethered to prevent her from andering into the vegetable garden. Nor did she resist being put eating down the unwanted herbage along the driveway. When e caught sight of us, she would bleat a cheerful greeting while isily nibbling at the spiky gorse bushes or the young tips of the awthorn and blackberry. I decided that 'the Mother-in-law', after hom she was named, must be an agreeable person.

The weeks passed, and Jan grew even more bulging so that the eight of her young began to drag her belly heavily downwards, posing the outline of her ribs and backbone, and when I thought e was about to burst, she managed to keep growing. I checked her several times a day, although she did not appear to be early as anxious as I was. She contented herself with chewing the d as she basked in the sunshine on the grass outside the barn, joying the delightful sights and sounds of the wildlife chattering isily on the sparkling blue waters of *Llyn Bwch*.

Then one day, it happened! I had just settled Saffron and Amber down for their afternoon nap and popped down to the lower fields to check on Jan, and there, peeping out from her rear end, were the tiny nostrils of her kid. I stood nearby and watched as she stopped walking around for a moment, stretched her sturdy white neck, lifted her chin to the air and uttered a slight grunt as she pushed out the little white head with its front hooves tucked under its chin. She then bent down and continued grazing while I dashed indoors to fetch a bucket of warm, soapy water to wash my hands.

Approaching her cautiously, I remembered my mistake with Snowy Lamb, but this was different; Jan was not a skittish young Welsh Mountain ewe, and I felt sure she had learned to trust me. So I drew nearer, calling out soothingly to mother and kid as I did so. Jan looked around at me with a heavy-lidded and nonplussed expression as though this was an everyday experience before repeating her previous performance as the next contraction took hold of her. At that point, I gently took the lengthening little forelegs of the kid in both hands and as Jan walked away, it slid out easily. I let it drop gently onto the grass, where its mother turned to inspect it, whickering lovingly as she licked its petite white body.

"Well, that was easy enough!" I exclaimed as I watched them bleating to each other and the newborn attempting to struggle to its feet. "I wonder if there are any more in there." Jan was too engrossed in grooming her firstborn to notice me gently slide my carefully washed arm into her gaping birth canal. And sure enough, there was the second little kid, only this time it was in the breech position. Fishing around for its hind legs, I pulled gently and then another white, mucous-covered kid lay on the grass beside its sibling. Jan looked surprised to see it, but she started licking it lovingly when it shook its little head and gave a pitiful bleat while the first one stumbled about on its wobbly legs. While

96

Jan was occupied I decided to try another internal investigation, and there was the third member of the group of triplets, with a facial presentation this time like the first one. Gathering the tiny front hooves between my fingers, I hooked my thumb carefully into its opened mouth to prevent the head from turning backwards and drew the creature towards its exit, where it slithered out to join the rest of the family.

With the appearance of the afterbirth, I felt reassured there was not another kid waiting to be born. I was rapt with the success of my midwifery, but I was growing anxious about my sleeping babies indoors. So I patted Jan on the head in congratulations, and she locked eyes with me briefly in casual appreciation before returning to her motherly duties while I returned to mine.

# 11 Heroes of the Moment

It was an exciting day at the beginning of Philip's university spring break when he and Gary started clearing the front garden, ready to build the extension. The long-awaited government-funded home repair grant was now available for Mynydd Mechell homeowners, and our old farm cottage was in dire need of attention as the thick stone walls were damp and their cement rendering cracked. The roof had been made from small, irregular slates from a local quarry more than a hundred-and-forty years earlier. However, it needed strengthening and re-slating since the weight of its gritty concrete covering, protecting it against the prevailing south-westerly wind, had gradually caused the ridge to curve downward like the back of an old donkey. It would have been pointless to have all the work done on the original part of the house only to have to undo much of it later, so it was the ideal time to build the house extension.

Our brother-in-law, Michael, was true to his word and had prepared blueprint drawings and arranged full council approval. It was a splendid architectural design incorporating a large lounge with views over *Llyn Bwch* and a practical entrance hall with curved stairs leading up to the bedrooms. There would be an office for Philip at the top of the stairs, where he intended to keep his new computer, and a passageway leading to the existing bedrooms and to our new bedroom with its ensuite bathroom. It promised to be a comfortable residence when finished.

With the precise dimensions of the extension marked out, Philip and Gary set to work scraping away the topsoil, ready to dig a trench for the concrete foundations. However, their spades immediately hit solid bedrock. The building inspector arrived a few days later to evaluate their work, and Philip was dismayed to see that he was the same man who had previously been responsible for delaying the building of our barn. The man pulled up in the driveway and, without knocking at the front door, headed directly to inspect the barn to ensure it had not been used for housing livestock. He jumped nervously when he noticed Philip, who had come quietly up behind him, giving the man a look of reproach.

"Ah, Mr Barlow, I was just checking to see that everything was well here," he explained.

"I guessed," Philip replied testily. "However, it is the foundations of our house extension I would like you to look at today if you will?"

"Yes, yes, of course," the man blustered, giving the barn roof a final appraisal before following Philip back to the house.

"We have cleared the area, but, as you can see, we have hit solid bedrock," Philip pointed out. "Surely, there would be no need to dig into the bedrock to lay the foundation?" The inspector frowned and referred to his clipboard upon which lay a copy of the plans.

"Hmmm...." he said several times as he picked his way around the perimeter of the excavated area. "No, unfortunately, you will need to dig the prescribed trenches into that bedrock and lay the foundation according to the plans," he stated decisively. The man tapped his pen firmly on the top of the clipboard the same way he had done when he had decreed that we should stop building the barn some months earlier. Philip was open-mouthed with surprise.

"You can't be serious!" Philip retorted and turned to Gary, who shrugged his shoulders and raised his eyes heavenward. "Look, this stone house has survived here on this bedrock for over a hundred and forty years, and now you mean to tell me it would not be good enough for our extension?" Philip swept his arms in a wide arc, taking in the old house to emphasise his point.

"I am sorry, Mr Barlow, but that is what is stipulated by your own architect," the man smiled insincerely at Philip, gave a cursory nod of farewell, strutted back to his vehicle and bumped back own the stony lane. He had the 'pen power' and he was etermined to use it.

"Mynydd Mechell?" The man from the tool hire company in mlwch grimaced when Philip arrived to order the required diesel-owered air compressor and jackhammer the following day. "You ill need at least six extra, hardened steel 'points' to get through e rock up there!" And he was right.

The robust, orange-coloured compressor shuddered into life the front driveway, sending black smoke billowing into the esh spring air. Philip and Gary attached one end of the rubber se to the jackhammer and connected the metal claw on the her end to the spigot on the front of the compressor. With a firm vist to the valve lever, the connecting parts locked together, and en a burst of air sent the hose thrashing about madly like an itated grass snake before it stiffened, ready for use. The sound the work shook the house and shattered the peace across the lley. The cat and the dog ran to hide in some remote corner of e farm, the men juddered, and their nerves shattered, but they ade minimal impact on the bedrock. After two hours, with all ven jackhammer 'points' blunted, they were feeling totally feated. So they were very pleased to see our builder, Chris, who rived to check on their progress.

"What are you doing?" he asked. "Why are you digging into lid bedrock?"

"That is what we would like to know!" Philip replied irritably. ry mopped his brow with a large handkerchief and sat down on dislodged piece of the garden wall.

"You don't need to do that!" Chris stated when he heard about e instructions from the building inspector. "All you need to do is ill one-inch diameter holes down to six inches deep and one yard art to take one-inch thick steel rods…….." After brief and freshing instructions from our capable builder, it was time for a *panad* and a little word with the building inspector at Llangef[...] County Council.

"No, no, no," countered the building inspector when Chr[...] made the telephone call. "Mr Barlow must have misundersto[...] me; of course, he does not need to dig into the bedrock; he on[...] needs to......."

"Yes, he agrees with what I just said and gives you the g[...] ahead," Chris assured us when he finished the call.

Thank you, Chris, our hero!

The foundation work then progressed at a rapid pace. Phili[...] returned the compressor and jackhammer in exchange for [...] powerful electric Hilty drill, and within two days, the who[...] concrete pad was laid and ready for the building work to begi[...] Chris brought his scaffolding, and Gary started stripping th[...] cement rendering off the front of the original house. A speciali[...] contractor arrived to install the damp proofing of the lower pa[...] of all the walls around the old house, and then it was time for Chr[...] and Gary to start constructing the extension walls with concre[...] blocks. Within just a few weeks, they had the walls built and th[...] roof covered in new slates that glinted smooth and charco[...] coloured in the sunlight.

Our carpenter, Greg, built the angled wooden staircase in th[...] new lobby, and then Philip fitted the newel posts and spindles [...] the stairs, ready for me to sand down and varnish. The prou[...] moment arrived when Chris and Gary opened the access to the o[...] part of the house and then dismantled and sealed up the site [...] the original staircase in the parlour. Our brother-in-law, P.J., wh[...] ran a double-glazing business in the south of England, drove [...] and fitted the windows. Glen, the electrician, started th[...] installation of the electrics while Gary engrossed himself [...] pebble-dashing the walls of the original house with attractive b[...] and brown-coloured Canterbury Spar. It was a task that to[...] enormous patience; nonetheless, Gary did it with a smile a[...]

102

cheerful words. Not that I understood what those words were; even though I had known Gary for some years by then, I was still struggling to make sense of his Manchester accent.

Wood featured throughout the extension, with pine-panelled doors, pine skirting boards, and wooden floorboards in the bedrooms. The mantelpiece over the stone fireplace, which Gary built in the new lounge, was a sturdy, weathered beam of Greenheart wood discarded from the old pier in Holyhead Harbour. A burst of captured sunlight warmed the room through the large picture window while the emerald feathers of the pine trees fluttered in the breeze and sent fascinating shadows rippling across the walls. Our new bedroom with its exquisite view over *Llyn Bwch* was so inviting that I could have moved in immediately, despite the small detail of having only bare wooden floorboards on which to lie.

"Tell me, have you ever used a bidet before?" Ernie, our plumber, asked tactfully when he arrived to advise us on the best arrangement for the ensuite bathroom fittings.

"Actually, no, we have not," Philip and I replied somewhat bashfully as we stood, looking down at the porcelain in the new bathroom together. "Why do you ask?"

"Well, I guessed you had not by the positioning you are proposing for the bidet. I hope you don't mind my saying, but it is obvious you don't know how to use it." He then proceeded to demonstrate, fully clothed, how to use the thing.

"Thank you, Ernie; you deserve a medal for all the helpful advice you have given us," I gushed with embarrassed appreciation.

"I did receive a medal once," Ernie replied, and he frowned as he considered some unsettling memory.

"Oh, was that when you rescued those people from that awful plane crash?" I ventured tentatively. (See the book A Handful of Toads by this author.)

103

"No, no," Ernie returned to the moment. "Very few people know about that; I have tried to put it to the back of my mind. No, this happened when I was just a boy."

"Do you want to tell us about it over a cup of tea?" I suggested.

"Yes, I was just a boy when it happened," Ernie repeated as he sat in his favourite chair at our kitchen table, holding his mug of tea between both hands and staring into the black depths of the chocolate cake in front of him. "It was a lovely sunny afternoon, and I decided to go and take a swim in the Stockport canal. I was just in my swimming shorts with my towel over my shoulder, walking along the bank of the canal, when I heard a lot of noise coming from the direction of the lock gate. A young woman was holding a baby in her arms; she was screaming and pointing to the river and calling out the name of someone. 'Help, help!' she shouted. 'He can't swim. Please help me!'"

"Oh, my goodness; how frightening. What happened?" I asked with my eyes riveted on Ernie's distressed features as he relived the event.

"Well, I guessed that one of her children had fallen into the canal, so I rushed up to where she was standing, and I jumped into the canal to the area she was pointing to and started swimming around and diving where I thought the little fellow might be."

"Did anyone else jump in?" I asked, thinking horrified thoughts of our own children being in that water.

"Yes, a few others also jumped in after me, I was pleased to say. As I said, I was just a boy at the time, and although I was quite a strong swimmer, the water was very murky, so it was impossible to see anything." Philip and I watched Ernie intently as his story unfolded.

"Then suddenly, I felt a hand grip my ankle!" A gasp issued from both of us at the terrifying thought. "Of course, my first reaction was to kick it off, but it took a lot of self-control not to do that. So I shouted that I had found him and called for help from the people

104

who had gathered on the bridge. Someone threw me a life belt; I grabbed it, and they pulled me in with this young lad still gripping my ankle until I reached the canal wall. A couple of men rushed down and pulled him up to safety." Shivers went up and down my spine at the horror of Ernie's story; it could have happened to anyone.

"Oh, my word, Ernie; was he all right? Were you all right after that?" I asked with genuine concern.

"We were both all right, thankfully," Ernie reassured us and took a long drink from his teacup. "Although his mother was a mess, the poor woman could not stop trembling and thanking me."

"I can imagine!" I let out a heavy breath of relief at that successful account of bravery. "So you were awarded a well-deserved medal, Ernie?"

"Thank you. Yes, it was an engraved shield, and it came with a Certificate of Gallantry," he smiled and reached for his piece of chocolate cake. "But I have never yet received a medal for teaching someone how to use a bidet."

# 12 When Giants Fell

"You don't look too comfortable down there; are you all right?" Philip was startled by my unannounced entry and peered up at me curiously for a moment or two. I guessed I had interrupted his train of thought, but I didn't dwell on the idea that he could have been somewhat shocked by my appearance. I must have looked rather strange in my dusty boiler suit with my hair embalmed in the pink scarf I kept for decorating purposes and my face covered in creamy powder from sanding the recently plastered walls of the new lounge.

"I am OK, thanks," he replied as he continued varnishing the skirting boards in the entrance hall. "I am just pleased to be able to do something to help." When he was on form, there was no stopping him in his energetic endeavours, but when he suffered from a flare-up of his chronic back pain, he would be incapacitated and needed to rest. As he lay there on the concrete floor, his mind wandered back to the childhood accident that led to his persistent back pain and difficulty performing everyday tasks.

Philip had spent most of his childhood living with his family in an old farm cottage near Knowle Hospital. It was one of southern England's largest hospitals, built during the Victorian era specifically for people with mental health problems. With six children to feed, life was hard for his parents, who both worked as nurses in the hospital. However, Knowle is in a wooded part of Hampshire, rich in wildlife, and Philip enjoyed a life of adventure and discovery.

The English Elm tree that had grown straight and tall from the top of a roadside bank overlooking his home had always seemed like an appealing challenge to him. A tangle of well-established ivy had wound itself around the Elm's 'invincible' trunk, where small creatures capered and peeped out mischievously.

Fourteen-year-old Philip had watched that tempting scene since being a small boy, so on that warm and sunny summer day,

with nothing to do but dream and explore, he decided that it wa
time to indulge his yearning to climb up into the tree. A pair o
Wood Pigeons flurried away as he clambered up that ivy-clad giar
and a Jay darted out from amongst the emerald foliage, like a blu
and buff coloured arrow, scolding in protest at this invasion of i
domain. A Woodpecker, clothed in olive-green plumage, took
undulating flight, chucking and complaining as it dipped an
soared across the Meon Valley.

Gaining confidence with every grasp of the sturdy vine tha
acted like his ladder to the heavens, he reached a comfortab
sitting position in the crotch of a branch that spread out hig
above the verdant, hummocky field below. As he straddled th
bough, Philip congratulated himself on achieving his long-he
ambition to conquer that towering Elm. Almost hidden from vie
he felt on top of the world, and although nervous, he could watc
unseen, the activities of any visitors to the meadow.

Doctor Robinson had come into view, engrossed in his regul
Saturday afternoon pursuit of archaeological discoverie
Formerly a university professor of History, he was one of th
hospital's friendlier patients. It was from him that Philip ha
learned the reason for the irregular mounds and hummocks in th
meadow. That erudite scholar, probably in his mid-sixties, w
convinced that the field was the site of a prehistoric Stone Age fli
quarry. His precious stash of flint artefacts that clearly showe
signs of being partially fashioned by human hand into arrowhead
scrapers and axe heads certainly contributed to the validity of h
hypothesis.

Philip had no idea why Doctor Robinson had been a patient
the hospital for so long; he appeared to be a perfectly norm
intelligent man, but that seemed to be the case with many
those living there. For example, there were a few Polish e
servicemen who were among those who had fled from the Na
invasion of Poland to England at the very beginning of the Secon

World War. They had fought courageously alongside the 'Allies' with the Free Polish Motor-torpedo Boats under the direction of the Royal Navy while others from their country flew Spitfire aeroplanes with the RAF. However, when the war in Europe ended, numerous Polish men were unwillingly deported back to Russian-ruled Poland to face summary execution at the order of the cruel Russian Dictator, Joseph Stalin. So, knowing the fate awaiting them, this small group of shrewd Polish warriors had escaped 'repatriation' by feigning madness. They had since resigned themselves to their lifelong occupation of working on the hospital farm in the peaceful environment of that red-bricked sanatorium. Each year on Armistice Day, they proudly displayed their medals as they paraded around the War Memorial in Knowle with the other War Veterans from the village. Philip reflected on how easy it seemed for people such as those soldiers and Doctor Robinson to reach positions of honour and then to fall from grace so swiftly.

Beneath him, the shallow, sparkling water of the River Meon tumbled clean and bright, weaving its way prettily through the valley. It swirled around the roots of the Alder trees and bubbled on toward the little wooden footbridge next to the old Funtley Watermill. Philip loved hiding in his secret den in the river bank under that footbridge, wearing his swimming goggles to peer through the lively, clear water at the mesmerising performance of life in another world. The pebbly river bed was alive with tiny freshwater shrimps, all intently absorbed in their own pursuits and unaware that they were being watched. Cadis fly larvae crawled slowly upstream, wearing a tubular disguise consisting of tiny stones cemented together. Occasionally a Brown Trout would swim by, twisting and rubbing its silvery-red spotted sides colourfully over the glistening river stones. Philip was often rewarded with the appearance of brown or black freshwater crayfish when he lifted some of the larger stones; they would wave their little pincers threateningly at the goggle-faced intruder like miniature knights in armour.

Laying his head back against the comforting strength of the Elm's trunk, Philip thought contentedly of what a good life he enjoyed in the countryside. With the jade green leaves fluttering in the warmth of a summer breeze and his face dappled with golden sunshine, he gradually succumbed to slumber. A tiny rodent ran across his hand, jolting him from drowsiness; he jerked his hand automatically, released his grip on the branch he had been clinging to, and suddenly he was falling down, down, down.

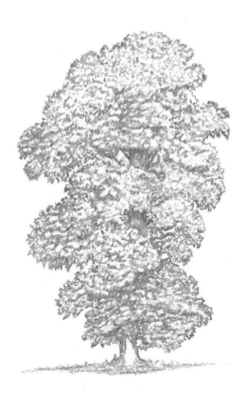

He had no concept of the time that had passed when he awoke to find himself amongst some rusted corrugated iron at the foot of the steep slope from where he had rolled after landing on the earthy bank. The blood that had poured from the gash on his head had dried hard, meaning that he must have been unconscious for quite a while. His mother was shocked to see his condition when he returned home, and his father had bathed and sutured the wound, giving him a shot of antibiotics. Besides a few bruises, the cut to the scalp was the only outward sign of his misadventure, although the resulting damage to his spine was to plague him for the rest of his life.

Philip had survived that fall, yet he had subsequently formed a reverential love/hate relationship with that lofty Elm. He once heard the tremendous crack as an Elm tree shed a massive bough. It happened without warning on a hot and windless summer day when one of those colossi discarded an unwanted limb without regard for any man or beast that may have been seeking shade beneath it. Living up to the nickname 'widow maker', those beautiful, towering giants deserved much respect.

About that time, Philip's Elm and all the others that skirted his childhood playground came under threat. Shipments of logs from the Netherlands carrying wood-boring beetles were responsible for introducing a deadly disease, with the local port of Southampton proving to be one of its doorways into Britain. Burrowing into the bark, the beetles infected the wood with lethal fungal spores, causing the demise of countless English Elm trees. It was the end of an era for those stately giants, the distinguishing mark of the English countryside proudly presented in the landscape paintings by the 'Masters' of the nineteenth century such as Constable and Philip's great, great uncle, John Noble Barlow. The trees were conquered by what came to be known as the Dutch Elm disease, and sadly, Philip's tree was among those

111

that were felled and left lying on the ground at the mercy of those tiny bark beetles that proliferated amongst their rotting carcasses.

By the early 1990s, when we were building our extension at *Ty'n Llain*, very few mature English Elms were left remaining in the British Isles or throughout much of Europe. Philip still bore the consequences of his unfortunate fall, but unlike his lofty Elm tree, he had survived to tell the tale.

# 13 Small Print

"Excellent report, Daniel! Linda 'Lipstick' writes glowing words about your Welsh language abilities." We liked Daniel's glamorous and good-natured Welsh teacher, and Daniel beamed as his father finished reading his school report on that summer evening in June. "Mr Evans reckons you are doing very well in French....English is good...but he needs to write more neatly and not with such small letters...Art is good, can select colours easily...." I was relieved to hear that last comment as I had fears of his having inherited colour blindness from my father.

"You are doing very well, Daniel, by the looks of it," Philip said as he reached for his cup of tea. "You just need to speed up and write with bigger letters, and your teachers have high hopes for you for the coming year."

"Thanks, Dad," Daniel smiled contentedly. It always meant so much to the children to have their father's approval, and it meant a lot to Philip that his children did not struggle with the same difficulties that he had suffered throughout his life with reading and writing.

"I was just thinking; maybe it is about time for you to have your own desk in your room to help you with your homework." Philip looked pensive, and Daniel looked up from his dessert expectantly. "Yes, now that I have my office with a big desk, I will not need my antique oak bureau; would you like it?"

"Really, Dad?" Daniel's eyes lit up at the suggestion.

"Yes, why not? We can move it into your bedroom this evening after dinner." Philip was pleased with the response to his offer. "We have had that bureau since we lived in Hampshire," he added thoughtfully. All the children paused temporarily in their absorption with their custard and strawberry jelly trifle and looked at Philip to see where he was going with this piece of information.

"It was while Uncle Paul and I were working on the threshing machine for Simon Collins." Daniel and Joshua started tittering as

113

they recalled the story of their uncle with the rat that had run u
inside his trousers while he was standing on the wheat rick. "Th
tractors played such an important part in the wheat harvest. The
were very smart John Deere tractors, just a couple of years ol
with air-conditioned cabs. They were Simon's pride and joy; h
washed them every week and parked them under the roof of th
big barn next to the wheat stack to keep them looking good. The
one Monday morning, we came to work, and there the
were...gone! We depended on those tractors as we could not wo
without them."

"What happened to the tractors, Daddy?" Amelia asked with
frown.

"We soon found out when Simon came out of his farmhous
with a piece of paper in his hand and looking very distressed; h
was hopping mad!" Philip answered.

"'Philip, I have a problem I need you to help me with,' he sai
'I found this note in my letterbox from the finance company c
Saturday morning, and when I looked, both my tractors we
missing!' All four of we workers gathered around as he showed
the contents of the letter, which read:

*'Mr Simon Collins,*
*RE: Lease hire agreement for two John Deere tractors.*
*In view of the fact that you were ten days late with yo*
*repayments for the month of May last year, we hereby inform y*
*that we have invoked clause 14c, which clearly states that we ha*
*the right to repossess the said tractors at any time before t*
*completion of the contract.'*

"No wonder Simon was so annoyed; he only had one mo
payment left on the tractors, and they would have been his!"

"That's terrible!" Daniel exclaimed. "Are they allowed to
that?"

"They say 'possession is nine-tenths of the law', Daniel. So un
the last of the payments had been made, the company were s

part owners, and Simon guessed they would soon sell them to someone else. If Simon had read the small print on the agreement, he would have known that to be the case. Even so, you would have expected the company to have written to him to let him know that he was likely to have his tractors repossessed so that he could remedy the situation or at least stop paying any further monthly repayments."

"That is so unfair!" Ever firm for justice, Amelia pursed her lips and smacked the table with her dessert spoon. Joshua took the opportunity while everyone else was distracted to ask for seconds of strawberry trifle.

"So what did Simon do, Dad?" Daniel asked, genuinely interested in how this story related to the desk he had just acquired.

"Well, that was when he came to ask for my help, Daniel," Philip continued. "As soon as he discovered that letter, Simon contacted a detective agency to locate the whereabouts of his tractors, and the detectives quickly tracked them down to an aerodrome near London, about fifty miles away. I was more than ready to help Simon retrieve the tractors as I was annoyed by the injustice; apart from that, my livelihood depended on finding them. Simon had the tractor registration papers in his name, so all he had to do was regain possession of the tractors, make the final payment, and they would fully belong to him. He knew the aerodrome, which was a well-known site for auctioning used cars, trucks and equipment. So straight away, with one of the other workers as the getaway driver, the three of us set off to reclaim what belonged to him.

We reached the aerodrome about an hour later and saw that the uniformed security man at the gate was occupied with several vehicles queuing up to go in and others waiting to come out. So we drove slowly past and peered over the earth bank that ran along the roadside, serving as a barrier. It was about three or four feet high and had recently been planted with shrubs. Our driver, Mike, was a tall man, so he could see over the bank, and there in one of the aeroplane hangars were Simon's two tractors amongst quite a few other vehicles. We guessed they had also been repossessed and would be sold at the next auction." With his eyes full of the exciting memory of his assignment, Philip related the next episode of his story.

"'Just here, Mike; pull over here,' Simon said. 'Here is the key to one of the tractors, Philip; I will point out which one when we get over the bank,' he said as we quickly got out of the car. 'I have the registration documents, and if anyone stops us, I will do the talking. Let's go!'" Apart from the two little girls, who had slipped down from the table to play with their toys, we all hung on Philip's words, watching the animation on his face as he relived his experience.

"Simon and I walked casually along the pavement, making sure the man at the gate was still occupied, and then we quickly clambered over the bank and into the car park of the aerodrome. Thankfully no one noticed us, so we walked smartly, without running, towards the hangar as though we had just come from one of the parked cars. 'The one on the left, Philip,' Simon whispered when we reached the hangar, and I pulled the key out of my pocket. We climbed swiftly up into the tractors and started up the engines. It was music to my ears to hear them roar into life! Simon drove out his tractor while I followed close behind in mine, and we headed towards the man at the gate, who was still dealing with the queue of vehicles coming and going. Then, Simon suddenly swerved his tractor to the left, mounted the bank, drove straight up and over it onto the road and sped off toward home. So I followed him, and Mike followed us."

"What did the man at the gate do?" I asked as gasps echoed around the table.

"I saw him in my rear-view mirror, standing in the middle of the road with his mouth open and his arms spread wide in disbelief."

"Did he send the police after you, Dad?"

"I was worried about that, Daniel, but bear in mind that these tractors had been stolen from Simon, and he had the documents to prove they were legally his. So I followed instructions and trusted that Simon would take the rap if the police did come after us. Well, it was getting near lunchtime, so after about an hour's drive, Simon abruptly swung into the car park of a country pub; we parked the tractors behind it and went in for a good lunch as Simon's treat." Philip's face broke into a victorious smile as the children watched him with amazement.

"You should have seen the faces of Uncle Paul and the other workers when we arrived back at the farm!" He chuckled at the memory. "Anyway, Simon made the final payment on the tractors that very day by recorded delivery, so there was no question as to whom they belonged, and we all got back on with catching up on our work of threshing the grain."

"Oh, wow, Dad. You got those tractors back!" Joshua had decided that his father was his new hero, a close second to his Uncle Paul.

117

"Simon certainly was pleased, Joshua; he came out to see me before the end of the day and said: 'I am really grateful for your help, Philip; you did a great job. I don't have the money just now to reward you, but I want to give you something to show my appreciation.' And that is where your bureau comes in, Daniel. The next day, Simon arrived at our cottage with the bureau and that lovely Renoir print that hangs in the lounge."

"Oh, my goodness; I never knew the story behind that desk and picture, Dad," Daniel said with genuine surprise. The value of his new gift had suddenly taken on new dimensions. "I will look after it, I promise."

"Did the people from the finance company come and try to take the tractors back, Dad?" Amelia asked.

"They did not have the right to do that, Amelia, since Simon had made the remaining repayment. But you can be sure he was not likely to take any chances, so he always stored them where they could not be stolen again. Apart from that, the law changed soon after that event, so now when people borrow money from finance companies, the companies are no longer allowed to repossess without allowing the borrower the opportunity to repay any outstanding payments." It was a story of justice and a lesson in the need for caution in this life, which I am sure, has stayed indelibly at the back of the minds of our children.

"So, what is the take-home lesson from Simon's story, Daniel?" Philip emphasised before everyone left the dinner table that evening. "Try to make your writing larger and tidier, and if you should ever take out a loan or make any other agreement, always read the small print!"

# 14 Wilful Wanderers

"Mrs Barlow, would you please come to fetch your goat from the school playground, as she is distracting the children from their lessons?"

"Oh, no! Not again?" Philip groaned as I attempted to imitate my sister Candy's rendition on the phone that day of a rather angry headmistress.

"Yes, it is the third time this month that Lacy has broken free and taken herself off to school to find Natasha and Hadleigh." In truth, we both thought it funny to imagine that mischievous black and white character saying "Me-me-merrh" through mouthfuls of geraniums as she peered through the classroom windows. However, Candy was very embarrassed by the antics of her now almost full-grown Alpine goat.

"They don't know how to contain her with her *Houdini* inclination for escapology and there being no fences around *Saith Ôr*," I continued while peeling the potatoes and dropping them into the pot of boiling water. "Apparently, quite a few of the neighbours in Pen Y Bonc have complained about her eating their flowers and vegetable tops."

"Doesn't do much for good neighbour relations, I guess," Philip agreed between sips of tea and a review of the Anglesey Mail newspaper at the kitchen table.

"Mind you, I can't say that goats are my favourite animals right now," I complained. "Jan's kids have been up to mischief all day. I had to chase them out of the vegetable patch again, and Jan broke free from her tether and tried to eat Amelia's pyjamas off the washing line."

"Oh dear, naughty," Philip muttered distractedly as he scoured the newspaper for temporary summer jobs.

"I mean, yes, they are cute and the children adore them, but I think we have bitten off more than we can chew with all our other responsibilities," I continued.

119

"Yes, true," came the comment from the depths of the newspaper.

"Apart from that, the kids managed to get up on top of the she today and broke a hole in the roof," I announced as a by-the-wa as I pushed a large steak and kidney pie into the Rayburn's oven

"What? The little terrors!" Philip exclaimed as he leapt from h chair and out of the door in a flash to investigate.

Jan, the goat, had seemed so mellow and likeable in the ear days of our acquaintance, so I had developed quite a respect ar admiration for 'the Mother-in-law' after whom she was named could only imagine that she and her son-in-law must have had warm and loving relationship. I had hoped to be able to milk Ja since I had learned that goat's milk was hailed as a healthf alternative to cow's milk and as a soothing balm for digesti disorders. But no, she was thoroughly uncooperative with n every effort. Just when I thought I had everything set up to be th successful milkmaid of my aspirations, she would kick out with h rear leg and knock over the metal pail I had hoped to fill. Or, i did manage to get the odd squirt into it, she would lift her gnarle hoof and stamp in the pitiful milk puddle that lined it.

She consequently cut a deep gash in her udder on one su rebellious action and was thereafter plagued with flies, whi gorged on her wound as though it were the local 'watering hol Despite my attempts to deal with it using homemade concoctio and frustratingly un-sticking plasters, the injury refused to he Philip sprayed the infected area with gentian violet, leaving hi with purple hands for some days, and Sally, the vet, took a look it, trimmed her hooves as best as she could and administer some treatment. However, nothing could prevent Jan fro reopening the laceration in her efforts to waft away her entoura of flies.

"I wonder what goat would taste like," Philip mused th evening after the children were all put to bed.

"You wouldn't?" I responded in surprise. "What would the children say?"

"I tell you, I am seriously thinking about it," he replied from under a dark cloud of irritation. "There is no way of controlling the little blighters; they can scale any wall, they have eaten the tops off all the flowers in the garden, and who knows how much it will cost to repair the hole in the shed roof!"

"Well, I must say, I am disappointed not to be allowed to milk their mother, and that was the main reason we agreed to take her on," I had to confess. "I wonder if we know anyone who might like to adopt an 'adorable' family of goats."

"I cannot imagine anyone who would be so foolish as to do that," Philip replied with a snort. "Only us, I am afraid."

A few days later, we received a visit from Greg, our carpenter, and his wife, Shirley, who seemed to have forgiven me for helping her drop her car into our neighbour's ditch during our last barbecue. (See the book A Handful of Toads by this author). Shirley was shocked to see the condition of Jan-the-goat and had no compunction in telling me so.

"How could you have let her get into this state?" she demanded as she examined that snowy-white casualty tethered to a clump of gorse on the lane leading to the house. Jan continued chewing on the yellow gorse flowers and eyed me smugly while I mumbled my excuses like an errant schoolgirl before an irate teacher.

"Well, she was pretty much like that when we first got her," I countered. "She must be quite old, and her hooves were already splayed and......waffle, waffle, waffle."

"That is no excuse!" Shirley contradicted authoritatively. "You should not take on an animal unless you are prepared to care for it!" As uncomfortable as I felt by my reproof, I knew Shirley was right. Perhaps we had been rather immodest to take on another responsibility when we clearly had quite enough to do. But then, the thought occurred to me that I could use this situation to my advantage.

"You sound very experienced in caring for animals, Shirley; would you like to care for Jan yourself? I am sure you could do an excellent job," I flattered. "She does a great job of keeping the weeds down, and she produces lots of milk for the kids; it just needs the right person to take advantage of that," I continued persuasively. "Philip has suggested taking her to the butchers, which would be such a shame for such a beautiful goat." Shirley, still crouched over Jan's udder to examine the offending, fly-infested gouge, paused in her scolding. And then, rising from her stance, she turned to face me, and a clear look crossed her face as though this was something she had not previously considered. I smiled a warm, encouraging smile at her with hope in my heart.

"Well, I had not imagined myself as a goat keeper," Shirley answered thoughtfully. She returned her attention to Jan, who paused in her innocent occupation of trimming the grass edging the lane and turned her large, slit, amber eyes to gaze appealingly into those of her new admirer. "But I suppose if the poor girl needs a good home......"

Shirley had not anticipated acquiring not one but four white Saanen goats that day. However, with the mother goes the kids, so we made hasty arrangements to bundle them all into our trailer, which Philip helped Greg attach to their car before she changed her mind. We waved a 'sad' farewell as they all disappeared down the lane, and then Philip started repairing all the damage. We did not hear any reports from Shirley about how she was coping with her newly-adopted goat family, but rumour has it that most of them found their way quite quickly into their freezer – but we did not like to tell that to the children.

Life began to take on a degree of normality after the departure of Jan and her little family, and Philip managed to repair the hole in the roof of the old barn. However, we started having problems with another member of our farm family. Our sheepdog, Jill, was getting bored. Philip was away at university every day, and the older children were at school. The sheep and lambs were replete with good grass, so they did not need to be moved so regularly. She no longer had her accomplice, Poppy, the Jack Russell, to go on illicit adventures with since that little rascal had gone to a new home. After accompanying Philip on his tour of the top fields first thing in the morning, the highlight of her day was joining us on our walk down the lane to meet the school bus.

When it was time for everyone to come in from the fields for dinner, I would ring the large brass ships bell, which I kept on the sideboard. Usually, Jill would be the first to come in response, followed soon afterwards by the rest of the family. Sometimes, however, the children would delay responding if they were too far

123

away or engrossed in building dens or carving little 'villages' amongst the tall summer grass in the paddocks. When Jill arrived obediently at the back door, I would send her off to round up the rest of her 'pack'.

"Children, Jill!" I would call, and she would run joyfully back to where she had left them, with her tail swirling in white-tipped circles. Within a short while, they would all appear hastily from wherever they happened to be, with Jill pretending to nip at their ankles in necessary discipline. Sometimes, if I was just too busy or the little girls were unwell or asleep, I would send Jill down the half-mile-long lane to meet the children from the school bus in my place, a job she did with enthusiasm and a sense of parental responsibility. It was amusing to watch the children hurrying over the ridge of the lane with Jill weaving from side to side behind them to make sure that none of them strayed.

One day, I was getting behind with my work at home. I would love to have lazed on my beautiful, inviting bed, where warm shafts of sunshine lay across it in swathes of golden gauze. But no, I had to keep pace with my daily routine, and it was normal for me to be running from job to job. So I decided to call on my dependable envoy and send her down the lane to meet the children; however, she was nowhere to be seen. I was becoming anxious as the children hated passing the unfinished house belonging to an absent English family. My overactive imagination attributed many sinister characteristics to that unattractive construction, half-hidden amongst the undergrowth and shrouded in mystery.

So, with Jill not responding to my call, I had to quickly gather Saffron and Amber and bundle them into the coach-built pram which bounced vigorously as I walked briskly down the stony lane. By the time I was within viewing distance of the main road, the children had already disembarked, and the school bus was pulling away. That was strange as Elaine would never allow her 'Mountain

124

ildren' to leave her care until she was sure they were in safe
nds. However, as they started walking confidently toward me, I
oticed they were not alone. Zigzagging behind them was our Jill,
ho I heard had been sitting waiting for them since lunchtime.
ter that, I found it necessary to keep her on a lead by the back
or so she did not get into trouble with the neighbouring
rmers. But there were many more times that I would call on my
usted advocate when the need arose to fetch the children, and
vay she would bound, not a wilful wanderer but a dog on an
portant mission.

Jill and Amber

# 15 The Auction

"I hate filling in forms! I hate form-filling at the best of times, but this is ridiculous!" Philip complained as he sat crouched over the kitchen table with the despised wad of forms before him. "I know it's necessary if we want to benefit from the government ewe premium subsidy, but with such a small farm, I wonder if the time it takes to fill out all these forms is worth all the effort. It takes just as long to report on two hundred sheep as it would if we had two thousand! It's no problem for the big farmers; they can afford to pass these complicated forms to their accountant, but we small-time farmers have to do everything ourselves."

I was more concerned about waging war with the green bottle flies invading the house.

"Where are they all coming from?" I asked rhetorically. In truth, those unwanted visitors were only the stragglers from the swarms of flies that had suddenly swooped down upon us during the warm days of summer. Most of them had focused on attacking our sheep, causing 'fly strike' from maggots eating into the flesh of the live sheep. So we needed to keep a constant vigil and dipped them twice a year in Dave and Molly's chemical bath at *Ty'n Gorse*. Philip paused in his battle with the paperwork and looked around the kitchen.

"You know what I think?" he offered. "I think they must be coming from that large sheep farm just over the hill on the road to Llandeusant. There are always dead sheep lying in those fields, just left unburied and covered in flies. It seems the new owner has taken on more farms than he can manage. These government grants were supposed to help keep small farmers viable, but instead, they are making big farmers rich. They are buying up all the smaller farms, but they don't have the manpower to properly care for all those thousands of sheep. That's why there are fly-ridden sheep carcasses all over that farm."

"Revolting!" I replied, genuinely repelled. "You could be right about that; I have noticed a lot of magpies and crows hovering over that way when I tour the top fields." As John Owen warned us just after we moved here, 'sheep die', which we had found to be so true, but we always buried them so as not to encourage flies.

"Yes, I noticed them too, but I suppose there is nothing we can do about it other than to make sure we don't contribute to the problem ourselves," Philip nodded in self-agreement.

"Well, we are doing our best, but I sometimes wonder if we are winning," I replied, swatting another fly with my tea towel with such annoyance that I managed to knock a cup off the draining board, which crashed to the floor and parted company with its handle.

"Oh, good grief!" I exclaimed with irritation, picking it up and examining it.

"Philip, you know those two identical cups that Terrie gave us last time she visited? Well yours has broken I am afraid," I informed him as I tried to assess the possibility of it being repairable. Philip looked at me across the kitchen and frowned.

"How do you know which one is mine if they are identical?" he asked.

"Oh, that's easy," I said simply, as though common sense had managed to elude him. "Yours is broken!" His eyebrows rose and a puzzled look crossed his face as he considered my logic, and then he returned to his form-filling while I returned to my fly-swatting.

Despite the unusual fly plague, the summer holidays passed happily, with many trips to the beach and enjoyable time spent with family and friends. We were appreciative of the government grants for renovating the old part of the house; the extension was developing nicely, and it was time to call in the building inspector again before Chris and Gary put up the ceilings in the new bedrooms. Philip and his workers stood nervously to attention awaiting the inspector's verdict. All seemed to be to his liking

# 17 Snake Bites

It was a warm morning in late April when Philip and Daniel finished helping Dave and Molly at *Ty'n Gorse* with the drenching of their sheep. It had been a physically demanding job since their flock comprised the large, strong, Llŷn Peninsula breed that, not surprisingly, rebelled against their dosing of that unpleasant anti-parasitic medicine.

"Eee, Dave, take Philip to see the adders in the wall," Molly suggested over tea and biscuits.

"Aye, coom and take a look at this, Philip," Dave responded as he led the way out of the kitchen while Molly cleared the table and continued preparing his dinner. Philip and Daniel were pleased they were wearing their 'snake-proof' rubber boots as Dave guided them across his fields towards one of the lichen-covered stone walls surrounding his property. Although he was fascinated by those elusive reptiles, Philip had a morbid fear of them, so he scanned the terrain cautiously in anticipation of being accosted by any snakes skulking in the grass. Thickets of tall, golden-flowered furze gorse filled the air with a strong coconut aroma while pea-green bracken croziers were beginning to unfurl amongst the layer of dry, brown fronds of the previous summer. Islands of knee-high heather and dwarf summer gorse surrounded the flat, rocky tableland, which had possibly been scraped clean of soil by Ice Age glaciers.

"There, look!" Dave whispered suddenly, bracing his strong arm across Philip's chest. There, warming themselves in the spring sunshine on a large, flat rock, was a pair of adders, the female a thick-set black and brown beauty of about two and half feet long and her male friend, a slim, black and white specimen of around eighteen inches in length. They raised their heads in sync at the sight of their visitors and then wove their way gracefully and unhurriedly back to their home, a mini cave in the side of the wall.

145

"Stand still; they might coom out again," Dave breathed. The group stood motionless, hardly daring to move as a brisk April breeze buffeted and cajoled them. After about ten minutes, a small, black and white head emerged, and then the female joined her partner to see if they were still being watched. Extending their long necks a little further from their home, their keen eyes with vertical slits regarded the intruders suspiciously while their split-ended tongues, like thin, black shoelaces, slicked in and out of their lipless mouths to test the air for signs of danger. Having inspected their visitors for a few moments, they decided there was nothing of interest outdoors, so they retreated harmoniously back inside.

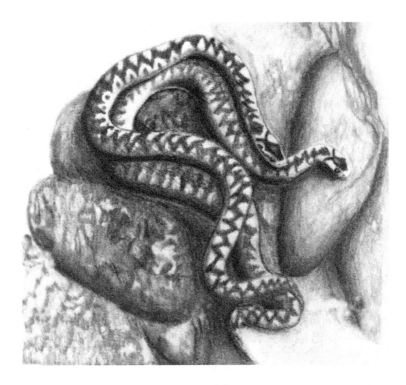

"Look at that; not a sign of aggression, like a scene from a Brambly Hedge book, eh, Daniel?" Philip suggested with a smile at Daniel, who watched the scene with rapt attention. "Mr and Mrs Adder from *Ty'n Gorse*; what do you think they will be saying to each other now over a cup of tea?" Our children loved to hear the stories from those beautifully illustrated children's books.

Despite that encounter, Philip continued to be wary of snakes, and with good cause, as we were about to discover.

"Judy is laid up with a snake bite," John Owen made the shocking announcement a few days later when he visited us to share a *panad* in the garden.

"No! Not Judy from *Bryn Hidil*?" I queried, although she was the only Judy I knew. She was a kindly lady with a cheerful, sunny outlook who lived in one of the houses up a small track that branched off of our lane.

"Yes, Judy was working in the garden when she noticed a snake in the flower border, but it looked as if it was asleep, so she didn't think she needed to worry about it," John explained.

"Did it come and attack her?" Amelia asked, and all the children looked around them warily as they sat at the garden bench with their biscuits and glasses of juice.

"They say adders will usually mind their own business unless someone attacks them, don't they, John?" Philip tried to calm the children as they looked disturbed.

"Yes, but you need to be especially careful at this time of year when they are still drowsy after their winter's hibernation," John answered. He hated snakes, especially as they often hid in the undergrowth, and we had noticed the rising grey smoke and crackling sound of burning gorse coming from the area near his home earlier that day. Everyone stared at John expectantly as he took a long draught of his tea and then gave a noticeable shudder as he dramatically related the event as he had heard it.

"Anyway, the adder woke up when Judy called out to her husband to come and look at the thing. It must have been surprised to see Judy there, so it struck out and bit her on the ankle!" Exclamations of horror rippled across the benchtop.

"Where is Judy now, John?" I asked.

"Dr Rob Owen phoned the hospital straight away and they sent out an ambulance to take her to Emergency in Bangor. She is back at home now and I saw her yesterday; her leg is all black and blue and she has to keep it lifted up for a couple of weeks until the swelling goes down," John replied.

"I am so sorry to hear that; poor Judy. I am no lover of snakes and I have had a few uncomfortable encounters with them," Philip confessed. "I had a close call with an adder when I was a boy, working in our vegetable garden. I was picking up a bundle of hazel sticks that my father needed to prop up the peas when I heard a loud hissing and wondered what it could be. Then I saw movement in the bundle, so I dropped it and jumped backwards as an adder, about eighteen inches long, slid out from amongst the bundle. It looked up at me and just slithered away. It could have bitten me, but it did not, so I learnt that snakes are not always aggressive."

"Oh, you were lucky!" John's eyes widened and the expression on his face betrayed his fear.

"And just a couple of years ago, I was working almost chest high in bracken in that field leading to *Bryn Llyn*, wearing my knapsack sprayer full of herbicide, when I heard the shushing sound of snake scales nearby. The bracken blocked my view of the ground, but I knew it was somewhere nearby. The sound was caused by the adder rubbing its scales against the bracken stems as it slipped out of the way, but where was it?" Philip rose from the bench and demonstrated how he had stood stock still, listening intently and waiting for the snake to attack him while we all watched him expectantly. "Well, after a while, the sound began to drift away into the distance, so I quickly ran to safety, and I never want to put myself in that situation again!"

Judy eventually recovered from her snake bite, and she bore the adder no ill will since she believed it was only acting instinctively on what it must have considered self-defence. But she was 'once bitten, twice shy', as they say, so after that painful incident, she always wore suitable protective footwear when working in the garden. However, a serpent 'witch hunt' ensued as the news of Judy's disturbing experience spread throughout Mynydd Mechell. Our neighbour, Leslie, managed to kill a rather long snake and hung its headless corpse triumphantly over the wire fencing of his pony paddock, and there it remained for several weeks. Meanwhile, the gorse burning intensified as though in an effort to eliminate the 'Black Death'. Young lambs who adored the taste of those golden, coconut-flavoured gorse flowers were ecstatic when they discovered the nutty flavour of *toasted* gorse flowers, their fleece and noses becoming sooty-black from foraging amongst the charred remains to find them.

"You know that Saint Patrick was famed for supposedly casting out all the snakes from Ireland, don't you?" Philip reminded me as we sat on our rock, watching the setting sun and breathing in the aroma of gorse smoke still clinging to the evening air.

"Perhaps he should have tried the same miracle when he came here to Anglesey!" I retorted.

"Well, I heard that there never were any snakes in Ireland in the first place. Apparently, they never made it from Britain across the Irish Sea!" Philip assured me. "But, as for Anglesey, I think John Owen is doing his best to keep the snake population down around here, so we don't need to worry."

# 18 Rescue Forces

Joshua was so excited when he leapt from the school shuttle bus clutching a crumpled letter inviting me to accompany him on his school trip to Mynydd Y Garn.

"There is a new catamaran coming from Ireland, Mum. Will you come and see it with me?" he asked enthusiastically. I thanked Elaine, the bus driver, and we started our walk back to the farm with Saffron and Amber.

We were familiar with the sight of Mynydd y Garn, as it formed the most distinct feature marking the western horizon as seen from our land. The view from the monument at the top of that mountain is spectacular! Low stone walls snake over a patchwork of green and golden, gorse-edged fields, while narrow country lanes meander like silty rivers through purple carpets of heather. Skirting around spinneys of ash and oak, they pass old cottages that have seen generations come and go while the sun reflects off slate-roofed farm buildings and sparkles on the little lakes. The standing stones of ancient Druid times are respectfully preserved, along with disused stone windmills, now stripped of their once magnificent sails. Having once earned a living for hard-working millers, but now replaced by modern, white, electrical wind turbines that flash in the bright sunlight as they turn with the wind in dance formation. A panoramic view includes the coast from Holyhead Mountain, towards the Skerries lighthouse and around Cemlyn Head to Wylfa power station, Cemaes Bay, Parys Mountain and on to the Snowdonia Mountains. On a good day, the circumference of that superb view can stretch even further across the Irish Sea to incorporate the Wicklow Mountains of Southern Ireland to the west, with the Isle of Man to the north and even the humpy hills of the Cumbrian Lake District in the northeast.

But that is on a good day.

July can usually produce some reasonable summer weather across the British Isles; however, Anglesey has a weather pattern that defies all rules. So on the day of our excursion, we were unfortunate enough to be treated to a stormy battering of whipping wind. From our vantage point near the top of Mynydd Y Garn, Joshua and I lay on our bellies beside the other mums and school children, clinging to the grassy tussocks with the savage wind beating at our faces and tugging at our hair.

"Mynydd y Garn sits between the village of Llanfairynghornwy and Church Bay on the west coast. It is 170m high and one of the high points on the Island of Anglesey," Mrs Levett, the headmistress of Llanfechell school, shouted above the roar of the ferocious wind. "This monument, erected in 1897, commemorates Sir William Thomas, a ship-owner and the High Sheriff of Anglesey." What a courageous lady, I thought as she clung tenaciously to the metal fence surrounding the monument with her tartan scarf tied tightly over her head and the collar of her Macintosh flapping wildly against her face. Peering over the brim of the mountain with our woollen hats pulled down hard around our ears and our eyes half-closed against that invisible onslaught, we watched as a yellow helicopter flitted, wasp-like, above the 'jigsaw'-patterned coastline.

RAF 22 Squadron - Sea King Helicopter

Undaunted by the elements in its intrepid journey toward a group of rocky islets known as the Skerries, it hovered valiantly over the turbulent, steel-grey waters, whipped up into white peaks like frosted icing on a cake.

"That helicopter will probably be the one your Uncle Paul will be working with, Joshua," I yelled.

"Is Uncle Paul in that helicopter?" Joshua shouted back with his eyes full of wonder. He adored his Uncle Paul and considered him the next best thing to Superman!

"No, not *in* the helicopter, Joshua, but he will be on the boat just around the corner waiting for the helicopter to arrive," I replied.

"Is it a big boat?"

"Not at all; about as big as the school bus there, it's called the Pinnace. I overheard Uncle Paul telling Dad about it; he says it was used to clean up the sea bed of mines and bombs from the Second World War, but now it has been brought here to Valley."

"What does he do on the boat then?"

"He works with the Helicopter Search and Rescue Team, helping to train the pilots to rescue people in trouble at sea," I was proud to explain.

"Wow!" Joshua uttered admiringly; his Uncle Paul had just gone up another notch in his estimation. "Do you think he gets scared being out at sea in storms like this?" he asked, returning his attention to that raging sea.

"I am sure he does from time to time, Joshua. When all the boats in the area are heading for the shelter of Holyhead Port, Uncle Paul and his team will be going the other way. They go out into the storm to get some real-life action and experience, and today would be perfect for those exercises."

"They are so brave!" Joshua shook his head as he watched that helicopter battling the tempest on its unwavering course.

"I think so too, Josh; those men don't need to put their lives at risk, but they do it to save people from drowning and will probably help rescue many people in the future, at sea or on land." (Interestingly, this was the same squadron that Prince William would be joining at a future time.)

"The Lynx catamaran will soon be arriving from Ireland," Mrs Levett announced. "Today is its first time doing the ferry crossing. It can travel at a speed of about 40 miles per hour, which is fast on the water for such a big boat. It can carry more than 500 passengers and almost 90 cars. Let's see who can spot it first."

I looked at Joshua, wondering if he could hear the full dialogue. I enjoyed spending time with my little 'ray of sunshine'. He has always been an imaginative and artistic boy, creating items from pieces of wood as small gifts, such as the little table he made for me to put in our new ensuite bathroom. It was the first project he had attempted without his father's assistance, and I loved it. I believe he originally meant it to be a high stool, but after several attempts to even the length of the legs, it ended up being considerably shorter than planned. Draped with a white lace handkerchief, it became an ideal stand for my aspidistra plant. Joshua shared his father's innate love of country things, exploring the nooks and crannies of the farm, making dens and 'villages' amongst the long summer grass with his siblings or mountaineering over 'unconquered' rock faces. He would spend hours with his brother, Daniel, engrossed in watching water boatmen insects skating on the surface of a small pond, while small diving beetles busied themselves in the water below, unaware of two pairs of bright blue eyes watching them from the sky. At that moment, I wished we were doing that together instead of lying prone and wind-battered just below the summit of the mountain and wondering when this school trip would be over.

The Stena Lynx skipped across the wild waves and bounced into Holyhead Port like a crisp, white, and navy blue dart. With its elevated sharp nose, it resembled an enormous blue shark. All the children attempted to run and watch, but the driving wind forced them to return rapidly to the lee of the mountain as papers and hats were whisked away, leaving only the very determined clinging to the railings of the monument. Gripping the coarse clumps of grass, Joshua and I slithered snake-like towards the mountain ridge and peered over it.

"Oh, look, the new catamaran!" we said, satisfied that we had accomplished our mission, and then we scuttled, with as much fortitude as possible, back down to the waiting school bus. No one had any 'cobwebs' left after that invigorating experience!

"We saw the helicopter that Uncle Paul was working with today, Dad!" Joshua announced proudly at the meal table that evening, and everyone focused attention on him as he related the exciting events of his day.

"Thank Heavens for those courageous men and their helicopters; they have been responsible for saving so many lives," Philip exclaimed.

"You have your own story about courageous men at sea, don't you, Dad?" I commented. Philip gave me a puzzled look.
"Canoeing in the Solent?" I reminded him.

"Oh, groan!" Philip uttered and buried his forehead onto the back of Saffron's blonde curls as he held her on his lap. "That was more a case of stupidity than courage."

"Tell us, Daddy, pleeeeease," chorused the other children.

"OK," their father yielded to the pressure to reveal his inglorious youthful adventure as they all held their spoons poised expectantly over their apple pie and custard dessert.

"My father had given me permission to use his two-man canoe, so my friend Neville and I decided to make a trip from Stokes Bay in Hampshire to Ryde on the Isle of Wight. Although it was a cold Saturday at the end of March, the day was bright and sunny, and the sky was a clear blue when we lifted the canoe off the top of the car and across the pebbly beach. A sea breeze blew the green waters into a choppy rhythm, and our canoe rocked from side to side as we climbed into it. That should have given us a warning but we were young and felt 'invincible'. Apart from that, we were wearing our life jackets, and we had our distress flares and a packet of biscuits tucked underneath the foredeck, so we thought we would be all right.

The Isle of Wight was only about three miles away and we could see it clearly in the distance over the glittering waves, so we were excited to be setting off on our first voyage together. I felt quite confident as my father had given me instructions on how to be a sailor since I was a little boy, and although Neville had never had any nautical experience, he was keen for a challenge. It took a bit of practice, but we soon managed to get some harmony in our use of the paddles, so we congratulated ourselves on doing pretty well. By the time we reached the halfway point, we were beginning to enjoy ourselves. Then the Sealink passenger ferry steamed out of Portsmouth Harbour and passed right in front of us on its way to the Isle of Wight. It took a little while for the wake from the ship to reach us, and Neville got rather agitated as the canoe began to rock and bounce. But I remembered my father's instructions to always turn the boat into the oncoming waves, which we did, so we felt we were coping with the situation. Unfortunately, an oil tanker passed us on our Starboard (right) side coming out from Fawley's oil terminal in Southampton Water. At the same time, a container ship coming into Southampton docks passed us on the other side. The wakes of all three ships came together, raised our canoe way up on the crest of a massive wave, and tipped us into the icy-cold water!"

"Oh, no!" everyone gasped; "what did you do?"

"Well, we sank at first, but our life jackets helped us to bob back to the surface. I tried not to panic and was pleased to see that the canoe was still upright, although it had almost completely filled with water and was barely floating with the waves splashing over it. So I swam around and gathered the two paddles, pushing them securely into its stowing area. Poor Neville looked so shocked; his face was as white as a snowdrift, and he started to panic, saying he would try to swim for the Isle of Wight as we could see the jetty at Rye only a mile away. 'Don't even think about it, Neville!' I said. 'One of the first things my Dad taught me about these situations is to always stay with the boat; the boat can be more easily seen than just a head, bobbing about in the water.'"

"And did he listen to you, Dad?" Daniel asked anxiously.

"Yes, he did, but it took some firm persuasion. I told him I would send up some flares and that we would be saved, which reassured him. So I reached into the front stowing area of the canoe, and the soggy packet of biscuits floated out. But I was more interested in finding the flares, which were still there, tied to a piece of rope and in a waterproof container. I undid the top and bottom caps of the flare and struck the bottom part against the top, a bit like striking a match. It was quite painful holding up that flare as it spat bright orange fire into the air and hot sparks all over my arm! When it finally died down I let off the two smoke flares the same way. The strong wind was travelling from the west and carried the bright orange trail of smoke in an easterly direction, so it would have been easy for any vessel to see where it came from. Within just a few minutes, a Wessex Search and Rescue helicopter was racing towards us from Lee-On-Solent and hovered above us; we were so relieved to see it! At about the same time, the Portsmouth to Ryde ferry had changed course to pick us up, so the helicopter turned back and left us to be rescued by that wonderful little ship, *The MV Brading*."

"Whew!" The eyes of all the children were wide and I noticed that much of their dessert was still in their bowls, which was most unusual.

"So, how did you get out of the water, Dad? Did they throw you a life belt or something?" Joshua asked.

"Well, a door opened in the side of the ship, and some men appeared and encouraged us to swim over to them. I would not leave my Dad's canoe there, so I dragged it toward the ship. The men threw us a rope with a loop around it, which I passed to Neville, as he had turned a sickly grey colour due to the icy water. He pulled the loop over his head and tucked it under his armpits, and then they hauled him up the side of the boat and into the doorway to safety. Then they threw the rope back to me, but I called up and said they had to pull in the canoe first as I was not coming on board without it. They shouted that I would have to let the canoe go, or I would soon freeze to death; but I yelled back, saying there was no point in saving my life now, only to have my Dad kill me when I got home! So they threw me another rope, which I tied to the 'painter rope' at the end of the canoe, then they pulled that in first, and I followed."

"You must have been freezing!" Daniel exclaimed.

"I certainly was, Daniel; I couldn't stop shaking. They wrapped us in blankets and gave us a hot cup of tea, but I was shivering so much that I slopped it all over myself to add pain to my discomfort. The ferry took us into Ryde, where an ambulance was on the pier waiting to take us to the hospital. Poor Neville was in a really bad way and they said he had hypothermia. When I saw the nurses taking all his clothes off to dry him, I ran into the toilets, locked the door and said I would not come out until they passed me a dressing gown!" I laughed at the thought of that scene, as I could so picture him doing that.

"I had some friends who lived in Ryde, so I phoned them to ask if they could bring us some dry clothes, but they only had a daughter, and I did not fancy going home dressed in pink. So they called a friend who had sons and he kindly brought us some of their clothes and then took us back to the port to catch the ferry for Portsmouth and then to Gosport where I had left my car. Captain Bligh was the name of the captain of the ferry.

"Of The Bounty?"

"Wrong story, Daniel. No, not Captain Bligh of The Bounty; Captain Bligh of *The Brading*. This captain was a very kind man, and he let us travel home for free as we had lost our wallets and one of my brand new leather boots in the sea, but thankfully not my car keys. And he even delivered our canoe to the quay for us."

"Did you know about this at the time, Mum?" Amelia asked.

"No, Dad and I had not met yet, Amelia; we met just a few weeks later. And Granny knew nothing about it until she discovered the remaining new leather boot in the dustbin," I prompted.

"My poor mother was mystified until my Auntie Hazel telephoned to tell her about the newspaper report she had seen on the incident, and then it all came out," Philip confessed.

SEALINK MV BRADING

"That was a close one," Amelia said as she rose from the table and hugged her father's arm. "What would we have done if you had not survived, Dad?"

"There would not have been an Amelia for sure, nor any of the rest of you," I reminded her.

"How strange that one near-miss could have changed history for us," I mused as everyone finished dessert and cleared the table.

"That is not the first time a near-miss has changed my life," Philip replied thoughtfully, and all the children wondered if another exciting story was about to be told before bedtime. "One day, I will tell you the tale of my father and *HMS Affray,* but that will have to wait until another time.

# 19 Crystal

Our niece, Crystal, loved the country life and always enjoyed staying with her cousins on our farm. At ten years old, she was close in age to Daniel and Amelia, and they always had a lot of fun when they all got together. She was so excited when her family drove up the long, bumpy lane to our house, especially having Jill, the sheepdog, and our children welcome them and announce their arrival. Crystal could not wait to get out of the car to see everyone, explore the farm or have a trip on the flying fox; it was a home from home for her, even though there were over 300 miles between us.

After a brief exchange of love and hugs, my sister, Terrie, our brother-in-law, P.J., and Crystal's elder brother, Kirk, left her with us and went to stay with my parents in Cemaes Bay. On their departure, Crystal ran into the sheep fields with Joshua, chased a lamb under a barbed wire fence and cut a long gash in her scalp! The other children brought her indoors to me with crimson blood streaming copiously down her long, blond hair. Thankfully, although I was horrified by the extent of the damage, I was clear-minded enough to address the situation in a deceptively calm manner.

"Oh, dear, Crystal, let's see what you have done," I crooned as soothingly as I could manage. I took a dark red hand towel from the linen cupboard in the bathroom and placed it over her shoulder to try to disguise the sanguine flow as it cascaded from her injury. Nonetheless, the moment she saw the basin filling with her blood as I rinsed it away with the tepid water, sheer hysteria set in!

Her loud wailing continued as the poor girl sat trembling and distressed in the doctor's waiting room. And then, in the surgery, the unfortunate Doctor, Rob Owen, the husband of our vet, took the brunt of her chagrin.

"You jab me with that needle once more, and I'll........," the threats issuing from our usually amiable niece shocked all of us as we huddled around her in an effort to calm her while our kindly doctor injected anaesthetic into her gaping wound to administer the necessary sutures.

"We have to live here after you have gone, Crystal!" I hissed in an undertone to quieten her understandable reaction to the pain. Meanwhile, Amelia vacillated between compassionate attempts to soothe her cousin and sheer distress at the sounds of her cries.

"Now, you will have to hold her down, Mrs Barlow, while I shave off the hair around that wound so I can stitch it up," Dr Owen instructed. The next thing he knew, he was flat on the floor against the cupboard door on the other side of the room. Our Crystal may not have been very big, but she could surely pack a punch!

"Do you think it would be possible to leave the hair and stitch around it, Doctor?" I asked the poor, dazed man, who picked himself up from the floor with his glasses askew and a look of astonishment on his face. In view of Crystal's threatening expression, he readily agreed and continued very warily with his surgery.

Summer holidays are far too short for energetic youngsters to spend wallowing in self-pity, and there was so much to see and do. So, the next day, with her mother's permission and a scarf tied comfortingly (comforting for me anyway) over her head to protect it from grit and debris, Crystal was away over the fields again, exploring and running happily with her cousins.

She loved sitting on the deep window sill of Amelia's bedroom, overlooking the fields and garden, watching the clean washing blowing on the line, smelling the tempting aroma of baking bread wafting up from the kitchen, and drinking hot chocolate by the Rayburn after bath time in the evenings. All this was her idea of bliss. She quickly established herself as the joker of the family and

162

sometimes the victim of her uncle's pranks, which had everyone laughing, but she took it all in her stride, knowing we loved her dearly.

As we went about our travels to the various points of interest on the Island, Crystal and Amelia would practice their rendition of a Welsh song, which they would sing together in the back of our seven-seater Volvo. She was not much of a book reader, but she enjoyed spending time with her uncle, learning from him and helping him with his work. She had the best of both worlds; the luxuries of town life in the south of England and then with us in the wilds of Anglesey each school holiday.

Although Anglesey could bless us with some beautiful weather in the height of summer, we rarely managed to visit the lighthouse at South Stack without being battered by fierce winds and the timing of our trip that week was no different. The wind whipped salty sea spray into our faces as we stood atop the cliff, and a ferocious storm from the Irish Sea sent huge waves crashing against the rocky perch of the lighthouse. I could tell from Crystal's broad smile that she found the experience exhilarating, as though we had arranged the trip to test her fortitude. I feared the wind would snatch us and cast us into the turbulent water below, so I retreated to the car with Saffron and Amber. But all the other children queued up to shelter behind Philip, who stood staunchly on the clifftop, absorbing the experience of being at one with the elements.

Back on the farm, the sun began to shine again after the storm, and then only when they were hungry and in search of a meal did I ever see the children. Crystal was a helpful and appreciative guest, and the household rang with her laughter as she teased her cousins, sang them her favourite little songs and generally kept us all entertained. She ate whatever we ate and some things we preferred not to eat…

Growing up on wartime rations, my mother had learned to value every crumb of sustenance, and she trained my sisters and I to waste very little when feeding the family. She also had an eye for a bargain, so when our small market in Amlwch started serving as an outlet for some supplies of cheap tinned and packaged foods from the European Union, my mother stocked up her cupboards, our cupboards and those of my sisters. Even though she and my father were seasoned travellers who had savoured the delights of various continental delicacies, some tins amongst her booty did not appeal to them, so those were the ones we came to acquire most.

"I am starving!" Crystal announced when she came in for dinner after a day of adventure on the farm. I was satisfied to see that her rosy complexion was turning into a golden glow due to the warm summer sunshine.

"Well, I am pleased to hear that, Crystal," I smiled at her. "Your Uncle Philip has prepared something special for dinner tonight."

We all gathered around the kitchen table that evening in anticipation of the meal Philip had cooked, and it was Crystal's turn to sit on the tall stool at the end, where no one else liked sitting. It was not the most comfortable position, but she did not complain as she had a good view of what was going on around the table. After presenting a delicious-smelling, steaming dish, Philip said Grace and the kitchen was free of conversation other than the sound of slurps, appreciative mumbling and the odd request for more bread rolls. In her enthusiasm for her meal, Crystal appeared not to notice that her plate was steadily becoming piled high with what she thought to be button mushrooms, which she consumed with relish as her cousins steadily slid their supply toward her.

"Doesn't anyone in this house like mushrooms? I love them," she stated as she piled a small heap onto her fork. Sliding it into her mouth, she closed her eyes and relished the tantalising flavours. Everyone watched as she opened her eyes and resumed

164

scraping up more of her stash until her plate became so overloaded that she could not keep pace with all the contributions.

"What is the matter, Crystal? Don't you like my casserole?" Philip said from the other end of the table with a straight face and a slightly stern manner. All the children then looked from Philip to Crystal.

"Yes, it's very nice," she replied, and all the children looked back to the other end of the table, awaiting their father's response.

"Then why are you not eating some of it?" Like spectators at the Wimbledon tennis courts, everyone turned to Crystal's end of the table, anticipating her next 'delivery'.

"Oh yes, delicious mushrooms," Crystal reassured her uncle and proceeded to eat more of the donated items she had moved to the side of her plate. "They are just a bit springy," she confessed, trying to be honest without offending him.

"They are not mushrooms," Daniel bravely offered and watched as Crystal chewed happily. Becoming aware that all eyes were upon her, she stopped chewing and looked from one to the other.

"Of course, they are mushrooms," she retorted; "what else could they be?"

"Snails," said Joshua honestly, his big blue eyes staring at his courageous cousin with admiration, just as they had been throughout the meal. Crystal looked down at the remaining 'mushrooms' on her plate.

"What? Are you joking? Mmm, delicious snails; you should try them, Amelia," she taunted. "If they were snails, I would not be able to pull them apart like this," she suggested and attempted to demonstrate her theory without success. "All right, if they were snails, I could cut them open, and you would see all their guts inside. Look." And everyone did so as she sliced through one of them, and then her eyes widened, her jaw dropped, and she screamed! She stared at her plate and then at her cousins, who watched her horrified expression, wondering what she would do next. Philip's face morphed from its mock austerity, and a wide grin began to form under his beard, which spread across his face, displaying a set of perfect teeth. His eyes steadily disappeared into his cheeks as he began to shake with suppressed mirth before he exploded with laughter, and apart from Crystal, so did everyone else.

"YUCK! I can't believe you gave me snails to eat; that is so gross! You rotten lot!" she exclaimed as she rushed to the kitchen sink to wash the taste of that shocking discovery from her mouth, swearing never to forgive us. However, that proved to be a short-lived promise as she was soon absorbed in preparations for the events planned for the weekend. But, as we were about to discover, some *unplanned,* potentially disastrous events were to assail the Mountain during her visit...

# 20 The BMX Rally

The BMX rally was to be the highlight of the holiday, especially organised to coincide with the visit of Crystal and her family. Terrie and P.J. had brought up Kirk's BMX bike and he and Hadleigh started practising for the big day on the field attached to *Saith Mor,* where Candy kept her beloved horse, Timmy. Timmy was a thoroughbred ex-steeple-chaser, and sometimes Candy would ride him all the way to our farm, where they would gallop to her heart's content. Our mother would say that Candy was never happier than when she was flying through the air with her hair on fire!

P.J. and Philip's brother, Paul, came up to the farm to help cut some racing tracks through the bracken across the far side of the top fields. The course would take the contestants around this gorse bush, over that rocky hillock, along the little dried-up stream bed and eventually back to base. They marked the route with bamboo canes topped with the colourful pennant flags that Amelia and Crystal had made from remnants of dress-making material. Meanwhile, Mum, Candy, Terrie, and I started preparing small wrapped gifts for all the participants, with something special for the winners. Since Candy and Terrie were both working as representatives for a chocolate company at the time, they could supply some scrumptious consolation prizes from merchandise left over from a previous campaign.

Happily, the day of the event was warm, dry and sunny, with only a light breeze. Vehicles started arriving shortly after lunch, unloading numerous excited youngsters. Almost everyone knew the routine since we had organised a barbeque most years since we had lived on the farm, and the kitchen again became filled with contributions of meat, onions, cakes, soft drinks, beer, cider and wine, along with many helpful cooks. I can say from personal experience that when times are tough, that is the ideal time to throw a party, especially when we have such generous friends, as there would always be an abundance of leftover food to share or to store for the next time. I did spare a thought for the poor old kitchen carpet, but as the weather was so kind to us that day, I hoped that most of the cooking would happen on the grill that Philip had made outside. Apart from that, I had learned not to stress too much and to leave the arduous carpet scrubbing for the next day.

The race was getting underway in the fields, and Philip started reading out the instructions for the course, which was to begin just over the stone wall by the back door. P.J. was sitting atop the wall, ready to log the departure times, thirty seconds between each competitor. Philip was to record the finishing times after the style of the Isle of Man TT motorcycle race. Paul held the starting flag aloft and began the countdown with about twenty teenagers watching him eagerly, geared up and ready for action.

"Are you ready? Five, Four, Three, Two, One, Go!" And they were sent off individually at the drop of the flag. Away they sped, through the gate to the top fields, with mothers, little brothers and sisters cheering them on encouragingly. They raced up and over the hill toward the far boundary, with their fathers placed at various intervals along the route to ensure no one took any shortcuts. The cheering escalated as the panting racers returned to the lower fields toward the disused 'piggie paddock', where they vaulted over a low stone wall, ran their bikes over the rungs of a recumbent wooden ladder and then home to the finishing line where the contest had begun.

Rounds of applause accompanied the participants as each one crossed the finishing line, with special congratulations to the winners in each age group. There were no silver cups nor bottles of champagne for the winners, but there were prizes for those who had come first, second and third, while everyone else was awarded small, carefully-wrapped gifts simply for their involvement. Some of those contestants became so hooked on the sport that years later, two of our nephews coached their sons to become keen bikers, competing in National Motor Cross championships.

After all the activity, anyone still fit and energetic gathered wood and any combustibles for the bonfire. As the youngsters achieved that assignment with the same vigour and competitive spirit as for the race, it was an effective way to get help to clean up around the farm. However, Philip had to intervene and rescue his old wooden ladder, and he made a mental note not to leave his wooden-shafted hoe and spade lying around where over-zealous fuel gatherers might discover them!

The little ones decided they wanted to have their own bike race, so Uncle Paul enlisted the help of some of the preteens, such as Amelia and Crystal, to supervise an event for them in a quiet corner of the field where they would be safe. Eight-year-old Joshua wowed the little girls with his skills on his black and yellow go-cart, but he had to fend them off when they decided they wanted to take a turn. Colin and Bridget's two youngest girls, Mandy and Jane, were meant to share a bike, which led to a few battles and little Mandy went off in a sulk. I knew nothing about this altercation until she asked if I had noticed her absence.

"Did you know, Auntie, I went missing over there?" Now that was a statement not to be taken lightly.

"Would you like to show me where you went missing, Mandy?" I asked. So, taking me by the hand, she led me to the spot where she had 'gone missing'. "Oh, dear Mandy," I consoled her. "It was just as well you found yourself again, wasn't it?" Mandy nodded gravely.

"So, what would you like to do now?" I asked. With a collection of little ones surrounding us to see what was going on, I suggested they all have a ride in the wheelbarrow, which Joshua agreed to push around for them. Problem solved.

"What a good idea!" Philip said when he saw the results of my suggestion. "We could have a wheelbarrow race, with husbands pushing their wives. What do you think?" I was about to say I had to check on the mountain of jacket potatoes cooking in the Rayburn's oven, but it was too late.

"Hey everyone, we have come up with a great idea," Philip called out, waving his arms to attract attention. "How about a wheelbarrow race with husbands pushing their wives, and we can time each couple to see who can do it the fastest." Everyone looked at me as though I was either very 'game' or simply crazy! I disappeared indoors rapidly; however, thinking better of it, I returned bearing two enormous cushions.

"OK, we will start off the race," Philip announced. Joshua tipped the little girls out of the wheelbarrow unceremoniously and wheeled it to his father. Philip set off at a rapid pace to demonstrate the route he thought manageable, with me trying to maintain a semblance of dignity in the wheelbarrow. We sped up

to the top fields, around our favourite 'sunset rock', followed the stone wall that divided the top fields from the lower fields and then we returned to the starting point. It was a very bumpy ride!

"So, who's next?" Philip looked around at the couples, some of whom smiled graciously and begged off due to their aching backs or problems with arthritic knees. Katherine replied that she would love to join in the fun but could not risk any broken bones as she had to work at the hospital on Monday. Her husband, Robert, nodded with feigned disappointment but looked somewhat relieved by her decision.

Carl tried to persuade Sandra to join in the fun; however, the look she gave him told him there was absolutely no chance of that happening! In truth, none of us could imagine our stately friend subjecting herself to such indignity. My mother said she was up for the challenge. Ever young at heart, she was always keen to try anything. Unfortunately, there was no hope of my poor old Dad even attempting that arduous endeavour; he assured us that his days of strenuous activity were over. To her delight, Carl jumped at the chance to run that race and volunteered to cart my mother himself. Her face was a picture of excitement as they took off from the starting point, and when they crossed the finishing line, she was absolutely exuberant!

"Come on, Terrie, we'll show 'em;" Terrie also tried 'the look' on P.J., but she succumbed to his cheeky grin and declared that she would only comply if she could have at least two more cushions to ride on. Actually, Terrie is a real speedster; I knew that from when we used to race each other to work on the busy A2 road up to London. There was me, in my little blue Ford Anglia with no seat belts, ineffective brakes and holes in the rusted floor, versus Terrie in her flash, white parcel delivery van. I did not stand a chance! I could tell she was just the same when they finished the course with P.J. puffing and laughing and with Terrie, flushed and cheerful, nestled comfortably in her multi-cushioned wheelbarrow.

Paul could not allow his elder brother to outshine him, and Candy had no excuse to avoid competing given her reputation for loving the thrill of the gallop. Several more couples then dared to participate, with Alys and Dafydd being the winners by just over a minute. Dafydd was a little younger than the other contenders and was driven by his love of a challenge, although Alys was not the least amused by the journey and needed to resort to a glass of sherry to calm her nerves afterwards.

It was Derek and Lorraine who stole the show, however. We could hear Lorraine laughing the whole way around the course, either due to exhilaration or pure terror. Derek had warned us that he was seriously unfit and may be unable to complete the course. So as he neared the finishing line and someone waved a can of lemonade in front of him, he instantly dumped his wheelbarrow with Lorraine still in it and reached instead for the drink!

Many packets of crisps and nuts, along with a few gallons of lemonade and a bucketful of nettle ginger beer, had kept the youngsters occupied while they waited for their parents to finish their antics, so a loud cheer went up at the long-awaited heralding of dinner time. The company fell respectfully silent while Philip asked my father to say Grace for the meal, and then, like a swarm of locusts, we devoured the food with the voracious appetite kindled by the energetic activities of a happy afternoon.

Our Mountain echoed with music and laughter as the barn dancing got underway. It was enjoyed by young and old, whether or not they knew what they were supposed to be doing. My Mum enjoyed herself immensely, dancing the Gay Gordons and the Virginia Reel with the rest of us while Dad jiggled Amber around the fields in her pram. Then, as the setting sun began to arc toward Cemlyn, the guests started to filter homeward. The lower fields steadily emptied of multi-coloured vehicles, and we found ourselves with anyone wanting to stay behind for a little longer.

The air was warm and inviting as we sat on rugs watching the stellar display that decorated the cobalt sky. As we began to settle, each of us into our blanket-wrapped cocoon of quiet

172

contemplation, we noticed a yellow glow developing along the gorse-lined ridge on the other side of the valley. Was it a bonfire? It could not have been a reflection of our bonfire since that had already burnt out. No, it was a gorse fire, which started to crackle fiercely, spitting orange and scarlet flames high into the darkening sky.

By the time the fire engines arrived, the flames had travelled along the ridge and danced furiously in front of the home of Tom Pratt. His silhouetted form could be seen arched over a tray of refreshments, which he carried to the firefighters. The bursts of burning gorse came and went in waves of intensity while the flames billowed before the night breeze. Colourful sparks shot upwards like exploding fireworks, eclipsing the stars before cascading prettily over the shimmering waters of *Llyn Bwch*.

I was becoming increasingly concerned as the barrage of fire began to creep steadily toward us, but Philip assured me that the lake would extinguish it before it reached us. If it were not for the courageous battle put up by the Fire Brigade, whose numbers appeared to be increasing as the fire intensified, Tom Pratt and his family would surely have lost their home to that inferno!

Greg and Shirley would have liked to start heading homeward, but, seeing the rapt faces of their four boys, they guessed they would be in for some mutiny if they even suggested it. Our children and their cousins nestled together, thrilled with the entertainment as they peeped out from the small tents Philip had set up for them to camp in that night. Crystal sat entranced, wrapped in her voluminous blanket like an indigenous North American at the entrance to her wigwam. Her eyes were riveted on the spectacle as flickering, fiery shapes reflected on her enthralled face. When she did turn toward us, she gave us a radiant smile of appreciation, as though we had put on this show especially for her as the 'Grand Finale' to an enjoyable holiday.

"I hear you had a bonfire on your property last night, Mr Barlow," the Fire Chief stated, rather than questioned when he arrived at the house the next day. He had come to investigate the cause of the wildfire, the extent of which could be clearly seen by the spiky, black, charred remains of gorse, still smoking on the opposite hillside.

"We certainly did," Philip concurred. There was no point in denying it; our bonfire had reached lofty proportions, viewable from some distance. "But our bonfire was out before that gorse fire even started. What's more, we were downwind of it, so it was nothing to do with us," he countered defensively. After examining the site of our bonfire, the Fire Chief seemed satisfied that there was no trail of blackened grass to suggest that our bonfire could have crept to the other side of the lake and ignited there.

"Do you know who started that gorse fire, Mr Barlow?" he quizzed Philip with a keen and suspicious eye, watching for his reaction.

"I really couldn't say," Philip replied innocently. And he guessed that the Fire Chief would have the same response from all the other villagers. They may have had their suspicions, but we felt sure that no one would voice them.

# 21 Life changes

The summer warmth delighted us for the duration of August, so we made the most of the school holidays by walking along the beaches and coastal paths whenever we had the opportunity. The Cemaes Bay clifftop walks were a family favourite, with the silvery, sparkling water in the bay and the summertime activity on the beach below. One day, when the sky was a clear, cerulean blue and a silken breeze gently caressed us, we stood amongst the perfumed clifftop flowers, breathing in the salty aroma wafting up from the harbour. The high-pitched yelping of the seagulls floating in the air with outstretched wings blended with squeals of delight from the children splashing in the rippling water while Wylfa power station stood humming monotonously on the other side of the bay. Commanding respect from its elevated position on the rocky headland, it reflected the afternoon sunshine with its steely-grey presence. Beyond the mouth of the bay, frothy waves skipped across the Irish Sea, whipped up and chased before the ever-present westerly breeze.

Continuing our walk, we noticed someone else appreciating that intoxicating scene. On the edge of the cliff path, as it curved toward Llanbadrig, was a lone figure with a canvas set on an easel.

"That looks very vibrant," Philip exclaimed. "I like it; it reminds me of the style of Van Gogh for its bold use of colour and brush strokes.

"Thank you," the man replied.

"Are you on holiday?" Philip asked as he scanned the vista the man was endeavouring to capture.

"Yes, we are staying in Marianglas," the man replied. "My family is down there on the beach."

"Well, you have chosen a good day to sit here and paint; this is a beautiful location, and the wind is not too strong today," Philip acknowledged.

"Yes, we love it here. My wife and I talked about the possibility of living here someday," the man disclosed, returning his attention to his absorbing project.

"That is lovely; I would like to have a picture of our farm painted in that style," I commented as I came up behind Philip with the children to see what was distracting him. The man turned to give us a gracious smile and a word of thanks, and then we bade him a good day and continued on our walk. He was still engrossed in his endeavours on our return journey, his tall, slim form and dark, curly hair outlined against the brilliance of the afternoon sunshine.

"It's coming on well," Philip noted, taking the man by surprise as we came up behind him through a carpet of purple heather.

"Thank you; I try to capture the atmosphere of the landscape rather than just trying to copy a snapshot in time," the man explained. "You cannot catch the effect of the shifting light and shadows with a camera, so if you look carefully, you should be able to see those changes." When Philip did as recommended, he understood what the man meant and was impressed by his capability to grasp something so elusive.

"If you like painting landscapes, we think you would like the view from our farm; you can see for miles from the top of Mynydd Mechell," Philip invited as he pointed towards the distant hills. The man's eyes narrowed against the sun's glare as he turned to consider the expression on Philip's face.

"That sounds interesting," he replied; "I am always looking for new scenes to paint."

"Then, why not bring your family to visit us before the end of your holiday?" Philip offered. The man nodded appreciatively, took out his pencil and hastily scribbled our phone number on his sketch pad.

'Colour' is the impression I got from our first meeting with David Weaver's family, not just due to his impressive artistic abilities. His attractive wife, Julie, had a distinct Australian accent, dark hair and was dressed head to toe in Bohemian vibrancy. I loved it, and they and their five children all loved our little farm. After tea and cake on the picnic bench, we took a tour of the top fields, where David decided on the ideal situation to set up his canvas and easel to capture our stunning views with the majestic form of Mynydd Y Garn in the distance. As they were of similar ages, all the youngsters soon befriended one another, and we all got along so well that Philip offered them the use of our old Bedford van to help them if they decided to move to the Island. Tempted by the offer, they soon found an advertisement in a shop window for a large farmhouse to rent in Cemlyn Bay.

After living in the city for so long, they were excited to have the prospect of living in that rambling old Welsh farmhouse in such a peaceful setting, which even had a barn for David's art studio. Their children were amazed by the size of the house, and the three older boys, Ishmal, Asher and Keemun, made a rapid exploration of the house, making claims on their bedrooms. Their two younger children, Naomi and Joshua, clung to their mother's side, wide-eyed and bewildered by all the activity. The garden was immense, and they were delighted to see that it contained a small orchard with lots of ripening apples already beginning to weigh down the branches of the trees. Closely followed by a small herd of curious cows, the landlord led the family through the bottom fields to a sheltered, almost private beach. They were all ecstatic with their rural find! So, they returned to Nottingham after a delightful holiday, having made new friends. Three weeks later, they had packed up and were ready for Philip to help transport their possessions to their new home on Anglesey.

It was still mild and summery when the family arrived, which is usual for September, and just before the onslaught of the brutal westerly winds of October that had caught us unawares when we first arrived on the Island six years earlier. However, the downside

177

to the farmhouse was that there was nothing more than an open fireplace in the living room to heat the entire house.

"How did you organise the heating of your house, Philip?" David asked when the family invited us to visit their new home. Philip was happy to explain where he had purchased our Rayburn multi-fuel burner on which we usually burned coal but could also burn wood and household rubbish, including the odd old welly boot. He also told David about our good friend and plumber, Ernie, who had advised and aided us on its installation with hot water and radiators.

"If you want to find yourself a Rayburn or an Aga, I will help you install it," Philip offered. So, with the acquisition of a second-hand Rayburn, their kitchen was soon throbbing with warmth, cosiness and plenty of hot water. The family quickly settled into a very different life in their new surroundings. David established himself as an art teacher on the Island and we were delighted to find ourselves the proud owners of the wildly colourful painting of our farm that we still treasure.

It was also a time of change school-wise that September. Saffron had rehearsed starting school for several weeks, imitating her siblings' conversations about homework and teachers. So, when the school holidays ended that year, it was time for her to start at Llanfechell Primary School. However, she screamed and clung to me when I was about to leave her and Joshua was eventually summoned from his classroom to keep her company. After a while, I left them digging in the classroom sandpit while I slipped away home. That procedure lasted for some weeks until Saffron decided she was in a safe place and started to make some friends in her class.

At the same time, Amelia's life also changed as she moved up to join Daniel at *Ysgol* Sir Thomas Jones Secondary School in Amlwch. Our children were growing up! Being a fearless young lady, she was a good supporter and protector of her big brother, which also meant some changes for him. One day they arrived home from school while I was sharing a *panad* in the kitchen with some friends who had come to visit. After politely greeting our visitors, Daniel asked if he could speak with me privately. We removed to the hallway, where I noticed he was not looking at his best; his hair was dishevelled, his tie was askew, there was a hole in his jumper and mud down his trousers.

"I have had a hard day," he said unnecessarily, for it was plain to see. Poor Dear!

"Whatever has happened to you, Daniel?" I asked.

"Well, there is a boy on the bus who is always taunting me for being English, and today, he really roughed me up!"

"What did you do about it?" I wanted to know, as this sounded like a case of racial prejudice.

"I did nothing, Mum; you and Dad have said we are never to get into fights. But Amelia grabbed him by the tie, held him up against the wall of the bus stop and told him if he ever tries that again, he will have her to deal with! So the boy went off in a sulk to the back of the bus." That young lad was unprepared for our daughter's hot temper that rises dangerously when she senses injustice. He never did it again!

# Summer at *Ty'n Llain*

By Daniel Barlow

The summertime is where I start
For that is the season close to my heart
I cannot even begin to explain
The beautiful colours down our long lane.

We like to sit beneath the trees
And listen to their whispering leaves.
Oh, what a joy it is to climb
Up to our tree house, from time to time.

As well as this I like to ride
All the way down our aerial slide.
And speedily through the air I fly
Imagining I am a bird in the sky.

The water sprinkler cools the heat
With water fights in our bare feet.
Bike rides, barn dances and barbecues too
Songs by the firelight with friends old and new.

Watching water boatmen that skim on the pond
While diving beetles scuttle in the black mud beyond.
As tadpoles wriggle quickly along
The buzz of the bees blends with the summer bird song.

Enjoying a walk in the faraway fields
A paddle in the lake to cool off our heels.
Or making a dam in the gurgling stream
Then having the time just to sit and daydream.

This is the time when the fruits start to ripen
And the midday heat even starts to heighten.
By now the days are longer than the nights
This surely is one of the summer's delights.

Tadpoles grow legs and so hop around
With the wet autumn season, their numbers abound.
The harvest demands so much of our time
Jam making, pickles and sweet hedgerow wine.

Summer holidays end with a stiff autumn breeze
Whisks up waves on the lake, and whips leaves from the trees.
Let's hasten to gather the fruits of our land
Make the most of the sunshine for winter's at hand.

# 22 In a Hole

Philip was pleased to have some time to work around the farm before starting his third and final year at university. The coming year would be quite a challenge as it was his last year of studies, with the anxiety of the final examinations.

It had not been in our plans that Philip should be a university student when we moved to Anglesey. However, it soon became evident that raising sheep on just fifteen acres of land could never provide the necessary income to care for our growing family. Unfortunately, the employment crisis afflicting the United Kingdom throughout the 1980s and 1990s forced many skilled tradespeople into severe difficulties. After many months of applying for local work, he was given the option to accept unemployment benefits or become a paid, full-time student with the hope of gaining the necessary qualifications to make him more employable.

For the study of Botany, Bangor is a first-rate university, situated on the Menai Straits at Treborth with beautiful botanical gardens and tropical greenhouses. Philip discovered that all the previous university graduates of Soil Science managed to find employment compared to very few who studied straight Botany. Therefore, he committed to doing a Joint Honours degree in Botany and Soil Science; consequently he had eighteen final papers to complete instead of the usual twelve. It meant so much to him to succeed, especially as he had struggled throughout his school life with the humiliating consequences of undiagnosed dyslexia.

However, he was about to discover another bonus from his studies at Bangor University.

It was a cold, grey January day when this aspiring group of Soil Scientists flew out of Manchester airport, heading for the sunny Island of Tenerife, the largest of the Canary Islands, located off the

183

west coast of Africa. Their mission was not to lie on the warm beaches but to dig holes in the soil across that sub-tropical island paradise.

Philip and his colleagues marvelled at the fascinating height and angular form of Mount Teide as they flew slowly around that snow-capped volcanic mountain and landed in the recently-built southern airport. They had come to examine and report on the diverse soil types and make comparisons of soil profiles, which would count as one of their final degree projects.

The Island of Tenerife has a distinct split personality; the lush, green northwest has more than double the rainfall of the dry, prickly pear cactus deserts of the southeast, where water conservation is a serious problem. After digging for an hour in the rock-hard, gypsum-cemented, and bone-dry desert soil, Philip thought of the copious rainfall at home on Anglesey and felt grateful for it. However, what that side of Tenerife lacked in freshwater, was compensated for in sunshine hours, with abundant fruit and vegetables produced wherever irrigation was available.

On the fifth day of their expedition, the team boarded the early ferry heading westward to the Island of La Gomera. The short journey over the deep, inky-blue water was smooth, and they were pleased to see a small pod of marine mammals, probably porpoises. The ferry docked at the little port of San Sebastian, the last port Christopher Columbus departed from in 1492 before his epic voyage across the Atlantic and his discovery of America. Palm trees lined the tar-sealed roads in the town, which divided into narrow, winding, sun-baked 'tentacles' that climbed up the hill sides. The Bangor delegation drove their two hired vehicles up between the white, stuccoed houses topped with colourful roofs that lined their route. The number of homes thinned and became more humble in appearance as they zigzagged further up the island, over rocky hills and down through winding valleys.

184

When they finally settled on a suitable place to stop, on the north of the island, the hot but excitable group left their cars on the roadside and walked along a narrow track that led into a gaping, disused quarry.

"Without going any closer, who can identify the type of rock over there?" quizzed Dr David Jenkins, the head of the Soil Science department,

"*Igneous*; yes, probably *Gabbro*," agreed all his students.

"Well done; now go over and pick some of it up, and then tell me what you make of it," Dr Jenkins instructed. The students did so and were astounded by their discovery. The dark, grainy, pink and grey rock they held in their hands crumbled and turned to dust!

"This is a rare situation where the rock has weathered but not eroded by wind or rain," Dr Jenkins explained to his surprised students. "The geology here is so ancient that we refer to it as *Saprolite,* meaning 'Rotten Rock'." Philip was fascinated by the specimen he held, which was so old it had lost all its solid strength. That experience compounded his awareness of our comparatively short life span, giving him a changed concept of time and the lack of permanency.

Doctor Jenkins was a tall, slim, dignified man in his early sixties who Philip considered a real gentleman. He loved nature passionately, particularly Geology and Mineralogy and would get very excited about looking at the composition of soil particles through a microscope. When Philip first looked through one of those microscopes he could fully understand the reason for that man's obsession. He discovered the wonder and beauty of soil mineralogy that many would simply refer to as 'dirt'. On close examination however, it is a treasure chest of minute gems of various vibrant colours, including zircons and garnets, which would be worth millions if only they were much larger.

Philip & Will Standring

After returning to the main island, they dug many more exploratory holes, for example in the soft, volcanic ash in a peaceful pine forest draped with long, hair-like grey/green lichen. Then, as their convoy drove to the far east of Tenerife, their tutor suddenly braked hard, parked up and led everyone into the centre of a lush, green alfalfa field. There was an ideal situation to see the bright red Oxisol clay soil, the last soil type on their list.

"But it was not as red as the face of the farmer who marched towards us, brandishing his stick and hurling angry insults that none of us understood!" Philip related to the family when he returned home. "Our tutor was so absorbed in digging a nice, deep hole in the middle of the field that none of us noticed the furious farmer striding towards us. When we looked behind, we could understand his anger as we noted the trails of downtrodden alfalfa, leading directly to our boots as damning evidence of our guilt. Despite the language difference, we managed to appease the farmer with much grovelling, apologies and several banknotes before tiptoeing back to our cars, following our trails of

186

destruction. Our tutor then decided we had dug quite enough holes for this expedition, and it was time to return home."

However, that was not the end of their hole-digging exercises; there were still plenty more holes to dig back in Wales before the upcoming exams. Half a day each week, they made field trips to various places of interest, from the farmland of southern Anglesey, to the high moorland of Clwyd and to a raised peat bog near Borth. Philip would always arrive home tired and muddy but happy. The photos showed nothing but holes in the ground; black soil, red soil, and brown soil, with several people looking down into them. I decided it takes a particular type of person to be a Soil Scientist taking such a dedicated interest in what goes on under our feet.

Ian Kelso, one of the tutors, was a slightly built, softly spoken Irishman with bright and shining eyes, a grizzled beard, thick and wild, dark grey hair and a permanent smile. He was a modest man who had graduated from Trinity College, Dublin and had gone on to study at Rothamsted Research Establishment, Hertfordshire, which is famed as one of the oldest agricultural research institutions in the world. His fascination with the soil was contagious.

One morning Ian Kelso led the group of aspiring Soil Scientists to visit our farm. En route they visited Mynydd Bodafon to examine the reason for the contrast between the natural soil fertility on Anglesey, which was evident from the differences in the species of wild plants. Gorse and heather are prolific in our part of Anglesey, typical of acidic, infertile soil, while Benllech and Moelfre produce a profusion of trees and plants not seen closer to home. What was the reason? Was it because that region was more sheltered, or was it to do with the soil? Their discoveries near Mynydd Bodafon would answer that question.

"Ah, here is what I was looking for!" Ian Kelso exclaimed as he lifted a dark red-coloured stone from a field about one hundred metres from the base of Mynydd Bodafon. "You see how the indentations in this stone are small, white pits of a softer mineral? It is known as 'corn stone', a kind of iron-rich limestone, and the parent material for most of the deep, rich soil found in this region. Wheat crops would have been cultivated here in years gone by, and if you look around, you will observe all the trees growing nearby and the lush colour of the grass. Now let's see if you can find any corn stone on the mountain itself."

By contrast, Mynydd Bodafon was a swathe of richly-coloured foliage of yellow gorse and purple heather, through which those intrepid scientists next rambled. Reaching the surveyors' 'Trig Point' at the top of the mountain, which is part of a network across the British Isles, a spectacular 360-degree view rewarded them, encompassing all of Anglesey and the stunning Snowdonia Mountains. But they found no sign of corn stone on Bodafon Mountain itself, which led them to conclude that gorse and heather will grow well on poor, acidic soil while good crops are more likely to flourish on earth that is calcium-rich.

Daniel, Amelia and Joshua stood looking down into the hole their father had dug in one of our fields at *Ty'n Llain.* It was one of several he had excavated on that balmy spring morning in May, and they wondered what could be their purpose. He was not holding any trees to plant, neither were there any dead sheep around to bury, and what was more, a group of people had come all the way from Bangor to also look down the holes. Very strange! They were sure the people would much rather have been playing on their aerial slide with them, and they had said so once or twice already.

"An excellent example of a *regolith*," and other strange expressions were said by one of the men who seemed to be the leader. However, the children had heard many confusing new words since their father had started studying at the university.

The group of knowledgeable professors and raptly attentive students kept us all suitably occupied on the subject of soils at lunchtime while one and all did justice to my hogget casserole and freshly-baked bread rolls. Since the dialogue around our kitchen table was well over the children's heads and, in truth, also over mine, I seated them at a small coffee table where they could have their own conversations. However, they decided to pay attention to what was being said by the adults when their father began to tell one of his stories.

"I remember my first encounter with a soil profile when I was about twelve years old," Philip contributed to the discussion. "It was early on a warm Sunday morning when I went to watch the wildlife in a nearby silvery spring in the water meadows of Great Fontley farm. Our house in the Dell sat under a chalk cliff, probably the most westerly point of the South Downs. The grass in the fields was always a lush green, which I now know would have to do with the calcium in the soil." Ian Kelso nodded indulgently, pleased that Philip had learned something from their morning's exploration. "Anyway, I came across a trench dug by a JCB digger to reveal a deep soil profile for the students of Southampton University. The trench walls displayed a rich, chocolate brown topsoil, red clay subsoil and an Ayrshire cow."

"A what?" Sarah, the lady student, asked.

"A cow," Philip repeated. "That cow had the most beautiful big brown eyes and long eyelashes as she looked up at me, and from the state of her, half covered in mud, she looked as though she had been there all night. I guessed she had gone into the hole to lick the mineral-rich clay and was stuck fast. I did what I could, of course," Philip continued, aware that his offspring sitting listening were anticipating a happy ending to his story. "I tried to coax her backwards, even pushing at her head, but I didn't fancy getting behind her in that hole; I thought I might get stuck myself if I did that! So after about twenty minutes, I decided to go and fetch the farmer, who was very pleased that I did."

"Was the farmer able to get the cow out, Dad?" eleven-year-old Amelia asked, her eyebrows furrowed and her eyes intense with hope.

"Not at first, Amelia; he tried to pull her out with a rope, but no, she was so deeply wedged in that trench that she was going nowhere." A chorus of disappointment shivered across the coffee table. "Well, something had to be done quickly, so the farmer returned home to collect his tractor while I stayed with the cow, which was getting understandably distressed. When he came back, he put a halter around her neck and attached the other end of the rope to the front end loader of the tractor. He then tried to lift her and pull her out as gently as possible from what would otherwise have been her grave. I was sure she would die from that experience as I could hear the cracking of all her vertebrae like the sound of snapping dry twigs."

"Anyway, he managed to drag her out, 'mooing' loudly as she came, with me pushing as hard as I could on her rear end. Eventually, there was a loud sucking noise as she was pulled free from the mud and set down on the grass. As soon as she was released from the halter, she staggered to her feet and wandered off shakily to join the rest of the herd as though she had just been for some gruelling treatment with the chiropractor! The next day, the farmer came over to our house with a big box of chocolates and said his 'Lady of the Meadow' was as right as rain, although still covered in her mudpack after her session at the 'Beauty Parlour'." Everyone laughed with relief and repletion while Philip was pleased to give his audience a happy ending to his story.

"I am sure that farmer would have been grateful to you, Philip," Ian Kelso congratulated him, and everyone agreed as they all started to rise from the table. "But, in view of your story, I think we had better fill in those holes you dug this morning."

"Yes," Philip agreed, as little Saffron wrapped her arms around his leg, and he lifted tiny Amber into his arms. "We wouldn't want any of these little 'toads' falling into those holes, would we?"

"Then we must get on our way to our next point of research; Parys Mountain. But there is just one more thing we have been invited to do before we leave," Ian Kelso added as the appreciative group shook my hand and prepared to depart.

"Wheeeeee!" The children were delighted to watch as their father's fellow students gained courage and shot past them on their aerial slide. Daniel, Amelia and Joshua, their eyes gleaming with delight, nodded to each other as if to say: 'There; we knew they would rather be playing with us instead of looking in a silly hole!'

# 23 Romance and Consequence

"I will have no Ruddy Duck hunters on my land!"

I winced when Philip related his conversation with the men I saw arrive in a Land Rover, who had driven off rapidly after a brief interlude. That word was the nearest thing to a swear word my grandfather could get away with using without my grandmother rapping him on the wrist for cursing in front of the grandchildren. On reflection, I suppose the word was quite moderate for an ex-Royal Navy seaman bearing fading tattoos on his forearms. In this instance, however, 'Ruddy', was the name of a duck species and not an insulting expletive.

When the men arrived, Philip had been sitting quietly in the field overlooking *Llyn Bwch*, revising for his upcoming final degree examinations and savouring the tranquillity of his surroundings. The bird life on and around the lake entranced him with its medley of songs and chattering and the *plooping* sound of the shy Ruddy Ducks as they dived.

"Why does everyone want to come and kill creatures on our land?" I asked, heaving an irritated sigh and raising my eyes to the kitchen ceiling. "First fox hunters and now Ruddy Duck hunters!" I might have known that Philip would have an answer to my rhetorical question. Since he had been given a computer as part of his dyslexia grant from the university, he would slip off to his office upstairs at every opportunity to research and keep us informed on current affairs.

"It is to do with the Andalusian White-headed Duck," he explained while I continued shaping and oiling the bread rolls ready to go in the oven. "The Ruddy Ducks were introduced to the UK from America in the 1940s, but they are making illicit trips to Spain and interbreeding with the White-headed Ducks, making them a threatened species. So, now a government-sponsored team of environmentalists is focused on eliminating all the Ruddy

Ducks here in the British Isles to help preserve the White-headed Ducks of Andalusia."

"Cheeky birds!" I replied. "So, what did the hunters want with our land then?"

"They wanted to set up a hide so they could spy on *Llyn Bwch* and shoot all the Ruddy Ducks!" Philip stated indignantly. "In my view, as we have no native diving ducks, they are filling an empty niche and doing no harm locally."

"With our children and animals all running around; I can understand why you said 'no', Philip. And with Jill's red colouring, she could easily be mistaken for a large fox."

"Just recently, there was a United Nations Conference called the Rio Earth Summit. I am sure their intentions were good, and I agree that the ecological balance needs to be protected," Philip said thoughtfully, looking out of the kitchen window at the lake, which was sparkling and clear on that sunny summer day.

"And?" I asked, half listening.

"The Earth Summit was intended to encourage international cooperation on ecological issues, and amongst those was the matter of preserving the diversity of species, animal and bird life."

"So, that is where the duck hunters came in today, I suppose?" I tipped out the hot bread rolls onto a board on the kitchen table and tapped the underside of one of them to see if it sounded hollow and well-cooked before putting the next two trays of risen rolls into the oven.

"You know, I believe that here in Wales the Ruddy Ducks are no competition to other birdlife because, unlike other British wild ducks, they dive to feed off the *bottom* of the lake. I don't like creatures being killed at the best of times, except for food of course, but not from our land," Philip stated.

"Fancy that; an international conflict right here on our little Welsh farm. No, no, Philip," I soothed. "I am sure you made the right decision, and we have to consider the safety of our family."

The duck hunters did not return to *Ty'n Llain,* but we heard frequent shots coming from the other side of the lake over the following few weeks with much flurry and complaint from the disturbed birds. Although they did not achieve a total eradication, the number of Ruddy Ducks was significantly reduced, and the Andalusian White-headed Duck has survived as a species despite our collusion with those feathered 'Romeos'.

As it was, we were having a bit of trouble with our own birds. Due to the scare involving salmonella in eggs in the late 1980s, it was a difficult time for poultry farmers as many people avoided eating shop-bought eggs. Consequently, the egg production industry in the United Kingdom suffered an enormous drop in sales, leading to the mass culling of many chickens.

So we bought some little Maran chicks and eventually started producing our own dark brown, farm-fresh eggs. However, our hens were barely paying their way in providing us with anywhere near enough eggs to sustain the family. Gruffydd, who had sold us the chicks, was a seasoned poultry expert who had raised many an excellent chicken to grace a Welsh dining table during his lifetime. He was a sage, elderly Welsh man with a freckled face, sandy-grey stubble, and an unruly covering of matching hair who spent much

195

of his time stooped over his cosseted mottled brood in his garden hen house in Carreglefn.

"If you want your chickens to lay good-sized eggs with hard shells, you need to crush oyster shells or even the shells of their own eggs and mix it into their mash of potato peelings," Gruffydd advised us. "And my little secret to keep the chickens laying their eggs throughout the winter is to mix a little curry powder into the mash," his cheeks folded into a conspiratorial smile, and his faded blue eyes twinkled under his shaggy eyebrows as he imparted that piece of vital information. And he was probably right; the egg yolks were a rich, dark yellow, and yes, the chickens managed to continue laying eggs daily well into the winter. However, we decided that curry-flavoured scrambled egg for breakfast was an acquired taste, and, in view of a few comments from our visitors about my 'curried' fruit cakes, we decided to give up on that idea.

Our scrawny young cockerel, Clarence, was always the last of the chickens to enter the coop every evening. We decided that his reluctance was most likely due to the fear of reprisals from his harem, which he bullied and harassed during the daytime. I felt very sorry for the poor hens, having to put up with the 'amorous' advances from that ungainly adolescent, and wondered how Clarence could possibly consider his methods acceptable. The poor hens were rendered partially bald by his frequent assaults since he ripped out their head feathers as part of his propositions. Those painful antics reminded me of the privilege of being a human being.

"I cannot stand by and watch those poor hens being so abused, Philip!" I blurted out when he came in for dinner one evening.

"Well, it's not my fault!" he retorted defensively.

"Of course not," I replied, calming myself and acknowledging that a brutish thug of a cockerel did not represent the entire population of males, whether animal, bird or human. "But, I think we should get rid of the beast. Although I must say he is very skinny, maybe we should separate him from the flock and wait until he is ready for the pot?"

"Probably, but Clarence will have to take his chances with the hens tonight and I will think about what to do with him tomorrow," Philip suggested, sighing under the weight of his responsibilities and anxious about his upcoming examinations. Clarence was particularly uncooperative about going into the coop that evening. All his balding wives had strutted resignedly into their henhouse, but Clarence was leading us a merry dance around it.

"Stupid cockerel!" Philip shot verbal daggers of exasperation at that silly bird as it ran in long-legged circles around the coop, with both of us chasing after it.

"Chickens are not known for being clever, Philip," I commented derisively, which only compounded his irritation.

"Oh, this is ridiculous! Let's just close the door on the coop; a night outside might teach him a lesson," Philip proposed after at least fifteen minutes of that 'circus act'. And it did; the following morning, Clarence was nothing more than a trail of jade and copper-coloured feathers across the field.

"Oh, so the foxes are still around," I said to no one in particular as I encountered that disturbing scene. Annoying as that little bird was, it was still sad that Clarence had such a tragic ending. There would be no hope of cockerel casserole for dinner, but the hens lived happily ever after.

School exam time arrived, with heightened tension in the home. Daniel had only one more year to go before leaving school, and Joshua was in the last few weeks of junior school before moving up to join his siblings at the senior school after the school holidays. Philip diligently studied and revised, ready for the climax of three years of study at Bangor University. The following week would be his final degree exams, including a three-hour exam on Ecology, the principal assignment being to write an essay

197

explaining the meaning of 'niche' and citing examples. So, having done much research on the topic, Philip wrote a detailed account of the Ruddy Duck and its dilemma, which won him a very high mark.

Bangor University was ahead of its time in understanding the difficulties of dyslexia, and they were very fair in marking the exams, making allowance for spelling and writing problems. As written notes were not allowed into the examination rooms, Philip had an advantage over most other students who depended on their lecture notes while he relied on his photographic memory.

While waiting for the exam results all the students attached to the School of Biological Sciences (SBS) were invited to make an oral presentation of their Honours projects, some of which were thought-provoking and well-presented. Philip's topic was 'Soil Variation and Plant Species Distribution in a Natural Pasture', for which he won a prize for the best presentation. He was stunned to receive such an accolade. It was so good to have his problem with dyslexia recognized and accommodated, and his painful school years were becoming a distant memory.

What a happy day it was when he received his exam results: A Batchelor of Science with Honours for a joint degree in Botany and Soil Science. Philip was delighted! He finally felt achieved and optimistic about finding suitable employment, and our future was beginning to look rosy.

# 24 Piggy Slippers

"Meadowsweet!" I exclaimed, and an audible groan issued from the back seat as I stamped on the footbrake and brought the car to a halt on that pretty, narrow country lane.

"Must we, Mum?" Daniel spoke up as the representative for the complaining collection of children.

"It won't take long; please all hop out quickly before a car comes and pick as many as you can reach." Despite their misgivings, they quickly leapt from the car and waded into the ditches to gather those delectably honey-scented roadside flowers. Like fluffy white candy floss on straight, thin stems, the soothing perfume of meadowsweet fills the car and the house with a calming fragrance. When infused in hot water, the heads make a delicious herbal tea, which country folk recommend as a remedy for many health problems, such as digestive complaints, stomach ulcers, colds, joint pain, arthritis, gout and even kidney disorders.

Meadowsweet champagne is the simplest of recipes and a potent, naturally fermented alcoholic beverage that improves with time. (For the recipe, see the book 'A Handful of Toads' by this author.) I often wondered why Philip insisted on trimming the tiny flowers into the brewing bucket with his dagging shears; perhaps there was some carefully guarded secret he had learned to improve the flavour. Nonetheless, we all lived to tell the tale, and so did our friends.

Our children were delighted with the gifts of chocolate and other generous offerings from their Auntie Terrie and Uncle P.J. when they came to spend a few days on the farm with us. Amber had been hoping that among her aunt's stash of goodies, there might happen to be a pair of Piggy slippers such as she had seen on the feet of her little friend, Mandy, and I am sure there would have been if she had let us know earlier.

199

After gift-giving, the children raced out to the fields to give their cousins a guided tour and show off their latest den-building projects. However, as the days passed, they exhausted the things of interest on the farm, so we decided it was time to explore new coves and beaches further afield. So we were delighted when Glen Howard invited us to join him, his wife, Megan and young Bethan for a fishing trip at Porth Llanelian, a secluded bay near Amlwch. In summer, the mackerel would come close to the rocky shores of Anglesey in their masses but only in localised, tight shoals so that one either had no rest between catching fish or caught none at all.

It was a relatively mild day when we arrived at the rocky coast, the sun was shining encouragingly, and there was a light breeze, which we hoped would not interfere with the efforts of our fishermen. The water was a calm and soothing blend of clear, azure blue that washed gently over the emerald green seaweed clinging to the rocks edging the pebbly beach. Glen and Megan had brought along Megan's visiting nephew, a 'delicate' young man inclined to poor health.

"How are you today, Steven?" was probably the worst question to ask if you were short on time, as it tended to lead to a lengthy explanation of the frailties and health issues he had endured in recent times. After an extended period of just such an interview with Steven on that particular day, I was slowly melting into a 'black hole' of transmitted depression. Thankfully Philip noticed my drained expression and rescued me by offering to loan Steven his spare fishing rod. So the day panned out happily, with Daniel, Joshua and Kirk getting into the spirit of angling and anticipating a grand catch while Steven started to relax and dwell on matters unrelated to his health. Terrie and Megan became acquainted with each other whilst keeping a watchful eye on the children for fear of them slipping down the rocky slope and into the sea. Meanwhile, Glen and I reached for our chilly bins to prepare for lunch.

"Oh, look at this; snow!" Glen announced as he lifted a large, misshapen block of ice from his chilly bin and threw it in the direction of the fishermen. The frozen chunk hit a rock behind them, showering them with icy particles. They all looked up at the sky in bewilderment before returning their attention to their fishing rods. For some reason, best known to no one, I decided to pull a similar mini iceberg from my chilly bin and attempted to copy Glen's trick. Unfortunately, just as I launched my ice block, a sudden gust of wind arose out of nowhere, it snatched my missile and hurled it at the back of Steven's head, and the poor young man collapsed into a groaning heap on the rocks. Philip and the boys turned to look at him and then at me with a look of surprise but were distracted by Kirk's fishing rod, which started dipping vigorously into the sea. The ladies rushed to Steven's aid, helping him drag himself to a comfortable grassy tussock, where he lay, grumbling and rubbing his head.

Feeling very guilty, I quickly searched for another lump of ice in the chilly bin and wrapped it in a tea towel to address the rising bump on his head.

"Strange how these lumps of ice are inclined to drop from the sky isn't it?" I commented unconvincingly. We gave Steven a sandwich, which he picked at unenthusiastically, and then he spent the next hour sitting on his grass tussock, rubbing his head as he gazed out to sea. Despite that little mishap, it was a reasonably successful fishing effort that day, with fresh fish filling the emptied chilly bins. Even Steven began to recover and took an interest in the fishing activity from his safe position, far away from dangerous chilly bins.

Amber had discovered the thrill of throwing stones into the sea and was impressed with the splashing effects when she reached her target. Picking up a large, sea-worn stone, she threw it with all her might; unfortunately, her missile fell far short of its intended destination and managed to whack Steven painfully on his elbow.

He emitted an agonised scream, and rolled around on the grass, clutching the injured limb. Poor Steven; it was not his day.

"Quick! We must get him to a doctor!" Terrie shouted.

"Let me look at him," offered Megan, a nurse at Bangor Hospital. "No, I think he should be all right; there is nothing broken here," she assured us as she manipulated the elbow with Steven wincing and complaining loudly.

"Let's look for some meadowsweet," I said, making our children also wince and complain loudly.

"This is not the time for picking flowers, Lynnette; the poor boy needs to see a doctor!" Terrie exclaimed. There was no point in telling her that the honeyed smell of meadowsweet acted as a good sedative, which would help with the pain. It suddenly dawned on me just how far apart we had drifted in our approach to life. Despite my original protestations, I was adapting to the country life, and over the next few days, our diverse values continued to reveal themselves.

Terrie has the reputation amongst our family of being successful in every way. A striking beauty like our mother but taking after our father for her shrewd business mind. She keeps an immaculate, well-organised home and garden, is frequently called upon to do the flower arrangements for special events and, like our paternal grandmother, cooks the tastiest of meals. We have all tried to emulate Granny's culinary achievements, especially Sunday lamb roasts with light and fluffy Yorkshire puddings. 'Toad in a hole' was one of the recipes she passed down to our mother and her granddaughters, and that Sunday, Terrie cooked us a wonderful meal that would have made our Granny proud. Fat, succulent Lincolnshire sausages embedded in sumptuous, golden-brown batter, served with crisp, gilded roast potatoes and salted cabbage covered in meaty gravy. I was more than happy to hand over the kitchen while she produced some gastronomic wonders.

One night, I carried a tray with a digestive biscuit and a cup of tea up to the bedroom. I did not have a side table, so I placed the tray on the floor beside the bed while I plumped up my pillows and made myself comfortable. Leaning over the side of the bed, I was surprised that the biscuit had disappeared. Had I already eaten it, I wondered? Had I imagined that I had put a biscuit beside my teacup? I climbed out of bed, got down on my hands and knees and peered under the bed, and there was my biscuit in the tiny paws of a little mouse, half the size of the biscuit, deeply engrossed in nibbling it.

Terrie's eyes widened with shock when I related that experience at breakfast the following morning.

"What did you do?" she asked, horrified.

"Well, I came downstairs and got another biscuit," I replied nonchalantly "And the funny thing is the cute little creature woke me up by running over my pillow this morning!" I laughed, but it was all too much for Terrie.

"Oh, dear; I have forgotten my tablets," she announced. "I will have to hurry back to Mum and Dad's home." And she did.

We soon caught the mouse using a live mouse trap, primed with another morsel of digestive biscuit, and released it back to the wild where it belonged. Well, even one little mouse can cause a lot of damage in a house.

Shortly after the departure of Terrie and her children, our little stone-throwing daughter made an alarming announcement. We were finishing a meal of hot, buttered sweet corn when Amber picked up a yellow kernel from her plate and looked at it intently as she rolled it between her finger and thumb.

"I put a corn in my ear," she said casually. I stopped chewing on my corn cob and held it in suspension as I looked over the table at our youngest daughter.

"I would not do that if I were you, Amber," I recommended, hoping I was mistaken in what I thought I had heard.

"No, I put a corn in my ear already," she corrected my misunderstanding patiently, holding her little hand up to her right ear.

"What, one like that?" I asked, pointing to the cooked kernel she was still rolling about between her fingers.

"No, a hard one like we give to the chickens," she said, taking a deep breath and looking like she was not sure whether she was wise to have made that confession.

"Let me have a look," I offered, leaning toward her and attempting to peer into the shadowy depths of her petite orifice. "Well, I can't see anything; when did you put it in there? Does it hurt?"

"It does a bit; I put it in there the other day."

"Oh, dear; what do you think we should do, Daddy?" I asked.

"Do about what?" her father asked, distracted from his conversation with Daniel about his schoolwork.

"About the corn kernel that Amber has put in her ear," I informed him.

"What did you do that for, Amber?" he asked indulgently. "It is meant to go in your mouth, not your ear."

"It's an uncooked kernel, Philip, and it is beginning to hurt her," I screwed up my face into a concerned grimace.

"Well, that was a silly thing to do, wasn't it?" Philip suggested, and Amber hung her head remorsefully. "I think a drop or two of warm olive oil in the ear tonight might dislodge it; if not, a trip to the doctor will be needed." So, just a few days later, Amber sat on her hospital trolley, watching the tropical fish in an oversized fish tank and waiting to go into surgery to have the foreign object removed from her ear.

"Why are you looking like a doctor, Mummy?" she whispered as I stood beside her, dressed in a protective gown, cap and mesh-covered shoes. I thought then how innocent is Youth; she was so trusting and seemed quite nonplussed about the drama in which she featured. Thankfully, she was soon back in the ward, wide awake after the light anaesthetic and asking for breakfast, which happened to be a bowl of cornflakes.

As a special treat for being such a good girl and not making any fuss over her operation, we bought her a gift of the coveted Piggy slippers. They were puffy pink with a piggy snout, little piggy eyes, a cheerful piggy smile, and even better, there were two of them.

Amber was in love! What Piggy slippers could not do was not worth mentioning. Piggy slippers could dance, Piggy slippers could hop, Piggy slippers could jump, Piggy slippers could skip, and Piggy slippers could run up and down the stairs. It was at that point that Amber stopped stock-still on her trot back down the stairs, looked down at her slippers, then up at Philip and I, who watched her with proud amusement, and then she declared:

"These slippers make me look stupid!" And that was the end of Piggy slippers.

# 25 Near Misses

Bang! Philip jumped in alarm at the sudden sound just as he was about to take a bite from his crisp and golden battered cod. He glanced at Ernie, sitting beside him, enjoying his fish and chips on a park bench in a suburb of Manchester.

"Someone's car backfiring, I suppose," Philip suggested.

"No," Ernie replied. "Didn't you notice those bullet holes in the walls of the apartment blocks we were cleaning this morning?"

"Gunshots? Are you serious?" Philip replied in stunned realization. "I wondered why so many of those windows were covered with metal sheets." He looked around him suspiciously, his anticipated peaceful lunchtime moment suddenly shattered.

A fearful and tense atmosphere existed nationwide at that time. The Northern Ireland war, known as 'The Troubles', was still raging, with frequent acts of violence and bombing involving both sides of the conflict. It was a grievous war that had dominated the news reports for almost thirty years. Although those disputes mostly took place in Northern Ireland, there were episodes of violence and bombing in the major cities of England, such as London, Manchester and Liverpool. Some citizens had become hardened and fatalistic, while others were nervous, checking under their cars for bombs before starting their engines. It certainly was a distressing era.

So far, Philip had no success finding employment with his newly-acquired degree, but he was pleased to get some cleaning work with our friend, Ernie. They had started out very early from home on this particular day, commencing cleaning the office blocks by about 7 am. Philip worked on the insides of the three-story buildings, cleaning the lobbies, stairwells and windows, while Ernie worked on the outsides, and they managed to clean four blocks before lunchtime.

'What a brave man,' Philip thought as he watched through the windows at his friend balancing on his extra-long ladders. Realizing that he had scaled those scary heights on a shaky ladder despite knowing about the violent neighbourhood, Philip's admiration for Ernie increased tenfold.

"You have a lot of courage to go so high on those ladders, Ernie," Philip stated as Ernie drove them homeward along the A55.

"I have been doing it for so long now that I don't even think about it," Ernie reassured him, with a cheerful smile spreading across his rosy countenance. Philip shuddered at the memory of his own uncomfortable experience during his youth.

"I did some window cleaning some years ago, but I developed a serious fear of heights due to a frightening experience," he confessed. "I was on a triple-extended ladder, cleaning a third-floor window for one of my clients when her husband came out of the house. He jumped into his car and reversed into the foot of my ladder, pushing it along the front of the house!" Ernie turned a shocked and expectant look briefly at Philip.

"What did you do?" he asked.

"Well, the same as anyone would do in that situation," Philip replied. "I yelled out, but he couldn't hear me, and he had not the least idea I was there. So I quickly pulled the top of the ladder away from the wall with one hand and worked along the wall with the other hand until the car stopped. I could feel its engine vibrating up the ladder with me shaking at the top, and then he moved forward and just drove off. I was a mess after that, I can tell you!"

"I can imagine; I would have felt the same," Ernie consoled, tapping the steering wheel in thoughtfulness as he drove along the road leading to the Conwy bypass. Philip hoped he had not shattered Ernie's confidence in his own expert ladder work, and he thought it best to change the subject.

"Bodelwyddan," Philip read aloud the sign-posted name of the town with the impressive white marble church, its tall spire clearly seen from the road as they passed.

"Pronounced Boddalwithan, I believe," Ernie corrected.

"Hmm, quaint," Philip acknowledged. "There were some very quaint village names around the area where Lynnette grew up, like Dode and Luddesdown; extremely ancient little places. Have you heard of Snodland?"

"Snodland? Ernie turned to look at Philip to see if he was joking.

"Yes, Snodland. She says she used to wonder what was so remarkable about a *Snod* to have had a small town named after him," Philip replied, and a wide grin appeared on Ernie's face.

"What about Llanfair PG on Anglesey?" He countered.

"Go on then; do you know how to pronounce the whole name?" Philip challenged.

*Llanfairpwllgwyngyllgogerychwyrndrobwllllantysiliogogogoch,* Ernie reeled off expertly.

"Impressive!" Philip congratulated. "So, what does it mean?"

"I believe it means: 'Saint Mary's Church in the hollow of white hazel near the rapid whirlpool of Saint Tysilio of the red cave.' I heard it is the longest official one-word place name in Europe."

"OK, you win," Philip ceded, returning his attention to the road ahead.

"Thank goodness for this new tunnel; it cuts half an hour off the journey, especially at this time of the evening with the traffic being so heavy around Conwy castle," Ernie commented as they drove down into the tunnel recently installed under the Conwy estuary.

"How on earth did they manage such an amazing feat of engineering, I wonder?" Philip replied, peering through the window at the concrete walls of that imposing structure.

"I heard it was the first immersed tube tunnel in the United Kingdom. They had to suck out tons of mud and sand to prepare a deep trench, and the tunnel itself was made from long, precast concrete box sections, which were floated down with the tide and then sunk in place and bolted together," Ernie explained knowledgeably.

"So, where did they dump all the mud and sand?" Philip asked.

"They used it to make a new wetland wildlife preserve for the RSPB, and the dry dock made for the casting of the tunnel sections has been turned into a yacht marina. So it was all very carefully thought out," Ernie concluded and then fell silent and thoughtful as they drove along the coastal A55 expressway. They passed through the Penmaenmawr works entrance, where a new tunnel was under construction through a precipitous mountain that dropped right into the sea. A powerful dumper truck was carrying away some enormous boulders, and a smile crossed Ernie's face as they watched that powerful vehicle at work.

"I had a go at driving some heavy machinery when I was young and newly married, and I had a near-miss with some huge boulders," he said. "I got to know a farmer who lived in Cumbria and needed someone to farm-sit while he and his wife went on holiday. Kath and I had not had much of a honeymoon, so this sounded like a good opportunity to make up for that. It was not a very big farm, just a few sheep and beef cattle and a recently harvested barley crop, so there was not much work for us to do. There was an old Fordson Super Major tractor the farmer kept in his yard, which I knew to be a good make for pulling logs out of the woods as it was powerful and had good traction."

"Did it need to be tow started?" Philip asked, thinking of the problems we were having with our tractor.

"No, it started with no trouble," Ernie laughed; he knew our tractor! "It had a beautiful sound to the engine, and smoke puffed out of the upright exhaust pipe as I played around with it for a bit, running up and down the farm tracks. I got to thinking about those huge boulders in the middle of one of the fields. I could tell from the furrows that the farmer had worked around them, and I wondered why he had never moved them. He was getting on a bit, so I guessed he didn't have the strength or energy to do anything about them. 'I think we could make ourselves useful around here

210

and help the farmer move that pile of boulders in the field; what do you think, Kath?' I said one morning."

"Well, maybe you could, but what could I do to help?" she said.

"As it happened, there was a big old Whitlock digger on the farm; it was a muddy yellow colour, with a good-sized bucket on the front and a 'back hoe' behind for digging out ditches, and I was itching to find an excuse to try it out. So I suggested I teach Kath to drive the tractor, and I would dig out the boulders with the digger."

"Did it work?" Philip asked.

"It worked like a dream!" Ernie exclaimed, enthralled by the memory of driving that digger. "It took me a couple of hours to get the hang of using all the knobs and switches, and I knocked over one or two fence posts that I had to quickly repair, but eventually, I was ready to use the thing. Kath is a fast learner, so despite the heavy steering, she found the tractor quite manageable. So we did a bit of practice, tidying up around the farm before tackling those boulders. I made up a sledge system using a trail of pine logs behind the tractor to shift the boulders onto, and then we were all set to go."

"The farmer must have been pleased when he returned," Philip suggested, but a dark look crossed Ernie's face as he turned briefly to face Philip.

"Not at all; he was horrified!" Ernie exclaimed. "The farmer telephoned the house the morning we planned to start work on the boulders to see how we were and to ask if there were any problems. I was pleased to say that there had been no trouble and that we had set ourselves the goal of helping him out by moving that pile of boulders to the edge of the field. 'What pile of boulders?' he asked, and I thought it strange that he should ask as it was so obvious which pile of boulders I meant. 'That pile of boulders in the middle of the field,' I answered, but I was getting rather worried."

"'That is not a pile of boulders; it is an ancient burial chamber!' he shouted down the telephone. 'It is thousands of years old and is a protected site!'"

"Oh, good grief!" Philip uttered, trying to look serious.

"Yes," Ernie replied and said nothing for a while as he pondered the memory of his embarrassing experience.

"So, what did you do?" Philip asked with a carefully contrived, sympathetic frown.

"Well, we put the digger and the tractor away and decided to go for a walk instead." Philip and Ernie looked at each other, and Philip tried to stifle a chuckle. Then Ernie's expression changed, and they both burst out laughing.

"Oh, well, it was a near miss," Ernie said after a while. "But all's well that ends well, so they say." And, as they crossed the Britannia Bridge to the beautiful, peaceful Isle of Anglesey and headed toward home, they felt their day had also ended well.

# 26 The Old Drovers' Route

Philip was in high spirits when he arrived home after visiting the Job Centre caravan in Amlwch in early September. Mrs Wyn-Jones had been surprised to see him again when he turned up after the four years since she had introduced him to the demanding task of demolishing the Rosgoch oil tanks. However, having attended the Centre every Thursday for the past few weeks since finishing at Bangor University, Philip was on the point of giving up hope of finding work, despite his new qualifications. That particular day though, he was in for a welcome surprise.

"I have here a new posting, Mr Barlow," Mrs Wyn-Jones said. "It is a temporary, part-time position as Horticultural Clerk of Works for the company, Travers Morgan, the supervising civil engineers responsible for the management of the entire A55 upgrade project. The successful applicant will oversee the tree planting, landscaping and rubbish control from Abergyngregyn to Bodelwyddan. Do you think this would interest you, Mr Barlow?"

Philip leapt at the chance to apply for the job; 'temporary' was a vast improvement on 'nothing'. He knew his training over the previous four years at Coleg Pencraig and Bangor University had prepared him well to meet the theoretical requirements and he already had plenty of practical experience.

"Finally!" I breathed a sigh of relief when he told me his good news. "That is wonderful! When do you start?"

"The interview is for tomorrow, and if I am successful, I can start next week," he said, hopefully.

"Well, I really hope you get the job, Philip; it sounds amazing!" I replied; the thought of him being employed and bringing in a good wage again lifted my spirits immensely. And, yes, the interview was successful and he started work within a few days.

The new expressway was the main highway across North Wales, linking the industrial cities of Manchester and Liverpool with the sandy beaches of Anglesey. The route included the new Conwy and Penmaenmawr tunnels, with which Philip had become quite familiar over the last few weeks due to his window-cleaning trips with Ernie. The company, Travers Morgan, were the supervising civil engineers for the entire project, and their Horticultural department drew up the designs and the tree planting specifications. Philip's responsibility was to ensure that those specifications were adhered to closely by the contract landscapers.

Marlene, the young assistant landscaping architect for the company, had made excellent designs for the six roundabouts at Caernarfon, each of them different and appealing. On some, she had recommended huge, quarried boulders nestled amongst plantations of shrubs and flowers, while others she decorated with an attractive scattering of grey slate fragments from the local quarry at Penrhyn. The contractors worked hard to represent her ideas to the minutest detail, and Philip felt pleased to work with such a team of skilled workers.

One day as he walked the miles along the A55, checking on the progress of the work, Philip stopped for lunch at a quaint old pub where he got to chatting with the landlord. The man told him some interesting details about travel between Anglesey and the mainland before the two bridges spanning the Menai Straits were built. Philip related his discoveries animatedly at the meal table that evening.

"What do you think? There were all these animals and geese that the farmers needed to get from Anglesey to the markets in England many years ago, long before they built the Menai and Britannia bridges crossing the Menai Straits. So, how do you think they managed it?" Our children always enjoyed their father giving them quizzes to test their common sense or general knowledge.

"I think they would have put them in a big truck and then….?" Ten-year-old Joshua's theory got a bit lost at that point.

"There would not have been any trucks at that time, Joshua," Philip replied, which was a staggering thought for a young boy who had never known a time when there were no trucks around.

"They would have had wagons with teams of horses to pull them, wouldn't they, Dad?" Amelia suggested, and I wondered if she had been watching too many 'Wild Western' movies.

"True, there would have been wooden carts back then, Amelia," Philip agreed. But many of the farmers would not have been able to afford carts, and what's more, it would have taken many of them to transport all the pigs, the herds of cattle, and the gaggles of geese."

"Gaggles!" Saffron giggled. She was only six-years-old, but already demonstrated a keen sense of humour.

"They would have to walk then," Daniel replied astutely.

"Exactly! But how did the farmers walk the animals and geese from Anglesey Island to the mainland without any bridges?" Philip watched the children's faces transform as they considered the answer to this puzzle.

"Catapult?" Joshua suggested with a cheeky grin. He was a real tease; no wonder I always called him my 'ray of sunshine'.

"Thank you, Joshua; any advances on the 'catapult' suggestion?" Philip chuckled.

"They could swim across, couldn't they, Dad?" Amelia had another attempt at the winning answer.

"They could swim, no doubt, Amelia, but have you seen how fast the water in the Menai Straits moves?" Philip asked.

"Ferry?" Daniel suggested.

"Good suggestion, Daniel," Philip commended. "There were several ferries across the Straits, some dating back hundreds of years. The Porthaethwy Ferry was one of them, which went from the little island that is now under the Menai Bridge. But it was expensive to cross that way, and the ferries were not large enough to take all the drovers and all their animals. But, as I said, the waters of the Menai Straits are dangerous, and there are two tides each day, coming from two directions. With the very strong currents and whirlpools, boats and ferries have been known to sink, and people have drowned.

"So, how was the crossing made then, Dad?" We were all stumped, but we knew Philip would have the answer.

"OK," he began. "Near Beaumaris is a spit of land that juts out into the Menai Straits, called the Lavan Sands or *Traeth Lafan* in Welsh. When the spring tides are fully out, the Straits are almost dry and can be walked across, although they would have had to go quickly as they would only have about an hour before the tide started to come in again. When they reached the other side, they needed to follow the old Roman Road from Abergyngregyn, all the way to England"

"That makes sense," I nodded, pleased to hear there was a practical solution to the problem.

"However, that long journey could take several weeks, and the feet of the geese and animals would have got very sore. So what did the drovers do to protect them?"

"They could wear shoes," Amelia suggested jokingly.

216

"That's right, Amelia! That is just what they used to do." Twelve-year-old Amelia looked pleasantly surprised.

"The drovers would herd the cattle into pens at Abergyngregyn, and the blacksmiths would nail metal shoes onto their hooves. They would have fitted the pigs with leather-soled woollen socks on their trotters, but the geese had another sort of footwear. They would have made them walk through a channel of warm, wet tar mixed with sand, and sometimes they would also have leather soles slapped onto their feet before the tar dried. So that is why Abergyngregyn was such an important village in days gone by.

As they enjoyed their fried eggs and oven-roasted potato chips, the children mused over that conversation, trying to imagine a strange world without modern cars, trucks or even a bridge connecting Anglesey with mainland Wales. In truth, it was hard for them to picture the area of Anglesey their father had been discussing as their world outside of the farm involved such a small circumference, spanning the more north/north-westerly part of Anglesey. That fact was likely also going through Philip's mind, for he made an interesting suggestion:

"I noticed the road sign for a place called 'Aber Falls' while at work today. How about we make a trip to explore it this weekend?"

So we arranged to meet with two other families in the car park at Bont Newydd, at the base of the walk to Aber Falls. Colin and Bridget, and Greg and Shirley, had recently become related by the marriage of their eldest children, Samantha and Jerome.

"I am sure that dog is more like a cat with nine lives; you just watch him; he has no fear of danger," Colin declared as he watched his collie dog, Jethro, rough-and-tumbling with the other dog, Teddy, the golden Labrador belonging to Greg and Shirley. Philip, Greg and Colin laughed at the antics of the dogs as the three

217

men kept the pace ahead of their wives and in pursuit of a swarm of children en route for the falls.

"He really should not be alive," Colin continued.

"Why, what has he been up to?" Philip asked

"He is very good at moving the cattle and not the least bit afraid of the bulls," Colin elaborated. "Any problem with them, and he would dive between their legs and nip at their heels until he had them hopping into obedience. But he is a compulsive tyre-biter, and one day when I was driving the tractor through a boggy field, he tried to bite the tyre. Unfortunately he got a bit too close to the wheel and his head went under it. I stopped the tractor and was horrified to see the poor dog with his head pressed into the mud; I was sure I had killed him! The next thing I knew, he had sucked his head out of the mud, leaving a perfect mould in the soft clay; he gave it a shake and got back on with his job like it was all in a day's work."

"I see what you mean," Greg said, issuing a low whistle.

We eventually arrived at Aber Falls, which was well worth the hike. It would have been informative to stop off and examine the Bronze Age settlements along the route and the standing stones that we spotted too. However, we were on a mission to reach the falls, which were of more interest to the young people, so we decided we would make that investigation on a future visit. The waterfall was quite spectacular and cascaded over the slippery rocks like silvery tresses from a height of about a hundred and twenty feet and ended in a deep, dark brown swirling pool of peaty water.

"Anyone fancy a swim?" Colin challenged.

"Not likely!" Bridget exclaimed, voicing the general opinion of we ladies; it looked lovely, but it would likely be icy cold, even on a hot day, and this was now late autumn. Colin and Greg's boys were up for it, however. They slid down over the slippery rocks with the two dogs, eager to be the first to take the plunge.

However, that was a quick burst of bravado that lasted only a few seconds. They all were back on the rocks instantly, laughing and shivering, blue with cold and with the dogs barking and shaking the water vigorously from their coats.

Back in the car park, everyone piled into their cars and headed back to share a *panad* with Colin and Bridget at their home on the edge of Parys Mountain, near Amlwch.

"Where is Teddy?" Shirley asked Samantha and Jerome when everyone arrived at the house an hour later.

"I don't know; I thought he was with you," Samantha replied.

"I thought he must have been with you in your car," Greg exclaimed, his face taking on a sudden greyness. "Come to think of it, I don't remember seeing him on the walk back down from the falls. Did anyone else see him back at the car park?" Everyone shook their heads worriedly.

It was late in the evening when Samantha and Jerome reached the Aber Falls car park again, and to their relief, there was one wet and lonely-looking Golden Labrador sitting and waiting, patiently for someone to come back to claim him. Teddy was ecstatic to see them, wagging his tail and yipping excitedly. How he managed to get himself separated from the group is still a mystery, but we were all so pleased to hear that he was safely returned home after his exciting day's excursion.

# 27 The Westerly Winds.

Duncan McFadden was a Glasgow man who had also come as an immigrant to Anglesey in search of a better, more peaceful life. However, his introduction to the Island was quite alarming...

Jennifer had come to live in Amlwch from Glasgow after her divorce three years earlier to be closer to her married son and hopefully start a new life. That evening she had filled the kettle in her tiny kitchen, set it to heat and heaved a sigh as she looked out at the garden, which was becoming shrouded by the descent of dusk. Rain beat fiercely at the window and the bare trees swayed, black and ominously, against the charcoal sky. She closed the curtains to block out the threat of a stormy night. The TV guide for the evening did not seem to offer any scintillating entertainment as she flicked through it while waiting for the kettle to boil, so she decided on an early night with a good book.

A sharp, heavy rap on the front door knocker made her jump, almost pouring boiling water over herself. Jennifer looked at the clock on the kitchen wall, it was five forty-five, and she was not expecting any visitors. She was pleased that she had taken her son's advice and had a security chain fitted on the front door. She was particularly grateful for that chain when she gingerly opened the door a crack and saw a tall, gaunt stranger peering back at her. His coat collar was turned up against the wind, and the cold rain beat against his high forehead, running down into his dark, deep-set eyes.

"Jennifer McAfee?" The man demanded in a deep, gruff voice. Jennifer's first instinct was to shut the door again and hide behind it, but he had a Glaswegian accent, and he knew her name.

"Yes," she replied timidly.

"My sister sent me," the man continued. "She said you would help me find some lodging. Margaret Broon." The reflection of the lights from passing traffic flickered eerily across his rain-lashed face as Jennifer considered that name.

"Just a minute, I will call my neighbour," she finally managed to reply and closed the door against that frightening figure. A few minutes passed before a familiar 'rat-a-tat-tat' came at the door, and opening it a crack, Jennifer was pleased to see her neighbour, Robert, from across the road.

"My sister sent me," the tall stranger repeated as he sat on the sofa opposite Robert, warming himself by the fire and savouring his tea while his coat dripped copious streams of water into the hearth where Jennifer had hung it.

"Yes, of course, I know Margaret," Jennifer was gaining a little courage now that she had her good friend with her. "But why did she send you here all the way from Glasgow?" Being suitably warmed and refreshed by his tea and biscuits, Duncan McFadden began to relate his story. He appeared to be a man in his early forties who had been in trouble with the law. His sister had been deeply concerned about his getting involved again with a powerful gang, so before his release from prison, she recommended that he get far away from Glasgow, and that was where Jennifer came in.

"Sorry to just turn up like this, with no warning," Duncan added. "It all happened very quickly, and Margaret only had your address but not your phone number." Robert and Jennifer looked across the room at each other and then pityingly at that bedraggled, homeless visitor.

"Well, you obviously can't stay here for the night," Robert stated decisively. "Let me ring Katherine to see if we can free up one of the bedrooms for you at our house, and then we can find you somewhere to live tomorrow."

Determined to change his ways and leave behind his dubious past, Duncan soon built up a business as a window cleaner and became a respectable member of society. He married a charming Welsh lady from Tregele named Carys, and they came to be amongst our circle of friends. So there they were, sitting at our kitchen table, eating homemade bread and cake and telling hilarious stories of his antics in Glasgow, many of which are best not repeated. Like most of our associates, they were a very resourceful couple, and Duncan could not pass a dumpster skip without rummaging inside, looking for usable or resalable items. Duncan related his latest experience of 'dumpster-diving', and Carys almost choked on her cake with laughter at the memory of that occasion.

"We were driving home from Holyhead, and I noticed a new skip in a layby," he began.

"I was getting tired and hoped he wouldn't stop," Carys interjected.

"But I just could not resist," Duncan continued in his rough Scottish accent. "So Carys stayed in the car while I jumped into the skip. It was mostly empty, but there were a lot of nuts, bolts, screws and nails covering the floor, good ones too. 'Well, I can use these for the building work I plan to do on the house,' I thought, so I started gathering them up and putting them in my bucket. It was getting dark, but I had a small torch with me, and I was concentrating so hard on gathering my treasures that I did not notice the truck that had pulled up in the layby until I was suddenly covered in grass cuttings!"

"Oh, no!" I exclaimed, trying not to laugh.

"Well, I stood up, with grass all over me and my torch in my hand, and I shouted, 'Oi! Do you no ken what yer doing?' You should have seen the expression on the face of that man when he saw me in the skip. He was so shocked that he jumped back into his van and drove off at top speed!"

Honestly, you had to have known Duncan to appreciate the shock he would have caused that poor, unsuspecting man. I am sure I would have reacted the same way if I had seen him rise from the shadowy depths of the skip, covered in grass, with his torch illuminating his skeletal-looking face. He must have made a terrifying apparition with his high forehead, deep-set, dark-rimmed eyes and gravelly voice reverberating around the walls inside that metal bin! We were all in hysterics at that mental image, and I can never now pass a dumpster skip without thinking of Duncan.

"So, do you like living here on Anglesey, Duncan?" Philip asked as the laughter settled down.

"Aye, and I am very pleased I met my Carys," he replied, putting his arm around her affectionately and making her giggle. "But this year, the wind has been oppressive; it was never like this in Glasgow."

"Yes, but it is not always this bad, Duncan; it has been unusually windy recently. Anyway, I have never known any different; I thought everywhere was like this," Carys confessed. Her comment reminded me that there were some people I had met who had never been off the Island or maybe had been no further than across the Menai bridge to the 'Great Metropolis, Bangor'.

"What about the cats the other night, Duncan?" Carys started laughing again, and Duncan's face creased with a broad smile. "We were getting ready for bed, and I went to put the cats out," she continued. "I tossed one of them out of the back door, but the wind took her, and she sailed away into the darkness! Meeeeeooooowww!" Daniel thought that was hilarious and could not stop giggling.

"So I said, 'Hey, Duncan, come and watch this; where is the other cat?'" Carys could not finish her story for laughing.

They were a happy couple and so good for each other. We spent many more pleasant times together around our kitchen table, enjoying the sound of Carys' rhythmic Welsh accent and listening to Duncan's tales of his errant youth. Then one day, they were gone! We never knew why or to where. Was it that Duncan's dubious past had caught up with him, or were they chased away by the invasive westerly winds of Anglesey?

"I don't know how much more of this I can take," Philip stated between energetic grunts and bat swings as he hit his squash ball against the wall.

"Come on, Philip, where is your spirit?" Glen Howard responded with a laugh. "We have only just begun."

"No, I mean this gale, 'grunt, puff'. It has gone on for almost two months without let-up," jump, whack. "I have never known it this bad."

"Yes, I must say it is a bit much; I don't remember ever having such a long storm," Glen agreed. 'Wheeze, swish, thump'. "Sometimes, I think of packing up and moving to Australia or New Zealand."

"Really?" Smack, thrust, crunch.

"Yes, I mean it; Megan is ready for a change as well," Glen replied.

"Ow!" Philip had stopped playing and was staring at Glen. "OK, your game. What do you plan to do then?"

"I am in contact with a firm of immigration consultants run by New Zealanders in London, Campbell and Hollings; they specialise in representing applicants for visas for the Antipodes. I have asked them to send me the application forms," Glen replied, wiping the perspiration from his face with his towel.

"When did you do that?" Philip was surprised by that revelation.

"Last week sometime; they said it would take about a week, so I expect them to arrive any time now."

"Well, you should qualify with no trouble, what with having a Master's degree and a trade," Philip assured him.

"There should be no problem, and of course, with Megan being a qualified nurse, I think it should go through pretty quickly." Glen picked up his racket and retrieved the ball from the far side of the court, ready to continue the game. "Do you think it would interest you?"

"You know, it has gone through my mind once or twice, not that I am unhappy living here, but I need permanent, full-time work. We could do with living where there is still a thriving agricultural industry, preferably English-speaking and with more gentle weather. I will have to chat with Lynnette about that," Philip said, resuming the game somewhat distractedly.

I had to admit that Glen's suggestion sounded very appealing, especially as the fierce gale, which started about New Year's Day, continued to assail us throughout January and February. It was not just a strong wind, It was in full-on battle formation, attacking us at every turn and driving everyone to distraction! One shopping day, I had the helpless experience of watching my lettuce whipped out of my grocery box and blown into the distance along Amlwch High Street, like tumbleweed in a desert storm, and I had to go back into Cefni Fruit shop to buy another one. We were becoming irritable, needing to steel ourselves to leave the house, and the children needed to cling onto the fencing to make their way up our lane each day after school. When it was time to empty the wood ash from the Rayburn, we barely made it through the back door before the wind whisked all the ash away into the distance. That was not too much of a problem, provided that our newly-washed car was not parked just around the corner of the house. Every day was much the same for seventy-two days until the gale suddenly stopped!

We ventured from the house furtively, like post-disaster survivors, and tested the air; all was calm, and the day was cold but bright, sunny and windless. But it was too late for forgiveness; we felt abused by the elements for quite long enough, and the seed of 'change' was now sown in our minds. But where should we go? Daniel was approaching the conclusion of his sixth form at school, and then what? He was an A-star student in the Welsh language, but would he be another country lad lured by the bright lights and opportunities of the big cities in England? Our dear,

226

appreciative children had never complained about our having so little money for luxuries, and it was not until later in life that they realised there had ever been a problem. They were never hungry and were always well dressed, thanks to the generosity of our friends and family and the regularly-gifted black sacks of hand-me-down clothes.

We had been full of dreams of an idyllic life when we had first arrived on Anglesey, and here we were, nearly eight years later. What a wealth of experience we had gained; we had learned so much about cultural differences, mortality, resourcefulness, success and disappointments, history, humour, sharing and sheer hard work. We knew that we would never be the same again.

However, as Leslie had warned, employment was a major problem for everyone on the Island, but especially for 'outsiders', and even the children born here were moving to the big cities of England for better work opportunities. The elderly were often tearful when they recalled the days of their youth when these ancient stone houses were full of the noise and bustle of family life. Now many homes inherited from generation to generation were empty, with few young ones to treasure them. Many were being sold off as holiday homes to city dwellers and remained vacant for most of the year, causing understandable resentment among some locals. As the old folks feared, with the demise of their generation and with very few youths to follow their ardour for the long-held traditions, some of the almost-empty churches and chapels were becoming used as shops, Bingo halls or sports clubs.

When Daniel was just a toddler, he had learned the names of many of the tasty English apple varieties that Philip brought home in crates for us to sell to the neighbours from our back door, such as Worcester, Discovery, Russet, Laxton Superb, James Grieve, and Lord Lambourne. However, these and other ancient English apple varieties could not compete with the French Golden Delicious that

227

dominated the supermarket fruit shelves since the decision to join the European Union. Sadly, due to the overly rigid application of European regulations, many of those English apple orchards of Kent, 'the Garden of England', where Philip had once earned his living, had been grubbed out, with few remaining. Generally, the agricultural sector of Britain was looking dismal at that time. The wealth of Britain shifted to banking and finance, and the commuter belt around London was ever widening, allowing city workers to buy homes further afield, so rural properties in southern England were becoming unaffordable for the average country person who wished to work in agriculture.

Philip enjoyed his work on the A55 development and felt privileged to be involved in such a worthwhile project. However, the job would end within three to four months, with no suitable permanent work on the horizon, so we decided it was time to consider Glen's suggestion. I have often had to tame Philip as he has always been very objective, dynamic and achieving, although sometimes impulsive. However, our experience of moving to Anglesey had taught us the need to give time, thought and thorough research to any new projects. Nevertheless, within a few weeks of deliberation, we decided to apply for a visa to immigrate to New Zealand.

## The Westerly Wind

It swept in from the ocean and raced up the hills.
It set sails in motion on stately windmills.
It shrieked around houses and screeched through the trees,
Callously stripping off crisp autumn leaves.

It ripped away roof tiles and tore at old slates.
It slammed into windows and rattled the gates.
It whistled through cracks it could find in the doors,
Causing flurries of dust as it whirled across floors.

It screamed to the beach and assaulted the tide,
Striking fear into hearts, driving creatures to hide.
It whipped up the waves into buff-coloured foam,
Which crashed into coves as their force was made known.

They lashed at the harbour and pummelled the beach,
Sending watery sprays to heights once out of reach.
They tossed up small boats and splintered their hulls,
While the wind hindered progress of seafaring gulls.

With enough damage done but its power unspent,
It sped back out to sea with no sign of relent.
Once again tranquil, as the gale did rescind
Peace reigned in the wake of that westerly wind.

# 28 Breaking Barriers

I was rather pleased that I had curled my hair and applied my make-up before answering the door to the handsome young farmer on that mild morning in May. It was a complete surprise to have such a visitor walk up to the door unannounced; he must have been a local person who I had not met before.

"Mrs Barlow?" The young man asked. "Colin Chambers," he continued when I confirmed my identity. "My cousin, John Owen, tells me you want to rent out your fields."

"Yes, that's right, we do," I replied. "Are you interested?"

"I could be; I have a small herd of bullocks. Is your husband around?" I was fascinated by the carousel of flies buzzing around his flat cap, and I guessed he had probably dropped it in a cow pat at some time.

"Er, no; he is not here at the moment," I brought my attention back to the subject at hand. The farmer smiled and leaned casually against the doorpost, evidently thinking he had won another admirer. "But if you want to leave me your 'phone number, I will pass it on to him." Pleased with the success of his mission, the man smiled again at me after writing down his details on the notepad I kept by the front door, and then he strolled off, jauntily down the drive again with his entourage of flies still dancing around his cap.

Another reason to be grateful to our neighbour, John Owen, for his help, I thought as I watched the farmer go and considered how this new turn of events would make my life so much easier. From the very start of our time living at *Ty'n Llain*, we had been able to rely on John for help, advice and support for our various causes. We had only to let him know of our needs, and John would put the word around.

The bullocks arrived the following Friday; it had been a wet week, and the ground had suffered considerably from an overdose of rain, leaving the fields quite muddy. However, the weather had improved slightly, and the sun managed to break through the

231

clouds when Colin Chambers, joined by his brother, Christopher, walked their young herd up the lane that afternoon and into the fields at the back of the house.

"The cows have arrived!" the children announced when their father came home from work that evening. They were so excited as they had not had dealings with bovines before, so it was a new experience for them.

"They are nice-looking bullocks, aren't they?" commented Philip at the meal table. "But I recommend you don't go too near them; cattle are not all docile like sheep, although these have been castrated, so they should not be as aggressive as a bull." I could tell that the method of castrating a young bull was about to be explained until I caught Philip's eye and shook my head warningly, and the conversation turned to other topics. He did not need to elaborate on the meaning of the word 'castrated' as the children had seen him use that nasty little tool with the rubber bands he kept as an almost constant feature in the pocket of his wax jacket. Although Philip only used it to dock the *tails* of the lambs, he had explained that many farmers used it to emasculate the male lambs. We pitied the poor young creatures we saw in the neighbouring fields that hopped about uncomfortably for a few weeks until their claim to *ramliness* had dropped off.

Saturday improved weather-wise, so the afternoon was devoted to gardening and weeding around the vegetable patch. Some time was then spent on homework or go-carts, depending on the age of the child, although the new herd in the fields seemed to take up quite a bit of attention. They were a docile collection of Hereford/Friesian cross-breeds with either black and white or brown and white markings and large, long-lashed eyes that watched us with mutual interest. I breathed a sigh of relief that, much as I had loved having our flock of sheep, I was no longer responsible for them. I could now concentrate on making preparations for the sale of the house and on sewing our dresses for an upcoming wedding.

On Sunday morning, I drew back the curtains in the bedroom occupied by Saffron and Amber to encourage them to get dressed for the Service that morning. A sense of foreboding overwhelmed me however, when I looked through the window; the fields were empty! I hastened to the boys' room at the other end of the house and asked them to look out of the window to see if they could see any bullocks in the fields, and no, they could not. Neither could they be seen out of Amelia's window. Could they have perhaps somehow wandered into the fields at the front, I wondered? Philip rose from bed and checked through our window, but they were nowhere to be seen.

"Oh, no!" he groaned, and we quickly dressed and ran outside to find that the gate to their field had been pushed wide open, and a trail of cow dung and deep hoof ruts led away down the lane.

"Look, one of them must have lifted the latch on the gate with its horns to escape," Philip exclaimed. Leaving the children with instructions to get themselves dressed and have breakfast, we climbed into the car and followed their trail. There was no sign of the herd in Arthur's field at *Pen Cae*, and thankfully, Mr and Mrs Case had firmly closed the gate leading to their immaculately kept garden. That was a relief! I had visions of our charges standing in their attractive little fish pond or vying with Diesel, the Shetland pony, for his sparse supply of grass on that rocky terrain.

There was no sign of our runaways having taken the lane to the right where David and Judy lived in *Bryn Hidil*, but the evidence of cow presence showed they had headed down toward the main road. Unfortunately, Rhiannon's house had no gate to the garden and she had made the mistake of leaving her washing on the line overnight. It was not hanging on the line any more, and the lovely clean washing she had hung out the day before now joined the trail of cow dung marking the progress of the perpetrators making their way toward greener pastures. We passed the partially built house belonging to an absent English couple, which the children and I all found to be quite spooky and past which, we always quickened our pace on the way up or down the lane. The overgrown gorse-edged entrance must have looked unappealing as there were no knicker-draped cattle to be seen on that property. The trail continued to the end of the lane and then veered to the right, indicating that our escapees had travelled toward Llanfechell.

"Oh, good Heavens; what a mess they would make of the village square if they managed to reach it!" I exclaimed. Thankfully, we did not need to worry too much about an invasion of Llanfechell Square, for just a few yards down the Mountain road, the trail we were following disappeared into a large field, and there was the owner of the field, leaning against the closed gate and waiting for us. We thought we were in deep trouble!

"Your bullocks?" The farmer asked with an indulgent smile as though restraining runaway cattle was a daily event.

"Yes, sorry about that," Philip ventured. "They belong to Chris and Colin Chambers but they are supposed to be in our field."

"Ah, yes," the farmer replied, "I thought I recognized them; I will give Colin a ring to let him know they are here."

"Did they cause much damage?" Colin Chambers asked when he and his brother arrived a few minutes later from the top of Mynydd Mechell.

"Not too much," Philip replied, but I wonder what our neighbour, Rhiannon, will say when she goes to check on her washing this morning!"

"Don't worry about Rhiannon," Colin laughed, "she is our cousin; we won't tell her."

While the Chambers brothers, aided by their two sheepdogs, walked the bullocks back up the lane to *Ty'n Llain*, Philip and I sped home ahead of them to make a more secure fastening for the field gate and to chivvy along our offspring in their efforts at preparing to go out to Amlwch. We wondered what had been the interaction between the cousins when they met near Rhiannon's home, but we heard nothing more about her laundry.

So we had learned some more lessons about the local people, about age-old relationships that led to trust and goodwill. We felt that our many experiences had broken down cultural barriers and allowed us to occupy a small part of their close-knit community, a circumstance we had hoped to achieve for the past eight years. At that moment, we were quite sorry to be leaving.

"A tragedy! Such a tragedy!" Philip lamented. "I was concerned that the man who took on that job might not have had the experience to care for such a responsible assignment, and now look what has happened!"

"What has happened, Philip?" I asked, bewildered.

"The pine trees around Cestyll garden were thinned out and cut back last autumn to let in more light. Without the protective barrier, the recent storm winds invaded the garden, taking down many trees and doing a huge amount of damage!"

To his surprise, the supervision of the repair work on Cestyll garden was his new assignment from Travers Morgan. I had never visited the garden as it was only open to the public one weekend a year, at the end of May, and I always managed to miss it. But, as Philip had given me such a comprehensive description of it when he had discovered the broken down back gate some years earlier, I could visualize it in all its enchanting glory.

"What a shame; is there anything you can do about it?" I asked hopefully; I hated to see him so upset and irritated.

"Well, after wanting to work in that garden for so long, I will certainly do my best to help repair the damage," he assured me. "The first thing we must do is to protect it from further wind damage, and the immediate plan is to replant with new pine trees to restore the shelter belt. But trees don't grow in five minutes, and they will have a tough time against the elements. It could take twenty or thirty years to grow big enough to make a suitable barrier again, and the project will be an extremely costly undertaking. I would have enjoyed caring for that garden, but I am only the Clerk of Works, just there to confirm that the work is done according to specifications," Philip frowned and shook his head. "Still, I am so pleased that I finally got to work there, and hopefully, we can begin to restore the garden to the glory that the Lady Violet Vivian originally intended."

# 29 Three Rainy Days in Dolgellau

July was promising to be a good month. The sun shone for days, the wind was just a mild and gentle breeze, and the strawberry plants had produced a bumper crop of heart-shaped scarlet berries. Having finished school and attaining remarkable grades in his GCSE exams, Daniel began to search for local jobs, and he was delighted when he was offered part-time gardening work on the grounds of the Gadlys Hotel. Our friends, Brian and Petula, had done a superb job of renovating the hotel and were now hosting clients, and it was to them that we sold most of our strawberries.

I guessed that Philip and Daniel had left in a hurry early one Monday morning when I came downstairs and discovered a note amongst the scattering of cornflakes and sugar on the kitchen table:

'Hello, Mum, we have gone to work in Bala,' Daniel had written on a small note left on the table, while underneath, Philip had written: 'Because we are big men.'

"Why do we have to bash these weeds, Dad? Couldn't we just use weed killer?" Daniel was beginning to swelter in the hot afternoon sun as he whipped at the weeds around the young Hawthorn hedge lining the walkway. His father stopped working and wiped away the perspiration from his forehead.

"You see this stream here, Daniel; where do you think it will end up?" he quizzed his eldest son. Daniel peered over the top of the low hedge and surveyed the tapestry of sunlit, lime, jade, and emerald-green countryside beyond it. There in the valley lay the still, dark blue waters of Lake Bala, or *Llyn Tegid*, upon which floated the reflection of fleecy-white clouds.

"Oh, I see; the weed killer would drain into the stream here and then into the lake and could poison the fish."

"That's right, Daniel. There are conflicting schools of thought on the subject, but if the label on the herbicide says: 'Do not use near waterways', which many of them do, I would not use it near

237

waterways. Think about this as well, breaking down the weeds and trampling them into the ground makes matting that will hinder the growth of more weeds. Also, as it is so warm right now, the thatch of weeds will help hold in any moisture to protect the young hedge from drought." Realisation dawned on Daniel of the importance of considering the ecology, so he decided to keep up the weed-bashing.

Apart from the thrashing sound of their occupation, nothing but the tweet, twitter and bird song mingled with the bleating of the sheep on the distant pasture. Then suddenly, they heard a tremendous roar overhead that ripped the sky asunder as two terrifyingly noisy jet fighter planes tore through the tranquil skies! Daniel and Philip were shocked by the unexpected, ear-splitting invasion of those great, grey *behemoths* that veered and darted just a few hundred metres above their heads. They were rooted immovably to the spot and could only watch wide-eyed until the noise faded into the distance, echoing off the valley walls.

"Good grief! I didn't even see them coming!" Philip exclaimed when he regained his equilibrium. "They must be on training exercises." Daniel was still stunned and silent. He had never heard such a loud sound before, and he looked around furtively to see if any more of those startlingly powerful monsters planned to surprise them. He did not appreciate sudden, loud noises under any circumstances, and there was no excuse for such a shocking intrusion into his peaceful day. Philip noticed him frequently pausing in his work to check the skies for the next onslaught.

That night, as father and son lay on the mattress in the back of the pick-up truck loaned from their employer, Anglesey Mowers, Daniel's attention was still transfixed on the cloudless, indigo sky.

"What is that group of stars called, Dad? Is it The Plough?" Daniel asked; he knew his father would be able to answer his question. They had spent many evenings together at *Ty'n Llain* with his younger siblings, peering through the eyepiece of Philip's telescope so he could identify many of the clusters of celestial bodies that decorate the firmament.

"Well done, Daniel; why do you think it is The Plough?" Philip asked.

"The shape, although it looks more like a saucepan with a long handle to me," Daniel confessed. The two star-gazers continued to discuss those sparkling jewels of the night until it was time to pull over the tarpaulin cover and sleep the sleep of the exhausted.

With the weed control along Lake Bala's walkway completed by late afternoon the following day, it was time for them to move on to their next project – attacking some Japanese Knotweed at Aberdyfi (pronounced Aber dovie) on the coast of Cardigan Bay. En route, they spotted a charming, whitewashed hotel named *Pen-Y-Bont,* which sat right on the edge of the rippling waters of the lake called *Tal-y-Llyn*. Tempting aromas wafted from the open restaurant windows, enticing the two hungry men inside for a meal of *Cawl,* a slow-cooked stew made with Welsh lamb, leeks and various other vegetables. Considered the national dish of Wales, *Cawl* is a one-pot meal, perfect for those cold, rainy days, somewhat usual in Wales, regardless of the season.

The low ceilings and blackened timbers inside the restaurant exhibited an inviting charm, and on the wall hung a picture of a barefoot young woman who had lived almost two hundred years before. Daniel wanted to know who she was.

"Ah, that will be Mary Jones," answered the restaurant owner with a cheerful smile on his radiant face. "Almost two hundred years ago, she walked barefoot all the way from here to Bala to buy a Bible. That was some big effort for a fifteen-year-old; you would not find many young ones today prepared to work hard and save up for months and then walk twenty-six miles barefoot to buy a Bible!" Daniel did not seem overly impressed; he had never considered the need to walk twenty-six miles barefoot to spend his pocket money on a Bible as he had always been used to seeing the Bible in our home.

"Her cottage is not far from here, about an hour's walk up the valley. Although there is not much to see of it, just the ruins but people even come from overseas to visit it," the man added.

"Maybe we should take a walk to see it one day," Philip replied. "In the meantime, we are on our way to a weed control job at Aberdyfi, and it is getting late; would you mind if we camp overnight in your car park?"

"No problem," the man agreed hospitably.

"You know, that was quite a feat that Mary Jones accomplished," Philip mused as he and Daniel lay in the back of the truck that night, watching the stars. "Today, books can be printed and distributed easily but two hundred years ago, it was a far more complicated procedure. And to walk barefoot over the hills amongst all that bracken, gorse and heather – ouch! What a devoted young lady. I would be interested in finding that cottage; maybe we should take a camping trip here sometime," he continued. However, Daniel, weary from his day of work, had already succumbed to the sweet gift of sleep.

"I know the owners of that hotel and restaurant; I am sure if I asked him, he would allow us to camp on his land," Glen Howard said when he and Megan called to see us with Bethan and little Bobi a few days later. And that was how we managed to find ourselves propping up our borrowed tent in a field beside the pretty lake, *Tal-y-Llyn*.

Now camping has never been my idea of a relaxing holiday, but I knew that Philip and the children found it an exciting experience, so I put my best efforts into the project. However, there was one thing I had neglected to consider while making preparations for the trip.

"Where are the toilets?" I asked, looking around, hopefully, for even the most primitive of toilet and shower blocks.

240

"No toilets," Philip replied as we erected the last tent pole.

"What? No toilets?"

"No; why do you think we brought the spade?"

"No shower block?" I was getting worried.

"There is the lake; it should be very refreshing to bathe in," Philip said over his shoulder as he hammered another tent peg firmly into the ground.

"You did not mention there would be no amenities!" I was struck with the realisation that we were camping, 'Philip style'!

"I can see this is going to be a very short holiday," Megan laughed as she threw her pop-up tent into the air and watched it expand and settle, fully erected onto the ground beside ours.

"Oh, joy!" I groaned, picking up my essential toiletry accessory and dragging it, reluctantly, into the adjacent forest.

As predicted, the lake was refreshingly chilly, so we put off bathing until later in the day when the sun had managed to warm it a little. The children then got into the spirit of the occasion and were soon splashing about happily. It was an enjoyable day spent lying out on the sun-warmed banks of the lake, enjoying the fresh air and even having the freedom of having no toilets to clean.

The next day, Philip and Daniel decided to walk up the valley to find the cottage of Mary Jones. It was a long, pleasant walk, and they savoured the moist atmosphere of the sparsely-wooded route and the babbling of the silvery brook that tumbled down through the undergrowth. Eventually, they stumbled across the ruins of the tiny cottage near the village of Llanfihangel-y-pennant. Apart from the base of stonework that marked its perimeter, little remained of *Ty'n-y-ddol* cottage, or 'House in the Meadow'. They were taken back in time, just standing in its presence and imagining what life would have been like for people back then and the hardships they must have endured. They thought of the determination, sacrifice and courage of the girl whose love for God and the Bible had moved her to put so much effort into obtaining a copy in the Welsh language.

A monument had been built in the centre of the ruins in her honour, which reads:

**ER COF AM MARI JONES**
**YR HON YN Y FLWYDDYN 1800,**
**PAN YN 16 OED A CERDDODD OR**
**LLE HWN I'R BALA, I YMOFYN BEIBL**
**GAN Y PARCH. THOMAS CHARLES, B.A.**
**YR AMGYLCHIAD HWN FU**
**YR ACHLYSUR SEFYDLIAD Y**
**CYMDEITHAS FEIBLAIDD**
**FRUTANAIDD A THRAMOR.**


**IN MEMORY OF MARY JONES, WHO IN**
**THE YEAR 1800, AT THE AGE OF 16 [15]WALKED**
**FROM HERE TO BALA, TO PROCURE FROM THE**
**REVD. THOMAS CHARLES, B.A.**
**A COPY OF THE WELSH BIBLE. THIS INCIDENT**
**WAS THE OCCASION OF THE FORMATION OF**
**THE BRITISH AND FOREIGN BIBLE SOCIETY.**
**ERECTED BY THE SUNDAY SCHOOLS OF MERIONETH**

As Philip and Daniel walked the route back to our camp, it was a time for contemplation and self-analysis and to ask themselves if their appreciation for the Bible would have moved them to make the same sacrifices as that exemplary young lady.

That evening Megan, the children and I all returned to the lake for a swim while Philip and Glen prepared the barbecue. Unfortunately, Daniel forgot that he was wearing his new glasses when he dived into the water, re-emerging without them. The water was so disturbed, and the bottom of the lake so churned up that there was no hope of finding them, so we did not expect to see them again. Poor Daniel; it put a bit of a damper on the day, and we returned to the camp feeling defeated. However, the smell of roasted sausages and onions cooked over an open fire was soothing, and the unexpectedly delicious taste of Glen's tin foil-wrapped jacket potatoes and salted, steamed cabbage made a sweet finish to the day.

I emerged from our tent the next morning, looking like some prehistoric monster! The midges had feasted on my face overnight, making it swollen, red and lumpy.

"You look a mess!" Megan exclaimed. "Yes, this is going to be a very short holiday!" I guessed that was one advantage of having no bathroom mirror, in fact, no bathroom at all; at least I did not have to look at my grotesque reflection. I decided that a quick dip in the lake should cool down the itchy redness. As I took my first tentative steps into that chilly body, there, sitting on a large, flat rock under the silvery, settled water, were Daniel's glasses; he was so delighted!

The skies began to cloud over soon after breakfast, and then it started to rain.

"No matter, we have brought some board games; they should keep us entertained until the rain stops," Megan announced cheerfully. So we all huddled into our tent and played board games until we ran out of enthusiasm for that diversion. The rain continued all day, and all the next day, so we decided it was time to tell some stories from our past. Glen related some fascinating tales of his adventures in the Middle East, while, with much prompting from his eldest son, Philip decided it was time to tell the story of the ill-fated *HMS Affray*.

"It was in the year 1951," he began. "My parents had been married for just a few months, and my mother was expecting my older sister, Anne. My father, Michael Barlow, was in the Royal Navy and assigned to the submarine *HMS Affray*. The submarine was due to be sent out on a training exercise, the objective of which being kept a secret. Oddly enough, many of the well-trained crew were taken off-board at the last minute, exchanging them for a host of novice officers, fresh out of Royal Navy training school.

My father was among those enlisted to sail in her, but just before the *HMS Affray* was due to sail, he was called off of her and reassigned to enter an Inter-Service Marksman competition between the Army, the Royal Navy and the Royal Air Force. He was a top-rate marksman, trained to shoot at the tips of the detonator horns of naval mines placed in the sea during the Second World War. Several of those ominous-looking metal spheres could still be seen bobbing around Britain after The War and his aim was so good that he could hit one of the explosive horns at a considerable range with his rifle, and he would rarely miss.

On the 16th of April 1951, *HMS Affray* went out into the English Channel and never returned. Seventy-five lives were lost on that mission; my father could have been one of them, and I would not have existed were it not for his incredible skill with the rifle." (See the book 'Subsmash' by Alan Gallop for more details.)

Everyone in the tent was speechless. A cold shiver went down my back, and I could see from the faces of Philip's audience that they all felt the same way.

"So, is that what you meant when you said one near-miss could have changed history for us?" Daniel asked.

"Yes indeed, Daniel. And what kind of a world would it be without all of you lovely children?" Philip smiled, and they all gathered around him for a reassuring hug.

It rained heavily all that night, and the following morning was cold and drizzly.

"Well, that was exciting!" Megan stated wryly as we packed up our soggy tents and wrung out our dripping clothing on the last day of our camping trip.

"Yes, exciting," I replied cynically. The thought of a soak in a warm bath in a BATHROOM with a MIRROR dangled like a carrot before my donkey-like eyes to hasten my packing progress.

"What shall we call this 'delightful' adventure?" she laughed. "How about: 'Three Rainy Days in Dolgellau'?"

"I think we shall, Megan," I agreed. "I think we shall."

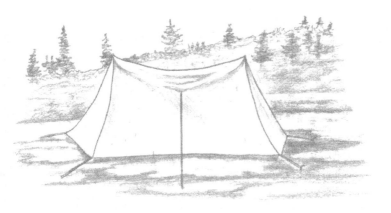

# 30 Heading South

The forms from the emigration consultants, Campbell and Hollings, had arrived in the middle of April, and we had duly filled them in and returned them. I then avidly studied a map of the world as I had no idea where New Zealand was in relation to Australia. I was also unaware that it was composed of two main islands, North Island and South Island, with similar land area to Britain and with several smaller islands coming under its domain.

Philip had done considerable research on the country during the weeks since we had discussed the possibility of moving there. I knew that Australia appealed to many Brits, but I heard that the country harboured scary animals, venomous insects and predatory reptiles. The thought of all those rapacious beasties skulking there was a definite deterrent for me, so I was delighted to hear that New Zealand had less than four million residents, very few poisonous spiders and NO snakes! It all sounded too good to be true.

Philip searched for the most well-suited region in New Zealand for us and pinpointed Tauranga in the Bay of Plenty, North Island. It seemed to be our ideal destination due to its high hours of sunshine, and a key fruit-growing region, which sounded promising for work prospects. The children were so excited, but the hard part would be how to tell our parents and extended family of our intentions. We knew it would be a shock since we had always been such a close-knit family. However, we had little choice but to go somewhere we could find work as we were getting ourselves into a financial hole. We tried to make light of it and reassured the family that it might only be a temporary measure, that they could be assured of a beautiful holiday destination and perhaps they would decide to join us as immigrants one day.

Philip's mother, Lucy, ever keen for adventure, was pragmatic about our decision when we visited her in her charming, red brick

Hampshire cottage to let her know about our plans. She was eager to be amongst our first visitors in the Antipodes and was already excited at the thought of eating New Zealand Green-lipped mussels. It was always a pleasure to visit her, and the children were excited when their Granny announced that she planned to treat us all to a trip to Marwell Zoo.

Situated in the rolling, wooded Hampshire countryside between Winchester and Bishops Waltham, we found the zoo to be fascinating, with a diversity of animals such as leopards, rhinos, zebras, gibbons and penguins. The antics of the meerkats were thoroughly amusing, and the children were intrigued by the giraffes with their long necks and tongues and huge, dewy eyes. However, the power and grace of the gigantic Siberian or Amur tigers caught our attention, so we decided to eat our lunch on a picnic table positioned at about ten yards' distance from their cage from where we could watch those magnificent, regal animals.

'Amur tigers are found in the Russian Far East and north-eastern China,' read the information plaque. 'They live in mountainous, forested areas and have been known to kill adult brown bears, but they mainly prey on wild boar, sika deer and red deer. They are opportunistic predators and will prey on a wide variety of animals, including birds, fish, rodents, insects, amphibians and other mammals such as primates, badgers and raccoon dogs.'

The plaque did not include human beings among the list of their gastronomic delights, but the look on the exquisite face of the 306-kilogram male as he lounged in his cage suggested that we would probably be on his menu if he were given the chance!

We were at the coffee walnut cake stage of our lunch when three adolescent lads arrived on the scene. They went right up to the wooden barrier, just two yards from the cage, and started to mock and jeer loudly at the stately tigers. The enormous male turned his head calmly toward them, and his amber eyes began to glow menacingly as the trio became increasingly raucous and insulting from what they considered their safe position.

"Call yourself a cat?" taunted the group. "Flea-bitten, mangy moggy. We are not frightened of you; you would make a nice rug for my fireplace!" The lads watched as that gargantuan creature rose to his feet and padded towards them languidly without a roar or a snarl. Their disrespectful mockery rose to a frenzied crescendo as they returned his steely gaze. Then the tiger turned his back on them, raised his imperial tail and issued a carefully-aimed high-pressure jet of urine, thoroughly soaking his tormentors so that urine covered them from head to foot and dripped off their chins and fingers, and they taunted no more. With his persecutors thoroughly drenched and humiliated, the tiger slowly returned to his previous position, laid his head down and dozed with a satisfied expression on his aristocratic face. We who had observed the whole scenario were in hysterics! We concluded that 'extremely intelligent, proud and vengeful' should be added to the description of the Siberian or Amur tiger.

Corina Atkins

The London Underground was crammed wall to wall, and the experience of being pushed, crowded and jostled into the trains before the doors closed unforgivingly was an overwhelming experience for our children. After the fresh, sweet Anglesey air, the aroma of hot and perspiring closely-packed humans was a shock to our senses. While we were there in that claustrophobic situation, Philip put his hand into the pocket of his waxed farm jacket in search of his rail ticket and produced a weapon-like instrument of torture.

"Oh, look what I have here," he exclaimed loudly, with evident amusement as he held up his evil-looking lamb tail-docking tool. I was anxious as I noticed several commuters moving a safe distance away in alarm.

"Put it away quickly, Philip," I hissed. "You will have the anti-terrorist squad swooping down on us!"

We were so proud of our children, dressed smartly to present to the New Zealand Immigration consultants in London. It was a warm, sunny day, and they all wore their best summer outfits and straw hats. I was sure they would make a good advertisement as an exemplary family who would be a valuable contribution to New Zealand society. The company of consultants, who were New Zealanders, had advised us not to visit New Zealand House in person as we could prejudice our application if we did. They assured us they had the right contacts to shepherd our application to a successful conclusion, and we could be confident of a favourable reply in just a few weeks. So, after being relieved of an exorbitant hard-saved four thousand pounds to cover their fees, we left their office, convinced that we would soon be on our way to our new country.

We made the most of our London trip, visiting the Science Museum and the National Art Gallery in Trafalgar Square. We walked miles and miles until poor little Amber grew extremely weary and needed carrying on the shoulders of her father or her big brother. After an exhausting day, we returned by train to the home of my sister, Terrie and her husband, P.J., in Kent, who kindly accommodated us for the trip. It was such a different world for our children; the weather was kinder, and chocolate flowed freely. Amelia's eyes grew wide with disbelief when her Auntie gave her a whole chocolate bar to herself, and she did not even have to share it.

The next day, Philip went to work with P.J. in the London suburbs, fitting double-glazed windows, and their work took them right under the flight path coming into Heathrow airport. Philip wondered how the London residents managed to cope with the sound of all that aerial traffic, but after two days of work, he almost stopped noticing it. That was until another 'bird' cut through the sky. The deafening sound reached them first; it was so loud that it rattled all the windows of the house they were working on and shook the men from head to toe. The sleek jet aeroplane soared like an elegant white paper dart overhead, so low that they could almost make out the passengers peering from the single line of windows along its side.

"What on Earth was that?" Philip exclaimed, wide-eyed with shock as the vessel descended gracefully into the airport.

"That was Concorde, coming in from the United States," P.J. laughed as he noted Philip's look of astonishment. They say it can go at twice the speed of sound and cross the Atlantic in just three and a half hours."

"Well, I heard that Concord was noisy, but I did not realise it was that bad!" Philip said as he began to recover his composure.

"Oh, yes, it is supersonic, but they are not allowed to really speed up until the plane is over the Atlantic," P.J. explained.

"Just as well; I could not cope with anything louder!" Philip stated. It reminded him that, even from as far away as our farm on Anglesey, we had often heard the sonic boom coming from the Ocean. **Boom-Boom!**

It also reminded him of the tremendous booming noise we had heard one day on our mountain. It was a beautiful, tranquil day; Philip had been repairing some fencing, and the children were playing outside while I prepared lunch. Suddenly, we heard a low rumbling that seemed to be coming from the rocky outcrops in the top fields, as though the rocks had begun to roar and bellow and were about to tumble down the hill. The rumbling had grown louder and louder, and I wondered if we would see a crashing aeroplane swooping over the horizon and heading towards the house!

### Rumble, rumble, rumble, rumble, Ka-Boom!

The house shook, I rushed to the back door to see all of the family standing stock-still with shock and bewilderment, and I noted that a fine crack had appeared in the wall of the house. Then we realised we had experienced the effects of an earthquake! It had only happened once during our time on the farm, and no real damage had occurred, apart from several repairs needed to the dry stone walls separating the fields, but the event had shaken us to the core and had made us quite jumpy for some time.

One evening while travelling home from working with P.J. in London, Philip noticed the sign on a restaurant that took his attention:

"Pete's Taverna," he noted, and P.J. glanced in the direction he was pointing. "Have you ever been there for a meal?" Philip asked.

"No, but it looks good. It must be Greek," P.J. replied.

"If you remember, we had a holiday in Athens, Greece, while Lynnette was pregnant with Daniel. We loved it; the atmosphere, the culture, but especially the food! We have often said we would like to return to Greece someday," Philip mused.

"Do you fancy going for a meal there before you go home?" P.J. suggested, and Philip's eyes lit up at the idea.

While the men continued their work in London, Terrie and I took the children for a boating trip on the canal at Hythe on the southeast coast. It was a calm and sunny day, and the children were so excited. Kirk and Daniel were proud to be in charge of their separate vessels and took care of Crystal, Amelia and Saffron while Joshua came in the boat with Terrie, Amber and I. Joshua was a capable boy at eleven years old and well-trained by his father in many different skills, including how to handle small boats. Philip had taught our children how to tie nautical knots, to understand river protocol and how to row. So, from the moment our little boat was pushed away from the jetty on the slick green waters of the canal, Joshua was keen to show off his rowing skills.

"I can row, Auntie," he exclaimed, tapping her on her shoulder. "Let me help, Auntie; I can row." Under normal circumstances, my sister, Terrie, is very objective and deservedly confident of her capabilities. However, it became apparent quite soon after our launching that rowing was not her forté, a circumstance causing her to be visibly annoyed with herself, and making Joshua certain of the need for his intervention. After about fifteen minutes of unsuccessful attempts at keeping a straight line and having the irritation of her young nephew persistently asking for a chance to row, it was all becoming an extreme test of her patience! Fixing me with her flashing green eyes and between gritted teeth she spoke very deliberately and in low, threatening tones:

"Tell him to stop, Lynnette. Please tell him to stop!" But I could not; I was in hysterics to the point that tears ran down my face, and I could not speak a word for laughing. After our allotted half-hour of mirth and endurance, while frequently untangling ourselves from the dangling webs of the weeping willows and dislodging ourselves from river bank to river bank, we zigzagged our way back towards the jetty. With my sister still tenaciously in control of the oars, if not the boat, and Joshua still dripping reassurances of his rowing skills in her ear, I finally managed to control myself and suggested to Joshua that it might be in our best interests to leave Auntie to row the boat. The man who helped us alight from the boat when we docked at the jetty was also laughing.

"It brought tears to my eyes to watch you weaving homeward like that," he said cheekily, adding to my sister's annoyance.

"I could have rowed," Joshua informed him with impervious innocence, and it was true; Joshua could row.

# 31 London Entertainment

The pungent aroma of traffic fumes filled the air; vehicles jostled, buses roared, and taxis hooted as they deposited two thousand excited and noisy concert-goers at the entrance to Crystal Palace Park. My sister Diane and her two children, Georgia and Joel, had come from Essex to join us for the event that Saturday evening, bearing heavy baskets full of goodies for our picnic. All our children skipped and danced excitedly ahead of we three sisters as we followed the crowds towards the Concert Bowl by the lake.

Terrie has always known how to give attention to comfort, even when attending an open-air concert. That evening, her accessories consisted of the essential bottle of chilled Prosecco, several wine glasses, a large woollen blanket and a few cushions, which she enlisted her children to carry. Diane, the Queen of all picnics and general culinary splendour, needed a *pantechnicon* van to transport her elaborate preparations, for which we were quite grateful as we were all beginning to feel rather hungry after our journey into London.

Mendelssohn's Hebrides Overture, Fingal's Cave, was already in full swing as we settled ourselves on Terrie's capacious blanket at the outer reaches of the excitable audience. That effervescent throng had spread itself from the lakeside as a happy, bubbling ripple of picnickers on the pristine, lush green grass. It had been quite a mission to save up the entrance fee of seven pounds, fifty per person, and I was savouring every unfamiliar experience. I was in euphoric bliss as I closed my eyes and allowed the music, the warmth and the atmosphere to wash over me.

"Cucumber sandwich, anyone?" Diane loudly broke into my trance, shattering my pleasurable experience. "Here, Georgia, take it carefully. Joel, Daniel, cucumber sandwich? Does anyone else want a cucumber sandwich? Bit of salmon? A drink, anyone?" I turned an irritated expression towards her for interrupting my reverie, but she was rummaging imperviously in her picnic hamper.

"Diane, we are trying to listen to the music!" I said with as much restraint as I could muster. Diane stopped short in her hospitable endeavours and graced me with a blank look.

"Oh, well, we are just enjoying sitting in a field and having a bit of fun," she replied after a brief moment of consideration, cheerfully oblivious of what a rare and cherished experience this was for me.

"Listen; if I just wanted to enjoy sitting in a field and having a bit of fun, **I would not pay seven pounds, fifty to do it!**" I retorted, returning my full attention to the divine strains of Bruch's Violin Concerto.

"Oh!" Diane was silent for a few seconds, and from the corner of my eye, I saw her look around as if she had noticed her surroundings for the first time that evening. She then turned to Terrie on her other side, who, entranced by the beautiful music, was singing along to the melody, swaying happily on her cushion with a glass of 'bubbly' in her hand.

"Hey!" Diane exclaimed. "If I just wanted to sit in a field, having a bit of fun and listening to some old lady singing out of tune, **I would not pay seven pounds, fifty to do it!**" Terrie turned Diane a non-fazed look, smiled dreamily and continued singing and swaying contentedly to the music.

As the evening slid into the night, the audience started to wave their multi-coloured glow sticks. The glittering lights from the platform reflected in the lake, while the full moon rose steadily above the orange city glow and hung in the blackness of a cloudless sky. The audience became rapt and deathly quiet as a solo pianist entranced us with a flawless rendition of Chopin's Nocturne 20 and a heron glided gracefully above the lake, wafting from side to side in sync with the music like a descending feather.

It settled on the shallow lake and ruffled its plumage contentedly, unaware that it was being watched by over two thousand people.

So captivating was that performance that the audience took a few seconds to rouse from the soothing finale, and then a tremendous applause burst from the appreciative crowd, and the startled heron flew off at top speed. The pianist stood up and bowed, the conductor took her hand and announced that she had informed him this was the first time she had performed before an audience of two thousand people and a heron!

The exquisite entertainment concluded with Tchaikovsky's 1812 Overture, accompanied by bolts of colourful fireworks shooting into the air at appropriate musical pitches to represent the cannon fire. The talented orchestra bowed and beamed with delight as the audience cheered and clapped enthusiastically. Packing up their picnics, everyone hummed and sang their way happily in a polite human stream that funnelled out through the gates of Crystal Palace. I felt my seven pounds, fifty, had been well spent.

It had been an enjoyable time spent in the south of England with our family. Nevertheless, it was nearing time to return to our farm to start preparing for our big move to the opposite side of the world. Before leaving, however, we decided that a special meal out was in order. Terrie and I were delighted when P.J. and Philip made their suggestion regarding Pete's Greek Taverna, so we invited our other two sisters and their husbands to join us for the meal.

Our winter holiday in Athens, Greece, all those years ago was a memorable experience, leaving us in awe at the history of the place. To walk in the footsteps of the ancients and sit on the Areopagus mentioned in the Bible was an event we will never forget. We explored the narrow, winding streets of the Plaka District in the cool evenings under the shadow of the illuminated Acropolis. The tempting aroma of meat cooked on glowing charcoal and exotic fare wafting from the abundance of restaurants still haunts our memories whenever we cook a barbecue today. Smartly dressed and smooth-talking men stood at the entrance of each restaurant, attempting to entice us inside, and we succumbed to the temptation several times during the week we were there.

The evening would start at around 7.30 pm, and the doors would be closed when the restaurant was full and until the feasting concluded around midnight. And what a satisfying repast it invariably was, with small dishes served at regular intervals during the evening. *Papoutsakia*, meaning 'little shoes,' which this dish resembles, consists of Aubergine halves stuffed with minced beef and topped with béchamel sauce and cheese. We were so hungry that we devoured it instantly and sat wondering when the main meal would arrive. The next dish consisted of a scattering of *Dolmades*, small parcels of cooked vine leaves stuffed with seasoned rice. All of them delicious, but they disappeared too quickly. Then there was *Skordalia*, a dip made from mashed potatoes and garlic served with pita bread or vegetables such as cucumbers or finely sliced carrots. We greedily ate through the small portions of *Saganaki, Souvlaki, Pastitsio* or *Moussaka*, with the dizzying offer of *Ouzo* and *Retsina Kourtaki* to wash down the fare for those allowed to imbibe. But we still sat looking like two starved street cats.

Seeing our hungry look, our host advised us to pace ourselves and enjoy the food slowly as these delicious dishes would be coming throughout the evening. And it was so true; there was no danger of our leaving the restaurant unsatisfied. We were eventually so stuffed full that we needed some exercise to survive the onslaught of dessert. So we were encouraged to join the dance of *Zorba the Greek*, with partly-baked clay plates smashed at our feet for authenticity. The linked line of sated diners danced out into the street, several yards past the rival restaurants. Then we skipped back into our own, where the doors were closed tightly behind us. Silence reigned outside in the darkness while the dancing, eating, and jollifications continued unabated inside. We enjoyed that delightful, innocent experience most evenings until the end of the week when we reluctantly returned to our icy English home.

So, with those delightful memories still alive, we had no hesitation in recommending that we book a table for eight at Pete's Taverna. Leaving our older children to babysit their younger siblings and cousins for the evening, we adults treated ourselves to some well-deserved self-indulgence. Sitting smugly at the head of the table in the restaurant and well-dressed for the occasion, Philip and I smiled at our group of beloved extended family. As they were self-proclaimed novice Greek meal eaters, we assured them they were in for a real treat. But we repeated the words of our restaurant owner all those years before with instructions to eat slowly. The evening progressed very enjoyably, and all was going just as we had anticipated, with multiple dishes arriving on cue with many compliments voiced to our hosts and we 'connoisseurs' of Greek cuisine.

And then it happened that our reputation was suddenly called shockingly into question. A cloaked and bejewelled apparition suddenly emerged from the kitchen to the roll of exotic music, commanding the attention of all guests, leaving many of them with forks part-way to their mouths in surprise. No one was more surprised than Philip and I when that mysterious creature suddenly threw off her cloak to reveal pastel pink and purple chiffon veils draped alluringly over her scant apparel. Everyone at our table turned from that voluptuous figure to look at us accusingly with shocked eyes almost as wide as their open mouths.

The gyrating belly dancer began to weave seductively around the various tables to the evocative strains of *Zurna* folk music, gradually removing her veils and draping them over gawping male clients. Then she spotted our handsome brother, Paul, against the wall at the far end of our table. As she danced purposefully in his direction, Candy shifted her chair as close as possible to his in a defiant gesture of possession. Undaunted, the exquisite dancer moved between them and, with one thrust of her hips, managed to evict Candy from his side, propelling her and her chair unceremoniously out of her way! Paul blushed beacon-red and sat resolutely on his hands until the woman had finished decorating him with the last of her seven veils. She then wiggled her way back to the depths of the restaurant, took an exaggerated low and revealing bow and retreated to the kitchen from whence she had come.

There was no point in explaining that we did not expect this performance and that we were never entertained that way during our visit to Greece. It was an event we have never lived down!

# 32 Eyes on the Ball

Whatever my father turned his hand to, he followed with passionate devotion. As a young man, he had perfected the skill of bar billiards, holding the title of Bar Billiards Champion for Kent at one time. He won several trophy cups and even trained one of the most talented players of the time to become Britain's champion during the 1960s. I remember peering over the rim of the billiard table and watching that man perform as we all crowded around him in the smoky depths of the Temple Farm Working Mens Club in Strood. He would set up two balls on the table and, using a wooden cue, he would pot them simultaneously and unerringly time after time, after time, taking care not to knock over the wooden pins stood in front of the holes while my father watched proudly at the achievements of his protégé.

Unlike the traditional English pub, the club was a family-orientated establishment that welcomed even small children. On Friday evenings, we would meet there with both sets of grandparents, and we children would run around the dance floor while the adults enjoyed a beer or a stout while playing a game of cards or Bingo. I remember the annual coach trips organized by the club to the sandy beaches of Margate or Broadstairs. Our grandfathers would lie back in their deckchairs, enjoying the sunshine with their trouser legs rolled up and wearing the obligatory knotted handkerchief on their heads. Our grandmothers would watch contentedly as we children dug in the sand and plied us with candy floss or ice lollies.

My father spent a great deal of time at the club, considering it his second workplace since he managed to procure a lot of his business while playing cards with other club members. He was a generous and enterprising man who could sell anything: central heating, electrical appliances such as washing machines, refrigerators, deep freezers, and in his later years, second-hand cars and double glazing. He also became an expert golfer, being a member of the Mid-Kent Golf Club in Gravesend, where he attained the enviable handicap of Zero/Scratch. Although we did not then understand what that meant, his broad smile said it must have been quite an achievement.

Usually, the golfer would need several strikes to drive the golf ball off the tee, down the fairway to the putting green, hopefully avoiding the rough or the bunkers and then putt it carefully into the hole marked by a colourful flag. So, to realize a 'hole-in-one', accomplished with just one strike of the club from 'tee-off' and then down the hole, gives evidence of incredible skill, accuracy and many hours of practice. Remarkably, my father managed not just one 'hole-in-one', but SEVEN! Seven ceramic plaques decorated the walls of our home to commemorate his incredible achievement, while the cupboards and dressers sported numerous silver trophies. The name of George William Baker Jnr must be engraved somewhere in the Mid Kent Golf Club archives as a talented and devoted member.

His seventh hole-in-one attracted the attention of Jack Daniels, the whisky distillers, which sent him seven bottles of their No.7 whisky as a congratulatory gift. Philip remembered that occasion with fondness as his father-in-law kindly shared his booty with his four sons-in-law.

Our Dad tried to include his family in his sporting hobbies, and we tried unsuccessfully to take an interest. Much as she would have liked more play time, our dear mother was too exhausted from fulfilling her household duties to join him. I take my hat off that wonderfully supportive lady.

"Always keep your eyes on the ball," he reminded us frequently as he introduced us to various ball games during our youth, teaching us how to throw and catch a ball. I am still hopeless at throwing, and I would never make a good bowler on the cricket pitch, but most of the time, I made him proud with my skills at catching. However, we girls were becoming less interested in

262

sports and more concerned with fashion and makeup, as young ladies are inclined to be. Nonetheless, our father did have some success teaching us golf swings, and when the sons-in-law joined the family, he was pleased to introduce them to the basics of the sport. Since his retirement, he had spent many pleasant hours on the Bull Bay Golf Club, on the clifftops overlooking the stunning views of the northern Anglesey coastline. When he grew older and too tired to manage the whole round of 18 holes, he found that the fields of *Ty'n Llain* were a perfect setting for him to practice his golfing skills.

On one warm and sunny Sunday, it was our turn to entertain my parents for Sunday roast dinner. It was a meal to be proud of, finished with my mother's famed strawberry trifle, her homemade wine for the adults, and nettle and ginger beer for the children.

"I think a good walk around the fields is in order," Philip suggested breezily. However, my father looked like he would have preferred to go for a short nap on our bed.

"How about a game of rounders?" Daniel suggested, and at the thought of a ball game, my father suddenly rallied and decided his nap could wait.

"So, who wants to be the bowler?" Philip asked after small piles of clothing had identified the four corners of the rounders pitch.

"Not me, for sure!" I affirmed. "Goodness knows where the ball would end up if I attempted to throw it, but I could stand at one of the bases."

"I can't run far, but I can bowl," my father offered, while my mother said she would also stand at one of the bases. That left Amelia and Philip to 'man' the other two bases, alternating with Joshua and Daniel as batsmen. Meanwhile, Saffron and Amber ran around in circles, looking down at their cupped hands and hoping the ball might just fall into them.

'How strange,' I thought as I watched them, realizing that we had not taught them the simple trick my father had taught us to look up and keep our eyes on the ball. I have frequently thought about that enlightening vision and considered how we need to teach our children the principle of looking up to see where the gifts in life are coming from instead of just  expecting them to fall into our cupped hands.

My father gained enough energy to get into the spirit of the game, and he and I took a turn at batting. That left only Jill, the sheepdog, as the fielder. She thoroughly enjoyed her assignment and chased after the ball to the furthest reaches of the field, returning it dutifully to the bowler, and she kept that up for the duration of the game. However, the afternoon was getting warmer, and she was beginning to tire and lag in efficiency and enthusiasm. So, after chasing the ball way down to the bottom of the field one more time and trapping it beside the gorse-edged wire fencing, she bounded back up again, bypassing the bowler and hopped into the sheep trough, still full of water, beside the new barn. With the ball still in her mouth, she sank into the water with an audible sigh of ecstasy. So that was the end of our rounders game for that day.

Having been informed of our imminent emigration, some of our good friends who had been meaning to visit us made a last-ditch effort to come to see us before we left. Among them were Philip's school friends, Nigel and Mark, with their families. Nigel and Mark are brothers, equally mischievous and talented, although very different in appearance and personality, and along with their sister Jenny, they were the children of Valerie and Keith Tovey who was a gifted and renowned artist. It was a delight to see them all, and as our children got to know each other, we mothers, Loren, Julia, and I caught up on what had transpired since we had last met in rural Lincolnshire. Laughter rang out from the living room as the men reminisced about the mischief of their youth and related old stories that never date.

"What about when you broke Nigel's leg, Philip?" Mark reminded him with a dimpled grin which I always found contagious.

Nigel          Mark          Philip          Jenny

"Oh, don't remind me," Philip groaned, and Nigel winced at the painful memory. "Well, if Michael Davy had not pushed me off the sea dyke, it would not have happened," Philip contested. The absent Michael Davy had been the other member of the youthful team of scallywags. He was tall and solidly built, with a rosy face harbouring twinkling eyes and a ready cherubic smile.

"I know, I know, Philip," Mark replied, but the grin on his face showed no evidence of genuine sympathy.

"I had to grab something to stop myself from tumbling down the bank, and Nigel's leg was the nearest thing, but I did not expect it to come off in my hand!" Philip protested.

"No one believed me when I said I thought it was broken," Nigel lamented. "You all told me not to make such a fuss and get back on my motorbike so we could go and get some chips to eat."

"Yes, I remember the doctor was not impressed when he heard you had just eaten before we arrived at the hospital," Philip acknowledged.

"I had to wait until the next day for the surgeon to reset the break!" Nigel shuddered as he recalled the pain of that night.

"The folly of youth," Mark conceded. "Do you remember when we went to see the movie 'Jaws' when it first came out?" Mark's face broke into that familiar cheeky grin as he prepared to relate the story to the rest of us. "I thought everyone already seemed a bit tense and jumpy in the cinema, but Philip was mesmerized, waiting for the man-eating shark to appear on the screen. And then suddenly, in one shocking scene, everyone in the audience gasped, but Philip stood up and let out a bloodcurdling scream, throwing back his arms and smacking us in the face. Then everyone else turned around and screamed because Philip was even more frightening than the movie!"

"Memories of that movie still fill me with fear even now whenever I go swimming in the sea," Philip confessed, despite the tears of laughter running down his face.

"What about when we all went camping in Cornwall?" Nigel added. "Michael Davy was with us and your sister, Diane, Lynnette. I remember it was a chilly night, and we had all gathered in your tent, Philip. We all took turns telling increasingly scary stories, which we recited with such believable embellishments that we were all getting worried about the thought of the night spent under canvas."

"Anyway, Michael's story was about to reach a climax with all of us hanging on every word when Philip suddenly let out another scream to rival the one at the cinema. He rushed out of the tent, shouting: 'It touched me; it touched me!' We all burst out of the tent, thinking that something weird was happening, when from the darkness, we heard 'Eeyore, Eeyore!' Attracted by the light in the tent, a donkey had wandered over from the next field and, wanting to be part of the party, had nudged Philip on the shoulder through the tent canvas to get his attention."

"You will never live that down, Philip," Nigel assured him between chortles of laughter, and it was so true.

We spent a pleasant week together, with all of us sharing in the cooking, eating delicious meals and relating hilarious stories as we sat together around the kitchen table or in our new, comfortable lounge. Daniel and Joshua entertained Mark and Julia's little Matthew and took him to play on their bicycle and go-cart. Saffron and Amber occupied themselves with his baby brother, Jacob, who had just learned to crawl. Amelia introduced Nigel and Loren's daughter, Abigail, to her good friend from the other side of Mynydd Mechell, who invited them to ride her horses with her. It was so rewarding to see the girls enjoying the freedom of riding the horses around the perfect setting of the fields of *Ty'n Llain.*

We visited all the usual places we took our visitors to, introducing them to the beaches, touring the clifftops and the fascinating points of interest, such as South Stack lighthouse.

However, we began to notice that Mark was becoming increasingly agitated.

"He is worried about our car-washing business that we have left in the care of one of the employees," Julia explained. "Mark is not sure he can trust him, so he keeps telephoning to check on him."

"Shall we see if we can get him to relax, Julia?" I suggested. "We have a hammock somewhere. I will ask if Philip can find it and string it up between the trees on the driveway." The hammock proved very popular with everyone except Mark, who continued to pace the driveway anxiously with his mobile phone to his ear.

"Come on, Mark, let me get you a nice glass of cider while you relax in the hammock," I suggested on one of the days when the sun shone warm and invitingly between the branches of the conifers to which the hammock was attached. Mark looked as though he might succumb to that appealing suggestion, so I quickly ran to the kitchen to pour him the cider before he was distracted by his next telephone call.

Meanwhile, Philip, Nigel, and the boys were in the field at the front of the house, overlooking the lake, where Philip was demonstrating some golfing swings with one of the golf clubs my father had given him. The shimmering blue waters of *Llyn Bwch* sparkled enticingly amongst the reeds as the ducks ruffled it and chattered loudly.

"My father-in-law was an amazing golfer in his time," Philip explained, and he related some of his achievements before attempting to instruct his audience on some of the techniques he had learned from him. "Now, first of all, you push your tee into the turf like this." Philip took from his pocket the small, pointed plastic item referred to, pushed it carefully into the ground to demonstrate and sat his golf ball into the small cup on top of it.

"You hold the grip on the club like this with both hands and place your thumb here and not too far down the shaft," he explained. Then you stand like this, with your feet apart, and wiggle your backside until you are comfortable with your position. Making sure there is no one behind you, you swing your club out to here, not too far, all the while keeping your eyes on the ball. Then you swoop it down and catch it just above the tee like this...."

Philip's golf club 'woofed' rewardingly as he swung it, sounding every bit as it was supposed to. With a loud CRACK!, it made perfect contact with the golf ball, which shot swift and clean into the air like every golfer's dream strike. No one was more surprised than Philip! Rising as straight as a rocket, it headed in its intended direction toward the top fields, with Philip and his audience watching in admiration, but then it began to change course and arched toward the house. No one dared to move, and all the admiring *oohs,* and *aahs* suddenly stopped as the group watched on helplessly.

Unaware of that drama, Mark was grateful for his glass of cider and agreed to try to relax. He was just melting into the hammock and beginning to enjoy the experience when suddenly, a golf ball soared across the clear blue sky directly above us. There was a tremendous crashing sound as our large, double-glazed bedroom window shattered, and shards of glass dropped to the floor below! Mark shot like an arrow from the hammock with cider dripping from his neatly-pressed shirt, and he stumbled around in shock! The culprit, still gripping his golf club, peered anxiously over the field gate surrounded by his golfing students, and everyone stared open-mouthed at the great hole in the bedroom window. At that point, Mark decided his nerves were beyond saving, and it was time to go home.

"Oh, dear, Philip, just wait until we tell Michael Davy about this," Nigel warned with a broad grin. "You should not have done that while we were here; you will never live it down." And he never has.

# 33 For the Picking

"Why is it that every direction to your house is determined by how many goats are in the field where we are supposed to turn off?" Our friend, Monica, made that observation when she telephoned from Hampshire to arrange her family trip to visit us. It is true that visitors needed guidance to find our house or any of the farms and dwellings off the beaten track on Anglesey. How a new postman manages to work out the destination of any missive in their care is a complete mystery to me. We were *'Ty'n Llain,* Mynydd Mechell'* with the relative postcode, which helped, but there was no way we could ever change our house name. Philip was locally known as 'Philip *Ty'n Llain'*, while the lane leading to our house was known as 'Philip's lane' to our friends.

It was a mild day at the beginning of September and just before the end of the school holidays when our visitors arrived, exhausted from their long journey. They were pleasantly surprised that they had managed to find our house despite my unusual directions, and they welcomed the sausage and onion hotpot simmering on the Rayburn's hotplate. Philip had known Monica since they were infants, just starting school, and he had been best man to her husband, Jack, at their wedding.

Monica is a petite, attractive blonde and a devoted wife and mother, the sort of person to cheerfully but firmly tolerate no nonsense. Conversely, Jack is an astute comic who could 'winkle out one's soul' with his deep and inquiring interest. With his crop of wiry black hair atop his beaming face, one could never be quite sure what perceptive observations he would make next. Their two pretty little girls, Sabrina and Jade, were of similar ages to our Saffron and Amber, and they took to each other instantly. That evening passed happily beside the blazing fire in our new lounge as the three old friends chatted and laughed over those

271

misdemeanours and shared experiences common to youthful friendships.

Saturday was a pleasant day, quite sunny and with only a gentle breeze, so we all went on a ramble to the extremities of the farm. The top fields provided an exquisite 360-degree view of the Island and beyond as we all stood atop a large flat rock, surrounded by shimmering purple heather, tinged with the toasted fringes of summer's demise.

To the east was Carreglefn, with Parys Mountain beyond and the route to Amlwch dotted with modern, electricity-generating windmills, which turned in sluggish synchronism. The mountains of Snowdonia presented a spectacular array, spreading along the south-eastern horizon. To the south, in the direction of Molly and Dave's farm, *Ty'n Gorse,* the patchwork of fields in various shades of greens and browns were framed by ancient dry stone walls and the occasional 'knitted' hedges of hawthorn. John Owen's farmyard at *Bryn Awel* stood just below the skyline marking the top of Mynydd Mechell, and to the northwest, Mynydd y Garn stood as a distant grey vision while tufts of white clouds scudded playfully above it. A large container ship glided slowly toward Cemlyn as though floating in the sky as the Irish Sea blended with the blue of the northern expanse while Wylfa power station basked in the morning sunshine as it presided over Cemaes Bay.

"Look at that 'fairy ring'!" Philip exclaimed.

"That what?" Jack and Monica replied and we all looked toward our neighbour's farm, *The Coeden,* in which direction he was pointing.

"You see that dark green ring of grass," Philip explained; "I am sure there will soon be mushrooms coming up over there." True to form, the fields of *The Coeden* were the customary luxuriant green that we had come to expect as Wyn Rogers always kept his fields in enviable good health. Nevertheless, the deep emerald circle of about twenty feet in diameter stood out clearly amongst its verdant setting. "That mushroom colony looks like it must be decades old," Philip stated.

"How do you know that, Philip?" Monica asked doubtfully.

"Well, the colony would have started at the centre, gradually spreading outwards just a few inches each year to benefit from fresh soil, forming a circle and leaving the spent soil in the centre. It has a symbiotic relationship with the grass, making it look lush and fertile." Everyone looked from the mushroom site back at Philip, our 'walking encyclopaedia'.

"Yes....I knew that!" Monica replied jokingly.

"But the important thing is, can we go over there and pick some?" Jack asked, turning our horticultural lesson into practical application.

"I don't see any sign of mushrooms ready for picking yet; they will probably appear in a week or two." Jack was disappointed by Philip's reply but we decided it was time to move along in further exploration of our land, with Jill bounding along before us.

"This pond here provided us with a dozen duck eggs last spring," I announced, and everyone crowded around to see how that could have been possible. It was just a small pond, set deeply into a crevice in the rocks, but it was a popular breeding spot for some mallard ducks and Philip had chanced upon it earlier in the year.

"Yes, when I discovered a broody duck there, I waited for her to fly off, and then I just took one or two of her eggs each day and marked the ones left behind with a pencil so that I did not take any developing eggs. That duck successfully reared a healthy clutch of ducklings," Philip assured us, pleased with himself for his resourcefulness. We had certainly enjoyed the product of his 'hunter-gatherer' efforts and the reward of watching the antics of those little yellow 'fluff balls' as they grew to maturity. We crossed the small stream that started at the top of the field and flowed beside the stone wall boundary, where the children gathered the

273

tiny, round, rubbery leaves of the pennywort from its niches and nibbled on them as though they were confection delicacies. The stream then changed course and trickled down toward the lower fields.

"Hey, look! Some creature has been making a track through the hedge here," Monica exclaimed, directing our attention to a small tunnel, worn away by tiny feet running under the dense hawthorn hedge.

"Looks like pheasants have been passing through here," Philip said as he bent down to examine the tiny prints embedded in the mud. We turned back toward the house at the forbidden kissing gate, set in a U-shaped iron frame that allows only one person at a time to pass, through which no young Barlow was allowed to venture without their father's accompaniment. Hopping over the little stream, which had disappeared underground and reappeared with a spurt and a burble before continuing down the hill toward the lower fields, we were delighted to find the answer to Jack's disappointment over the mushrooms.

"Field Blewits!" Philip announced.

"Are they edible?" Jack wanted to know; his gastric juices had been working overtime since the mention of mushrooms earlier in our journey.

"Yes, we can pick these, and they are delicious," Philip reassured him.

"How do you know they are not poisonous?" Monica was justifiably sceptical since it was so easy to misjudge and end up being seriously sick, or worse, from eating unsafe mushrooms.

"Mostly through having eaten them on several occasions," Philip replied with patient indulgence. "You see, the colour of the cap on the smaller ones is a bronze-brown with white gills, and these larger ones are creamy coloured and a bit domed with dusky pink gills. The stems are bulbous at the base and are a mauve colour; you have to cut off the roots quickly to stop any maggots from climbing up into the rest of the stems and making them inedible. Yes, definitely Field Blewits and you can have them for breakfast tomorrow, Jack."

"After you, Philip!" Jack replied unconvinced, although he was happy to gather them with Philip and carry them homeward for further examination.

Bath time that evening was an entertaining event, as always, with Monica overseeing the soggy activities of the little girls.

"This bathroom is enormous!" Monica commented as I opened a cupboard door and showed her where to find the bath towels, ducks, boats and bubbles.

"Yes," I replied proudly, "there were no cupboards when we first came here, just a freestanding bath, a sink and the toilet. Philip panelled the side of the bath and built the tall cupboard at the end and this shorter one I used for the nappy changing mat."

"Impressive," Monica replied admiringly before returning her attention to the little girls spreading suds up the wall, intent on rubbing off the pretty stencilled patterns with which I had decorated it.

"Our children believed that ducks, boats and bubbles were an obligatory part of bath time fun, thinking they were doing me a favour by adding them to my bath water," I told her. I then related the poem I had written for Daniel, Amelia and Joshua when they were little:

275

## Ducks, Boats and Bubbles

It occurred to me in my bath one night,
Children to bed and out of sight,
Story read and turned out the light.

It occurred to me, and I had to laugh,
As I soaked in 'Miss Matey Bubble Bath'
Surrounded by boats and by ducks beset,
That it's good to wallow a bit, and yet...

It seemed to me that it used to be,
When I was young and children-free,
That baths were once predictable;
I turned off the taps when the tub was full

I undressed and returned, and it looked just as clear,
No bubbles or boats or ducks would appear.
So now I have noticed, I really must mention.
Please note all you children, I call your attention.

If my bath shows a lack of aforementioned toys,
Don't deem it a duty of good girls or boys,
To repair the omission and save me some trouble
By adorning my bath with the odd duck or bubble.

Such items are added on *your* bathing night,
These optional extras are *your* great delight.
Though hard to believe, these are NOT what I'd choose
To accompany me in my bathtime recluse

Ducks, boats and bubbles,
Though it shocks you to know,
Are *not* standard fittings
And really MUST GO!

Your loving Mother X

The following morning Monica discovered another use for the tall cupboard at the end of the bath.

"Oh dear," she sighed as she seated herself at the kitchen table and dropped her head onto her hands.

"Are you all right, Monica? Did you not sleep well?" I asked concernedly, drawing the kettle onto the hot plate to make a pot of tea.

"Yes, I am fine, thanks," she confirmed, looking up and trying to appear serious. "I went into your bathroom and was just about to settle myself comfortably when suddenly the door to the cupboard burst open, and three children leapt out and said, 'Surprise!' And it was!"

Thankfully she had a good sense of humour, but a strict word and an apology from the children were in order before breakfast, which consisted of Field Blewits, hot bread rolls and farm-fresh fried eggs. Philip's demonstration of survival after consuming the first mouthful of those wild mushrooms was encouraging, so everyone gradually succumbed to their tempting aroma.

As the day looked promising weather-wise, we decided on a trip to the beach after the Sunday Service. With a picnic packed and everyone suitably well-wrapped against the expected windy onslaught of Anglesey's north-western coast, we set off for the beach at *Ynys y Fydlyn.*

"Oh, look, Philip! We could have a good meal from these pheasants!" Jack exclaimed as we walked along the footpath leading to the beach, where a bevy of pheasants ran colourfully before us like a burst of feathery fireworks.

"No, Jack, don't even think about it," Monica scolded. "This is private land and these are tame birds, no doubt raised by the land owner for the shoot." Jack knew that would be the case, but he loved to tease her.

"Perhaps we could coax them onto land that is *not* private with some breadcrumbs, and then they would be easy picking," Jack goaded. Monica's reproachful glare just made him chuckle mischievously.

"Now, here is something free for the picking, Jack; mushrooms! Ceps even," Philip announced excitedly as he rummaged in his pocket for the plastic bag he always carried for finds such as these. Those coveted and elusive delicacies are what every mushroom hunter dreams of finding. We collected a good amount from the roots of the forest that lined the fields en route to our destination, and Daniel carried the bulging plastic bag with due reverence. Several healthy-looking cows reposed on the lush grass, chewing the cud contentedly while watching our progress. It was tricky to hopscotch over the cow pats while cautiously looking around for any bulls, but Philip assured us that no farmer would even consider putting a bull in a field with a public footpath running through it. So we gradually settled into a pleasant stroll, admiring the views of the sea toward which we were heading.

We had not paid much attention to the 'pillbox' on the top of the hill on our previous visits, but Jack pointed it out. It rose from among a tangle of brambles as a large, hexagonal stone building with a flat roof and holes in the walls, likely for weapons against wartime invaders. It was an anachronism in that peaceful setting, and we suddenly considered ourselves the privileged generation that had not known the terrors our parents and grandparents had experienced, living in fear for their lives and the lives of their loved ones day and night during the two World Wars.

"Come on, Jack; race you to the top!" The temptation to explore that wartime edifice got the better of Philip while Jack, not wanting to be outdone, rapidly joined him as both men ran like impish schoolboys up the gorse-strewn hill toward it. The view it commanded from its vantage point took in the approaches to Holyhead Harbour. Philip guessed the soldiers would have scanned the rough seas for sightings of submarines and the skies for German bombers.

278

"I can't imagine it would have been too exciting being stuck in this building day after day," Philip suggested as they examined its weather-stained walls. "I should think they were a bit out of the way of the action up here."

"Just a minute Philip, what's that?" John's attention was riveted on a small metallic object partially hidden amongst the gorse. "It's a bullet case by the looks of it!"

"It is too, and here's another one over here. It's a 303 rifle bullet casing, I am sure," Philip replied. John gave Philip a look of scepticism.

"You are just making that up, aren't you?" he said with a grin and with that familiarity permitted between old friends.

"No, really," Philip assured him earnestly as he rubbed at his fascinating find to reveal the gleaming brass beneath its verdigris patina. "I recognise them; they are the same as my Dad used to use when he was a marksman in the Royal Navy. He should have given in his rifle when he left the Navy, but he kept it for a long time because it saved his life," and then Philip repeated the tragic account of the sinking of the submarine *HMS Affray* from which his father had narrowly escaped.

By the time the men had navigated a route through the gorse and brambles to join the rest of us, Monica and I had set up our blanket and picnic on the pebbly beach and we had a surprise to show. In the bay, not even thirty yards away, the large, black, shiny head of a seal was bobbing about just above the water line. Turning his great head towards the two new additions to our 'pod' the creature seemed just as fascinated to watch us as we were to watch him, and he stayed there in the same spot for the entire duration of our sojourn on his beach.

The afternoon was an enjoyable experience, with the little girls engrossed in digging in the gravelly beach while Philip, Jack, Daniel, Amelia, Joshua and Jill scampered over the slippery, black boulders to investigate the rocky caves, which would soon be

279

inundated at high tide. They all clambered up onto the little island that jutted into the sea and found it covered in a verdant baize with pompoms of pink thrift fluttering in the gentle sea breeze. It had been a bonus to gather some warmth and sunshine to reminisce on before the cooler days of autumn engulfed us.

About a month after Jack and Monica's departure, Philip was able to supply us with more country bounty. There was still dew on the ground as he made his early morning rounds of the top fields where he discovered an abundance of mushrooms like white-domed marshmallows, ripe and ready for the picking in the 'fairy rings' we had seen in *The Coeden*. Philip climbed over the stile and filled his plastic bag with them while our dog Jill watched him raptly from our side of the boundary. Philip knew those puffy white delicacies would have gone to waste had they not been 'rescued', as Wyn Rogers rarely walked that public footpath.

With the success of his foraging, Philip remembered Monica's discovery of the little tunnel and the tiny footprints under the hawthorn hedge. Lifting his eyes to the field where we had seen those tracks, he spotted about a dozen pheasants grazing busily about fifty yards beyond the kissing gate. He stealthily approached the field and crouched down behind the four-foot-high stone wall and Jill did the same, which was unnecessary, but she was always eager to please. Thankfully, the direction the wind was blowing meant that the pheasants would not have had the whiff or sound of man and dog. However, Philip knew that the moment he was seen, they would make a run for the tunnel at the base of the hawthorn hedge, which was now festooned with ripe, scarlet berries, set amongst the scant yellow and brown leaves still clinging to its barbed branches. Gently placing his bag of mushrooms on the grass, he peered cautiously over the wall and was pleased to see that the birds were still oblivious to his presence, and Jill did the same.

"Down, Jill!" Philip whispered, and Jill dipped down again into a low crouch and followed closely behind him, her front paws outstretched and her back legs tucked under her red-brown haunches as they both made their way toward the gate.

'This is no good; if I run toward them, they will take off in the other direction,' Philip thought. He turned to look at Jill, who was all ears and anticipation, and then he jerked his hand commandingly back toward the far end of the wall that ran up to the topmost perimeter of our land. Jill instantly scuttled off as instructed, still keeping low against the wall and hidden from view. She stopped halfway and looked back toward her Master, her tail twitching excitedly as she awaited his next directive.

Philip jerked his hand again to send her further, which she happily obeyed. He repeated this several times until she reached the furthest point from where she could still see him, and Philip motioned to her to stay still. He poked his head just above the wall again and was pleased to see that the pheasants were still unaware of his presence.

'Over, Jill!' Philip's hand signals commanded, so Jill leapt over the wall, then stood stock-still and threateningly where she landed. The pheasants raised their heads in unison at the sight of her and instantly made a dash for their escape route under the hawthorn hedge, heads thrust forward like well-aimed darts, legs stretched in long swift paces and feet tearing at the muddy ground. Philip raced through the kissing gate as fast as he could and sprinted towards the tunnel in the hedge. The sprightly males reached the tunnel first, and, one by one, ten birds disappeared through it, leaving two plump females until last. Philip made a full-on dive, skidding painfully through a patch of stinging nettles and caught both birds by their feet, one in each hand. He held up his prey triumphantly, with Jill bouncing up and down ecstatically on her hind legs to examine the results of their successful mission, her tail swishing wildly with delight.

"Well done, Jill!" Philip exclaimed. "There will be roast pheasant for dinner."

And there was.

Phasianus colchicus mongolicus —
(hat.)

Keith Tovey.

# 34 Contemplation

"God must be on your side; no one manages to sell their house quickly here," Dewi, the *postmon*, stated with a smile when he arrived one day with a water bill and our eagerly anticipated reply from the emigration consultants in London. We had not considered that it would be such an unusual event to sell a house on Anglesey; after all, we had bought the place after only one viewing eight years earlier and the new owners had done the same when they came to view the property. They were a pleasant couple, newly retired from their relative practices as doctors in Shropshire, who were looking forwards to enjoying the peace of the country life.

As we were confident that our application to immigrate to New Zealand would be successful, we had gradually returned responsibility for the small parcels of sheep-grazing land belonging to our friends. One of our neighbours heard from John Owen that we wanted to sell off the top nine acres of our fields, and he snapped them up. It was also due to John's good advertising on our behalf that we sold our flock of sheep, so it had been a reasonably smooth transition from the farm being a going concern of fifteen acres to just six acres.

We hurried back to the kitchen and carefully opened the letter, imagining that it contained the expected visas. However, our plans and dreams were blasted into little pieces with the devastating news that we had been rejected!

"What! I don't believe it! The consultants said there would be no problem!" We were understandably shocked and disappointed. Our children had looked so appealing on the day of our interview with them and Philip now had many qualifications to support his application. We were sure it would all go without a hitch.

"It says here that I needed twenty-eight points to qualify, which I thought I had, but I was one point short because I had my work

283

experience *before* I gained my qualifications, instead of the other way around." Philip's face looked drained as he placed the letter on the kitchen table.

"So, now what?" I asked as I stared dejectedly out of the kitchen window at the pine trees on the driveway, waving to and fro in the wind. We had put so much store by this application and made arrangements based on its success.

"Can we ask for our money back?" I suggested.

"I think that is unlikely," Philip gave a half-hearted laugh. "No, we will have to accept it is gone for good. I wonder if we would have done better if we had gone directly to the New Zealand Immigration Office instead of using the agency. Glen's application to immigrate to Australia was unsuccessful too; he is hopping mad!" As it turned out, yes, we could have filled out the forms and sent them directly to New Zealand House without involving the consultants and saved ourselves £4,000 in consultant fees. We stewed over that result all evening and did not want to tell the children or our parents the disappointing news. Two days later, Philip came home from work with a startling proposal:

"Let's go!" he said with gusto. "Let's just go. We have nothing else now; we have sold everything, and we have no hope of being able to afford anything nearly as wonderful as this place in the south of England. So why not pack up and go to New Zealand as planned?" I did not know what to say; I stood in the middle of the kitchen holding a pan of boiled potatoes and stared at him.

"Do you think we could do it?" I asked after a few moments of contemplation.

"Why not? We took a chance on moving here, and it has been a wonderful experience, but now we need to move on," he stated. I transferred the potatoes to a serving bowl with careful deliberation as I considered the possibility of that decision being a wise move.

"But that would mean we would be moving to the other side of the world where we have no family, no house, no job and no visa," I reminded him.

"We can do this, Lynnette; we have no better option," Philip assured me in his typical dynamic and persuasive way. "I hear people are offering what they call 'Farm Stays' in New Zealand, where you can work on the farm in exchange for board and lodging. We could travel around the country until I find a permanent job, and then we could decide where to settle."

"With five children, Philip?" I thought that to be an appropriate question.

"They are good children, Lynnette; the New Zealand farmers will love them." He was aglow with exuberance and contagious enthusiasm.

'Well, here we go again, another leap into the dark unknown,' I thought, but I had to confess to a certain thrill at his suggestion. For Philip, however, it was far from unknown; he had thoroughly studied the geography of New Zealand and done all the necessary research on the region most likely to suit our requirements. Good weather was high on my priorities while Philip's requirement was a healthy agricultural economy where he could use his practical skills in Horticulture and his recently earned Honours degree in Soil Science and Botany. For our children, we needed to consider living where there would be good work opportunities when it was time for them to leave school, although we had heard that the unemployment rate in New Zealand was very low. Philip pulled out his map of New Zealand and drew a large circle around Tauranga in the middle of the Bay of Plenty, North Island.

We could hardly hear the lady on the other end of the telephone, not just because she was twelve thousand miles away on the outskirts of KatiKati, but because of the intensity of the bird song and the resounding orchestra of cicadas in the background.

All my doubts melted at that sound and the reassurance of her welcome.

"There will be plenty of work for you to do here, and the schools are just a short journey into town," she assured us, in an accent that sounded like she was speaking English but was rather hard to understand. Having become accustomed to the Mancunian accent of our friends from Manchester after the last eight years, I thought I would eventually attune to the accents of New Zealanders.

So that was that; all organised. Philip booked our plane tickets for mid-February, and I set to work packing up enough suitcases for each of us for the six weeks of travelling ahead of us. We would need warm clothes for the three weeks we would be tripping the length and breadth of England as we visited our friends and relatives to say our goodbyes during one of the coldest winters known in recent times. Then we would need to change to clothes suitable to enjoy the following three weeks in the height of a sizzling New Zealand summer while we awaited the arrival of our shipping container. I confess to being thoroughly overwhelmed! However, during those preparations, we were introduced to someone who was to change our plans.

"You see that lady over there?" Lorraine whispered in my ear after the Service that Sunday morning. "She has just returned from visiting friends in Tauranga, New Zealand. Isn't that where you were hoping to go?" My eyes lit up as I thanked her and asked for an introduction to the visitor. Tugging Philip along to meet the lady named Carol, we discovered that her friends had recently moved to New Zealand from London and were a very hospitable family.

"Would you mind asking if we could contact them, please?" Philip asked Carol excitedly. And the next thing we knew, we were invited to stay temporarily in the basement apartment of the Hyatt family in Cherrywood, Tauranga.

One cold and dark Friday night in November, the children and I sat, watching the flames in the open fire and thinking how pleased we were that it was now the weekend, when suddenly a strange man burst into the room! Saffron and Amber screamed and leapt from playing on the floor to bury their little curly heads under my arms. Amelia and Joshua stared open-mouthed and bewildered by the audacity of this intruder coming into our home, while Daniel was shocked and rooted to the spot. It took me a little while to compute this strange situation, but that cheeky, dimpled smile eventually gave him away. I had not seen this man for more than eleven years, and now he appeared unexpectedly, as if through locked doors and invaded our lounge.

"It's all right, everyone," I tried to calm them all. "It's your Dad, without his beard!"

"Whatever made you decide to shave it off?" I asked after all the children had quietened down, and some of them had become brave enough to go up to him and touch his face to confirm that he really was their father.

"Well, we will be moving to a new country with a new culture, and I have no idea if beards are well-accepted in New Zealand," Philip explained. "Apart from that, we will need to appeal to the New Zealand Immigration office for residency when we arrive, so I don't want anything to prejudice our application. I can always regrow it once we know where we fit in."

"I don't know; I quite like you without the beard; it takes years off you and reminds me of when we first met," I smiled.

Our friends threw us a farewell party in the village hall, and all my sisters and their families came to join us for the event. The hall rang with some of my father's favourite jazz music, and some young ones played beautiful music on their guitars and keyboard. It was all so well done. Our father had always danced with us as children; he would stand still and hold our hands, two of us at a time, while we twirled and jived. He taught us to waltz, sometimes

287

with us standing on his feet so we could learn the steps. Seeing our parents dancing together was always a delight; they could dance the night away in their younger years, and that evening they danced together like old times. I wrote a song of appreciation for our parents that I planned to sing at the party, but I knew emotion would overcome me, so our friends, Bridget and Anita, took to the stage and sang it for me:

## Rocking Chair Blues

For Mum and Dad

You sit there in your rocking chair; you raise a little smile.
Thumbing through old photographs, you're back there for a while.
Life used to be much simpler then, your children by your side,
How quickly time has slipped away, like waters with the tide.

But,
You were the first love we ever knew,
You cared for and loved us as we grew.
You bathed our wounds, and you dried our tears,
Shared our laughter, our joys and fears
And we love you, now and forever,
Although we leave you, we love you still.

Life used to be all sunshine then, all visits to the zoo.
All party frocks and seaside trips, where did those years go to?
You taught us how to walk and dance, cook and sew and be ladies.
Then one by one, we all were wed and came those little babies.

But,
You were the first love we ever knew,
You cared for and loved us as we grew.
You bathed our wounds, and you dried our tears,
Shared our laughter, our joys and fears,
And we love you, now and forever,
Although we leave you, we love you still.

The shipping container arrived one frosty day in late December and was set down on the driveway of Roy and Millicent's house at *Hafod Las*, about a mile away on the Mountain Road. We were very grateful for their assistance as there was no hope of such an outsized transporter accessing our lane without crushing a few drainpipes or demolishing one or two fences. And we were so appreciative of our friends and family who arrived to help ferry our sparse belongings from the house to the container.

Paul, Philip, Daniel and Joshua did a final tour of the remaining fields of *Ty'n Llain* before standing together, somewhat tearfully, under the conifers on the driveway, looking out at the low, iced mist that hung over the silence of *Llyn Bwch*. It was a painful moment, and I felt for them. Paul hugged me before taking our children and Jill to my parents' home, where we were to spend our last few days on Anglesey. Philip and I stood at the front door and watched them drive off down the lane.

The house was empty and cleaned from top to bottom, and we were satisfied that the new owners would be happy with its presentation. There was one thing left to do, and we both knew what that was. We looked at each other and then dashed into the kitchen. We pulled, we heaved, we huffed, and we puffed, and we ripped up that wretched kitchen carpet!

Muffled against the cold evening air, we sat there, just the two of us, on our 'sunset' rock, peering through the diffusion of smoke rising from the burning carpet on the bonfire, each of us lost in contemplation as the sun began to set behind Mynydd Y Garn. Philip grieved to be leaving his beloved farm on which he had worked so hard for the last eight years, while I was wondering if we would ever own another home as grand and as comfortable as this one. Although we had been through some tough times and had overcome many challenges, we had countless good memories to take with us of our wonderful years spent on the beautiful *Ynys Môn*.

"I will miss this place," Philip said eventually, with a quiver in his voice.

"I know you will; you have put so much work into it," I replied sympathetically. "Look at all the fencing you have done, the trees we have planted, and such a beautiful barn and home you have helped to build for us."

"If it were not for the unemployment situation, we would probably not be sitting here looking at our empty house right now," he said wistfully.

"Yes, but it will make an ideal retirement home for the new owners, with no need to find work and to just cosy down until the rough weather passes and the sun shines again," I offered. "They could turn it into Bed and Breakfast accommodation if they wanted to; it would be very popular."

"Maybe we will come back here one day when we retire," Philip suggested.

"Maybe we will," I agreed. "You know, I can't say this has been the easiest eight years of my life by any stretch of the imagination. But I was thinking, we have had some good times here. When we were learning the skills of shepherding, lambing in the cold, dark winter nights and trying our best to integrate and learn the local language and culture, could we possibly have imagined just how contented we would become? Sometimes we need to colour our past with the cream of today's palette rather than muddy it with negativity." Philip turned to look at me and frowned at my philosophical observations as I gazed meditatively into the distance.

"Quite," he replied indulgently and continued to sit quietly, absorbing the atmosphere. I looked across the fields, recalling the music and laughter that had rung through them over the years and reflecting on the friendships, adventures and learning curves that had shaped our memories. While we both felt the sadness of leaving behind dear friends, good neighbours and precious family, we knew we would make new friends and a new life on our next adventure in New Zealand.

"I mean, problems can be like a large boulder that rolls into our river," I mused. "You can't get under it, you can't go around it, the only way is over it, and then it becomes a beautiful cascade that people come from miles around to sit beside." I nodded in self-congratulatory concurrence, and Philip looked at me sideways before returning his attention to the darkening sky, where we watched for the last time as the cool, white winter sun slid behind the distant hills.

# Toad-in-the-Hole Recipe

## The batter

400g/14oz plain flour
Salt and black pepper
4 free-range eggs
200ml/7fl oz milk

Whisk all the ingredients together until a smooth, lump-free batter with the consistency of double cream is formed (if the batter is too thick, add a little water). Cover the batter and rest in the fridge for one hour.

## The meat

2 tbsp sunflower oil
8 sausages

Preheat the oven to 210C/190C Fan/Gas 6/7.

Pour the oil into a large, deep roasting tray (about 30x20x6cm/12x8x2½in) and place in the preheated oven. Add the sausages and brown, turning until coloured on all sides (they do not need to cook thoroughly).

Whisk the rested batter and pour it into the hot tin between the browned sausages. Return to the oven and cook for 30–35 minutes, or until the batter is risen and golden-brown.

## Onion gravy

1 tbsp good oil
2 onions, finely sliced
½ tsp made mustard
Salt and pepper to taste
500ml/18fl oz meat stock

Heat a heavy-based frying pan over a low heat. Add the oil, onions and a pinch of salt. Cook gently for 15–20 minutes or until dark, golden brown. Stir in the mustard, pepper and stock. Bring the mixture to the boil, reduce the heat, and simmer for 10–15 minutes until the liquid has reduced and thickened. Taste and adjust the seasoning as necessary.

## Garlic cabbage

1 Savoy cabbage, shredded, with the core discarded

½ tbsp. good oil

Salt and pepper to taste

2 garlic cloves, peeled and finely chopped

Braise the shredded cabbage in a high-sided frying pan or shallow saucepan with 3–4 tablespoons of water over medium-high heat for 6–8 minutes, stirring occasionally. Once the cabbage is tender, pour off any excess water into the gravy and add oil to the pan along with the garlic. Fry over a low heat for 1 minute or until the garlic is softened and aromatic. Season the cabbage with salt and pepper and keep warm.

Reheat the onion gravy and serve the Toad-in-the-Hole in wedges with the cabbage alongside it.

# Tŷn Llain Bed & Breakfast

**TYN LLAIN B&B**

Come and enjoy a peaceful break nestled in rural
Anglesey just 10 minutes from the sea.

**BOOK DIRECTLY** via our website:

www.tynllainbandb.com.

Printed in Great Britain
by Amazon

38443101R00169